NEW PROCLAMATION

NEW PROCLAMATION

Year A, 2004–2005

Advent through Holy Week

Herman C. Waetjen

Jack Dean Kingsbury

Dale P. Andrews

Alice L. Laffey

Harold W. Rast, editor

Fortress Press

Minneapolis

NEW PROCLAMATION
Year A, 2004–2005
Advent through Holy Week

Cover design: Kantor Group, Minneapolis.

Illustrations: Tanya Butler, *Icon: Visual Images for Every Sunday*, copyright 2000 Augsburg Fortress.

The Library of Congress has catalogued this series as follows.
New proclamation year A, 2001–2002 : Advent through Holy Week / Francis J. Moloney . . . [et al.].
     p. cm.
Includes bibliographical references.
ISBN 0-8006-4245-7 (alk. paper)
     1. Church year. I. Moloney, Francis J.
BV30 .N48 2001
251'.6—dc21   2001023746

New Proclamation, Year A, 2004–2005, Advent through Holy Week
ISBN 0-8006-4251-1

Manufactured in the U.S.A.
08   07   06   05   04   1   2   3   4   5   6   7   8   9   10

CONTENTS

THE SEASON OF EPIPHANY
JACK DEAN KINGSBURY

THE SEASON OF LENT
DALE P. ANDREWS

Holy Week
Alice L. Laffey

PREFACE

New Proclamation continues the time-honored Fortress Press tradition of offering a lectionary preaching resource that provides first-rate biblical exegetical aids for a variety of lectionary traditions.

Thoroughly ecumenical and built around the three-year lectionary cycle, *New Proclamation* focuses on the biblical texts, based on the conviction that those who acquire a deeper understanding of the pericopes in both their historical and liturgical contexts will be motivated to preach engaging and effective sermons. For this reason, the most capable North American biblical scholars and homileticians are invited to contribute to *New Proclamation*.

We have asked the contributors to follow a similar pattern in their presentations but have allowed them to alter and improve that pattern in ways they think might be more helpful to the user. For example, one of the authors in a previous volume began each discussion of the Sunday lections with the Gospel rather than the First Reading, since it is assumed that most users preach on the Gospel reading for the day. In other instances, some authors have chosen to combine the interpretation and response to the texts into one section rather than separating them into two distinct sections.

In general, *New Proclamation* is planned and designed to be user-friendly in the following ways:

- *New Proclamation* is published in two volumes per year, designed for convenience. The present volume covers the lections for the first half of the church year, Advent through Holy Week, which culminates in the Great Vigil of Easter.

- The two-volume format offers a larger, workbook-style page with a lay-flat binding and space for making notes.
- Each season of the church year is prefaced by an introduction that provides insights into the background and spiritual significance of the period.
- The application of biblical texts to contemporary situations is an important concern of each contributor. Exegetical work is concise, and thoughts on how the texts address today's world and our personal situations have a prominent role.
- Although the psalms ("Responsive Reading") are infrequently used as preaching texts, brief comments on each assigned psalm are included so that the preacher can incorporate reflections also on these in the sermon. The psalms, for the most part, represent the congregation's response to the first reading and are not intended as another reading.
- Boxed quotations in the margins help signal important themes in the texts for the day.
- The material for Year A is here dated specifically for 2004-2005 for easier coordination with other dated lectionary materials.
- These materials can be adapted for uses other than for corporate worship on the day indicated. They are well suited for adult discussion groups or personal meditation and reflection.

It is important to keep in mind that the Gospel is the formative principle of the lectionary and that most sermons are based on it. From the First Sunday of Advent to Trinity Sunday of each year, the Old Testament reading is closely related to the Gospel reading for the day. However, from the first Sunday after Trinity Sunday to the end of the year (Christ the King), provision has been made for two patterns of reading the Old Testament in the RCL: (1) paired readings in which the Old Testament and Gospel readings are closely related, and (2) semi-continuous Old Testament readings that are not necessarily related to the Gospel.

We are grateful to our contributors—Herman C. Waetjen, Jack Dean Kingsbury, Dale P. Andrews, and Alice L. Laffey—for their insights and for their commitment to effective Christian preaching. We hope that you find in this volume ideas, stimulation, and encouragement for your ministry of proclamation.

Harold W. Rast

THE SEASON OF ADVENT

HERMAN C. WAETJEN

Introduction

The entrance into the hermeneutical circle of interpretation is that place at which the reader or the interpreter is located. Biblical interpretation begins very simply with a reading of the text in order to have the *experience* of interacting with the text in the fullness of consciousness that unites the heart and the head, the emotions and the intellect. It is analogous to the experience of sitting in a cinema and interpreting the scenes of the movie that are unfolding on the screen by means of the fullness of the understanding that the viewer brings to bear on the story into which he or she has been drawn as a participant.

Commentaries and such exegetical-homiletical helps as the New Proclamation series should always be secondary, following the personal encounter of heart and mind with the text. Although the Bible is distanced from us by 2,000 years and more, the initial experience of projecting one's own understanding onto the text is quintessential. Questions will arise from this initial interaction, and many of them, perhaps, will have to be answered by expanding the horizon of understanding through the appropriation of the historical, religious, socioeconomic and cultural information that biblical scholars produce through their critical research. The hermeneutical circle, therefore, moves from the interpreter's location in the early twenty-first century back into the past in an effort to uncover the original context of the text and to integrate the new insights with the earlier experience of the initial interaction with the text. But, even as the Old Testament is not interpreted validly from the perspective of the New Testament and its thought-world, the traditions of the past 2,000 years of Christian history and interpretation do not bear the necessary and appropriate theological, sociological, anthropological, and historical types of meaning that will open the texts of either testament of the Bible.

This hermeneutical process, then, begins with the projection of the interpreter's understanding and continues with the employment of the historical-critical method and social-scientific theory in order to bridge the distance between the interpreter and the original context of the text. Such an approach to the biblical text prioritizes the postmodern philosophical orientation "I am, therefore I think" in place of the centuries-old Cartesian formulation "I think, therefore I am." The experience of a human being's "I am" precedes the subject-object analysis of the scientific methods. It is vital that the interpreter embraces the biblical text and its history as personally and existentially as possible. Israel's history in all of its changes down through the centuries is our history. The stories of the creation, the fall, the exodus, the Sinai covenant, etc., are our stories. The stories of Jesus' career and the women and men who followed him are our stories. The history of early Christianity in which the writings of the New Testament were composed is our history. We should be drawn into them as vitally and existentially as we are drawn into the "world" of a movie in the cinema. The biblical text—with all of its truths that have been so profoundly inspirational and with all the untruths of its interpretation that have produced so much injustice and evil—tells our history, our story, leading us through prophetic judgment, the anticipation of a new creation, the birth of the pioneer of a new humanity, Good Friday's redemption and Easter's salvation, and therefore also into an empowered commitment to act on behalf of God in the exercise of God's rule.

> IT IS VITAL THAT THE INTERPRETER EMBRACES THE BIBLICAL TEXT AND ITS HISTORY AS PERSONALLY AND EXISTENTIALLY AS POSSIBLE.

The Season of Advent

Advent is the season of "coming." It is the beginning of the liturgical year of the church, and therefore it is very appropriate that it is a time of anticipation, a time of waiting and watching for the coming of Jesus the Christ. The lectionary texts for the four Sundays of Advent place Christians in an eschatological double bind. On the one hand, there is the more immediate prospect of the first coming of Jesus the Christ at Christmas. Our expectation of this eschatological reality, however, is based on the Christ event that occurred almost 2,000 years ago. In Advent we look forward to the fullness of all that Christmas means, the beginning of the good news of God's salvation in and through the Lord Jesus Christ.

On the other hand, there is also the prospect of the "last things," when history reaches its divinely appointed goal, and the present reign of God that was inaugurated by Jesus of Nazareth is culminated by the parousia, the so-called second coming of Jesus as "the Son of the Human Being," when God finally is "all things in all things" (1 Cor. 15:28).

Both of these orientations, the prospect of celebrating the beginning of the salvation event and the prospect of the future that culminates the salvation event, are accentuated by the summons to a conscious and attentive integration of Christian identity and activity. The texts of the Hebrew scriptures, especially Isa. 2:1-5 and 11:1-10, offer glimpses of the expectations that constitute the new age, the new moral order, and the new humanity that God wills to be actualized. In this time of world chaos and upheaval, these texts should be interpreted with a pronounced emphasis on the divine-human collaboration that the ministry of Jesus discloses. Advent is preparation time for the forthcoming celebration of the "Word made flesh." But unless that Word continues to be made flesh in the lives of Christians today and tomorrow, the prophetic visions

> IT IS REUNION AND REUNIFICATION, NOT SEPARATION AND REMOTENESS, THAT ADVENT ANTICIPATES AND THAT CHRISTMAS CELEBRATES.

of Isaiah and Jesus' delivery of God's reign to his disciples (Luke 12:32; 22:29) will never be actualized. Consequently the syndrome of passivity that is characterized by Samuel Beckett's *Waiting for Godot*, which represents the faith and lifestyle of many American Christians, must be avoided in the preaching of these texts (John 14:12).

The gradual intensification of the eschatological realities that are inaugurated by the birth of Jesus the Christ should make the eventual arrival of Christmas a powerful emotional experience. John the Baptizer proclaims the eschatology of separation (Matt. 3:12), but Jesus, who as Emmanuel is "God with us," introduces the paradigm shift of reunion and with it the unification of all humanity. The magi, who come from the East, and the Roman centurion, who comes from the West, will feast at the messianic banquet with Abraham and Sarah, Isaac and Rebecca, Jacob and his wives in "the kingdom of God." Christmas establishes the beginning of the actualization of the possibility that the paradigm shift of reconciliation and reunion will result in beating swords into plowshares and spears into pruning hooks. In the secularism of American culture, God is remote or absent. Jesus, as the incarnation of the Word, makes God present in the flesh and blood realities of historical existence. It is reunion and reunification, not separation and remoteness, that Advent anticipates and that Christmas celebrates.

FIRST SUNDAY OF ADVENT

NOVEMBER 28, 2004

REVISED COMMON	EPISCOPAL (BCP)	ROMAN CATHOLIC
Isa. 2:1-5	Isa. 2:1-5	Isa. 2:1-5
Psalm 122	Psalm 122	Psalm 122: 1-2, 3-4, 4-5, 6-7, 8-9
Rom. 13:11-14	Rom. 13:8-14	Rom. 13:11-14
Matt. 24:36-44	Matt. 24:37-44	Matt. 24:37-44

FIRST READING

ISAIAH 2:1-5 (RCL, BCP, RC)

Jerusalem has a destiny—indeed, a consummate destiny, pivotal for all the nations of the world! For the northern kingdom of Israel has been destroyed by the Assyrian armies of Shalmaneser V (726–722 B.C.E.) and Sargon II (721–705 B.C.E.). Judah and its capital city, Jerusalem, have been spared, but as a tributary of Assyria. Nevertheless, in spite of these stark realities, God's covenant with Israel—now represented alone by the southern kingdom—remains irrevocable and will continue to guarantee God's faithfulness into the future. In the context of two great crises, Isaiah offers a glimpse of Jerusalem's future. Mount Zion will become a new Sinai, an *axis mundi* for all the peoples of the world. "All the nations shall stream to it."

The first crisis was the formation of the Syro-Ephraimite coalition against Judah and Jerusalem in 734–732 B.C.E. that attempted to force King Ahaz to join in an alliance against Assyrian hegemony. Isaiah's oracles of judgment and salvation were spoken in this context, addressed primarily to Ahaz who, out of a lack of faith, had paid tribute to the Assyrian king, Tiglath-Pileser III (744–727 B.C.E.), for protection and consequently had reduced Judah to a vassal state. Shalmaneser V defeated the Syro-Ephraimite coalition and destroyed the northern kingdom after a three-year siege of its capital, Samaria.

The second crisis occurred when the Assyrian king, Sennacherib (704–681 B.C.E.), invaded Judea and besieged Jerusalem in 701 during the reign of Hezekiah (715–687 B.C.E.). Throughout this period, Isaiah counseled Hezekiah not to submit to the Assyrians. Yet, according to 2 Kings 18:14-16, Hezekiah paid a large tribute to Sennacherib in order to have the siege lifted. After the apparent elimination of the Assyrian threat, Hezekiah fortified Jerusalem with an enormous wall and at the same time allied himself with Egypt. In the face of this defiance, Sennacherib led a second campaign against Hezekiah, but his army suffered a major calamity that, according to the account of 2 Kings 19:35, may have been a plague. Both Isaiah 36–38 and 2 Kings 18–20 are related to the events of this second crisis.

The vision of Isa. 2:1-5, placed at the beginning of the presentation of Isaiah's prophecies, emphasizes its centrality in his forty-year career under four Judean kings, especially Ahaz and Hezekiah. Its significance is accentuated by the superscription of 2:1 that introduces it, a superscription that parallels 1:1, but which in that form occurs nowhere else in First Isaiah. In spite of the judgment that the prophet pronounces on the vineyard of Israel, the people of Judah and above all their rulers (5:1-30), he nevertheless "sees" a future for Jerusalem. In spite of the oracles of judgment which he has directed against the nations in chapters 13 to 23, he also "sees" a destiny for them, even for those despotic powers, like Assyria, that threaten the future of God's people. Mount Zion will become the architectonic center of the world that will draw all humanity to it. Like Mount Sinai, at which Israel was born as a nation by entering into a covenant with God and becoming God's unique offspring, Mount Zion will become the navel of the earth at which all human beings will enter into covenant with God and be born as God's sons and daughters. At this one universally acknowledged center of the earth, where God's name resides and where the presence of God would be experienced as an existential reality, all humanity will enter into a reciprocal relationship with God, embrace God's ethical instructions embodied in the law, and live according to God's will.

God will be the international arbiter and judge of all conflicts and disputes. War will no longer be the recourse by which disagreements are resolved. War will no longer be the strategy that the rich and the powerful employ in order to increase their wealth and power by subjugating and exploiting the weak. Consequently, the manufacture of weapons for warfare, whether for conquest or defense,

> WAR WILL NO LONGER BE THE STRATEGY THAT THE RICH AND THE POWERFUL EMPLOY IN ORDER TO INCREASE THEIR WEALTH AND POWER BY SUBJUGATING AND EXPLOITING THE WEAK.

will naturally end. "They shall beat their swords into plowshares and their spears into pruning hooks. Nation shall not lift up sword against nation, neither shall they learn war any more" (v. 4). A new age of agricultural production will initiate the equalization of goods and services for all people. There will be no more dominators or dominated, and justice and peace will finally have been actualized. Isaiah calls upon Israel to embrace this vision and live according to it: "O house of Jacob, come, let us walk in the light of the Lord!" (v. 5).

In this context it must be remembered that Jerusalem and its temple were superseded by the New Israel that Jesus constituted during his ministry and that God established by resurrecting Jesus from the dead. Mark 15:38 and Matt. 27:50 are especially decisive in this respect. When Jesus died and the veil of the sanctuary was torn in two from top to bottom, God abandoned the temple forever. Jerusalem, therefore, can no longer serve as the architectonic center of the world. In its place the people of God embody the future of Jerusalem that the Old Testament envisioned. God's house is no longer a building of any kind but the living body of Christ, the worldwide community of human beings who gather in Christ's name and constitute the union between heaven and earth as they worship, pray, and, in their commitment to the fulfillment of God's will, engage in the work of justice and peace.

RESPONSIVE READING
PSALM 122 (RCL, BCP);
PSALM 122:1-2, 3-4, 4-5, 6-7, 8-9 (RC)

This song of ascent, like Psalms 120 through 134, was sung by Israel's pilgrims as they journeyed to Jerusalem, the city of "shalom," their architectonic center of the world, in order to celebrate the great religious feasts that reinforced their covenantal relationship with Yahweh. Standing within the gates of the city, they remember the joy of anticipation they felt as they planned their pilgrimage to "the house of the Lord" for the festival they would memorialize in community with their fellow Israelites. Already here, on the threshold of the navel of the earth, they experience the solidarity that Jerusalem infuses in them under the rule and judgments of the Davidic dynasty. But their objective is the temple, "the house of the Lord," where a greater solidarity will be expressed in their worship of God as they offer up their sacrifices and, in their prayers of thanksgiving, remember to "Pray for the peace of Jerusalem" (v. 6).

The worship of God in the temple, prayers for peace offered during that worship, and the just rule and righteous judgments of the rulers of the Davidic dynasty—these are the necessary collaborative acts and the actions of all God's people, the rulers as well as the ruled, that will establish the "shalom" that the very name of Jerusalem incorporates. The thrones of the house of David were set up for judgment. Because God decreed that it should be so, the expectation is that the judgments will be equitable and just for all the people. To love Jerusalem, therefore, is to make a commitment to the future that God wills for it by praying for peace, presupposing that those who rule will also be committed to that same future. The outcome will be prosperity and "peace . . . within your walls and security within your towers" (v. 7).

SECOND READING
ROMANS 13:11-14 (RCL, RC); ROMANS 13:8-14 (BCP)

In the third major section of Romans, chapters 12–15, the apostle Paul summarizes the ethics of Christian life and discipleship. The opening summons of chapter 12, "present your bodies as a living sacrifice to God," indicates that the animal sacrifices at the Temple Mount of ancient Jerusalem have been superseded by a discipleship that follows Jesus into death and resurrection. Membership in the body of Christ establishes the equality of all believers, while the differences among them is distinguished by their individual gifts that enrich their community and the global world in which they live. From within the Christian paradox of freedom and indebtedness, Paul offers guidelines in chapters 14–15 to resolve the problem of the differences of individual piety within the Christian community, differences that so easily generate conflict and alienation within the body of Christ.

In the middle of this section on Christian ethics, the much misinterpreted chapter 13, Paul clarifies the Christian's relationship to the authorities of government within that same paradox of freedom and indebtedness. Christians are exhorted to subordinate themselves to the state by obeying its laws. They are obliged to do that! At the same time, however, they retain their moral independence in their subordination to the state, and their conscience always remains under their own sovereignty and jurisdiction. The boundaries of their freedom and indebtedness are determined by the divine love that originates from their membership in the body of Christ: "Owe no one anything, except to love one another" (v. 8). Love, therefore, is the only debt, the only obligation, that is given in freedom without imposing any limitations on when, where, how, and to whom it is expressed. "Love is the fulfilling of the law" (v. 10). In love one also fulfills the laws of the state. Within its boundaries there is no place for retaliation of any kind, neither toward other human beings or toward the institutions and offices of the state: "Do not be conquered by evil, but conquer evil by the good" (12:21). Since this verse is the transition between chapters 12 and 13, it also pertains to the Christian's relationship to the state, especially when Christians suffer evil at the hands of the state.

The foundation and the basis of this ethic of love that establishes the boundaries of both freedom and obligation in relationship to all human beings and human institutions is the eschatological reality of a new creation, a new moral order, that has been actualized by the death and resurrection of Jesus Christ. Eschatologically speaking, the vision of Isa. 2:1-5 has been inaugurated. The birth of Jesus, which Advent anticipates, marks the beginning of a new creation, a new humanity. According to Paul, this new time, the *kairos*, has only begun to dawn. It may be nearer than it was when we first believed, but it is visible only as the first glimmers of dawn, nothing more perhaps than that first orange-purple glow in the eastern sky. For us 2,000 years later, the brightness of this new dawn seems to have become shrouded by clouds. Whether the present reality of God's rule is viewed with the optimism of Paul or with a muted realism that is based on 2,000 years of the apparent continuing domination of the old moral order, the revitalization and reinforcement of this eschatological reality of a new creation depends on the fulfillment of the apostle's exhortation in vv. 12–14, "Let us put off the works of darkness and put on the weapons of light." The concluding imperative of this text employs the analogy of reaching adulthood and its responsibilities in Roman culture by putting on the *toga*, the garment that represents the coming of age, "Instead put on the Lord Jesus Christ" (v. 14). The only material evidence that our society and our world have of the reality of this new creation and its new humanity is its embodiment in the lives of those who regard themselves to be disciples of Jesus Christ. Advent is a time of preparation to determine how the birth of the Christ can be celebrated by a greater awareness of the very concrete responsibilities that arise out of "putting on the Lord Jesus Christ" and embracing the freedom and the obligations that God's love in us imposes upon our discipleship.

> THE ONLY MATERIAL EVIDENCE THAT OUR SOCIETY AND OUR WORLD HAVE OF THE REALITY OF THIS NEW CREATION AND ITS NEW HUMANITY IS ITS EMBODIMENT IN THE LIVES OF THOSE WHO REGARD THEMSELVES TO BE DISCIPLES OF JESUS CHRIST.

THE GOSPEL

MATTHEW 24:36-44 (RCL);
MATTHEW 24:37-44 (BCP, RC)

The fifth and final of the five great discourses of Jesus in Matthew's Gospel is divided into two parts. It begins with an indictment of the scribes and Pharisees, 23:1-39, and continues into a lengthy exposition on eschatology that culminates in three parables of warning, 24:10—25:46. Jesus is seated on the Mount of Olives, and he addresses all of his disciples, not merely the four named in Mark 13:3. The crowds are excluded. The mountain, the only one named in the Gospel and located in Jerusalem, has an eschatological character. From it the apocalyptic event of Jesus' entry into Jerusalem took place (Matt. 21:10); on it he will instruct his followers in the "last things"; and at this mountain, after his institution of the Eucharist, he will announce the beginning of the end when God will strike the shepherd and the sheep will be scattered (26:31).

The disciples' question, "When will these things be *and* what is the sign of your parousia and the consummation of the age?" (24:3), serves as the point of departure for Jesus' teaching. Only Matthew, among the evangelists, employs the term "parousia" as well as "the consummation of the age." The conjunction "and" that separates them in 24:3b implies a direct relationship between them. The first question, "When will these things be?" relates to the judgment Jesus pronounced on the temple in 24:2. Jesus poses many signs, one of them being the destruction of the temple, but all of them are no longer indications of the imminent end but only the commencement of the birth pangs of the new age.

The climax of Jesus' eschatological teaching and the explicit answer to the second half of the disciples' question, "What is the sign of your parousia and the consummation of the age?" comes in 24:29-31. "Immediately after the suffering of those days," when the birth pains have become almost unbearable, is the time when the new age will finally emerge from the womb of Mother History. There will be a dazzling display of apocalyptic phenomena that will plunge the world into a primeval condition of chaos: "the sun will be darkened, and the moon will not give its light; the stars will fall from heaven." Last of all, "the powers of heavens will be shaken" (v. 29). This collapse of the heavenly luminaries corresponds to the quake that will reduce the earth to its original state of chaos at the time of Jesus' death. In the future, after the cosmic prelude and after "the powers of the heavens have been shaken," the new creation will finally come into full being. Then the community of the New Human Being, "the Son of Man," will be born. Its birth, Jesus declares, will be marked by "the sign of the Son of Man" in the sky (v. 30). Since all the luminaries have been extinguished and the cosmos has been reduced to primordial darkness, "the sign of the Son of Man" must be a great light signaling the dawn of a new day. The sign of the birth of the Messiah was a star which, when it reached its zenith point in the sky and stood directly over where the child was, announced the beginnings of the messianic age. For the appearance of the New Human Being, " the Son of Man," to inaugurate the full-term birth of the community of the New Human Being, the same identification between the sign of the star and the reality it represents seems logical and appropriate.

This Gospel text for the First Sunday in Advent returns to the first part of the disciples' question in 24:3, the question of "when." The metaphor of the fig tree sprouting leaves and bearing fruit hints at a means of ascertaining the nearness of the end. "When you see *all* these things, you know it is at the gates" (v. 33). That "all these things" will take place is certain. The goal will be achieved! Heaven and earth will be dissolved, but Jesus' words will never pass away because they already are the reality they project. Yet no one knows the precise time of the dawning of this new day, "neither the angels . . . nor the Son, but *only* the Father" (v. 36).

Various analogies give warning of the style of life that this eschatological reality proscribes. A characterization of the time preceding the parousia is derived from the story of the flood. In that time of crisis, those who were completely absorbed in selfish and self-indulging pursuits, "eating and drinking, marrying and giving in marriage" (v. 38), were swept away by the great cataclysm. People will be engaged in their vocational activity: "Two farmers will be working in a field, one is taken and one is left. Two women will be grinding at the mill, one is taken and one is left" (vv. 40-41). It is vigilance that is required, because no one knows the time of the end. "If the housemaster knew at what hour the burglar comes, he would watch and not permit (him) to break into his house. On account of this, at an hour you do not suppose the Son of the Human Being is coming" (vv. 43-44).

> IT IS VIGILANCE THAT IS REQUIRED, BECAUSE NO ONE KNOWS THE TIME OF THE END.

SECOND SUNDAY OF ADVENT

DECEMBER 5, 2004

REVISED COMMON	EPISCOPAL (BCP)	ROMAN CATHOLIC
Isa. 11:1-10	Isa. 11:1-10	Isa. 11:1-10
Ps. 72:1-7, 18-19	Psalm 72 or 72:1-8	Ps. 72:1-2, 7-8, 12-13, 17
Rom. 15:4-13	Rom. 15:4-13	Rom. 15:4-9
Matt. 3:1-12	Matt. 3:1-12	Matt. 3:1-12

FIRST READING
ISAIAH 11:1-10 (RCL, BCP, RC)

Isaiah opens another window onto the future of Israel that has consequences for all the peoples of the world. It is a vision that is congruous with the oracle of 2:1-5. When swords are beaten into plowshares, and nations no longer make war against each other, the realities of paradise will have been restored to human existence. Therefore, if the human disease of alienation is eliminated from historical existence, it must necessarily have a corresponding affect on the world of nature and its creatures. "The wolf shall live with the lamb" and "the lion shall eat straw like the ox" (vv. 6, 7). That is also the conclusion that is drawn by the apostle Paul in Rom. 8:21, "the creation itself will be set free from its bondage to decay and will obtain the freedom of the glory of the children of God." Although the prospect of Isaiah 11 is oriented to the future of God's elect people, Israel, v. 10 explicitly includes the nations of the world in this reconstitution of all things. In this context a literal translation of the Hebrew text is more apposite than the rendition of the NRSV: "It will be on that day that the root of Jesse, which stands for a sign of the peoples, to him the nations will seek, and glory will be his resting place."

The agent of this reconstitution of all things will be a shoot from the stump of Jesse, a king from the house of David. He will be the ideal king, empowered by God's Spirit, and therefore he will rule as God's surrogate. Endowed with the gifts of the Spirit, he will be equipped with paramount qualifications to govern beneficently on God's behalf. His divinely endowed intellectual capacity will enable him to grasp comprehensively the realities of his kingdom and to respond with wisdom and understanding. His administrative capabilities will disclose judicious counsel. "He shall not judge by what his eyes see or decide by what his ears hear; but with righteousness he shall judge the poor and decide with equity for the meek of the earth" (vv. 3b-4). The power that he exercises in his rule will not be based on military equipment and weapons of war. The authority of his person and the words that he speaks will be sufficient to subdue those who oppose him. For his spirituality will be reinforced by his knowledge and fear of God (v. 5): "Righteousness shall be the belt around his waist, and faithfulness the belt around his loins" (that area below the waist that is considered to be the seat of physical strength and generative power).

It appears to be impossible to determine at what time in Isaiah's career this prophecy was spoken, but it may not matter. Isaiah was not only disillusioned by the rule of Ahaz. Even his anticipation of the birth of a new child in 7:14 (who would be Immanuel and who, according to 9:6, would become "Wonderful in counsel is God the Mighty, the Everlasting Father, the Prince of Peace") was not fulfilled in the person and reign of Hezekiah. Ultimately, therefore, the vision of 11:1-10 looks beyond both the new child and Hezekiah to a descendant of King David who, because of his divine empowerment and divinely endowed rule, will inaugurate a new age for Israel and the nations of the world. The strong will no longer prey on the weak, either in the realm of human relationships or in the realm of wild beasts and domesticated animals. "They shall not hurt or destroy on all my holy mountain, for the earth shall be full of the knowledge of Yahweh as the waters cover the sea" (v. 9). The human disease of alienation will be healed, and the resulting reconciliation will enable human beings to relate to each other equitably for the mutual establishment of justice and peace.

ISAIAH'S VISION MARKS THE INAUGURATION OF THE TRAJECTORY OF THE SON OF DAVID CHRISTOLOGY THAT CULMINATES IN THE EARLY CHURCH'S INTERPRETATION OF JESUS AS THE MESSIAH, THE ANOINTED SON OF DAVID.

Here is the beginning of messianic eschatology! Isaiah's vision marks the inauguration of the trajectory of the Son of David Christology that culminates in the early church's interpretation of Jesus as the Messiah, the anointed Son of David. The Christmas stories of Matthew and Luke feature this christological perspective, and Mark and John incorporate it into their individual presentations of the good news of Jesus Christ. As significant as it is for the interpretation of Jesus' person and work, it must not be forgotten, even in Advent and at Christmas, that Jesus did not want to be a king and therefore rejected Simon Peter's confession of him as the Messiah. Mark 8:29-33 and 12:35-37 are decisive in this respect. It is the prophetic act of an unnamed woman (Mark 14:3-9) who anoints Jesus for his burial with a very expensive nard perfume that enables him at his trial before the Sanhedrin to acknowledge his identity as the Messiah (Mark 14:62), but as the Messiah in death. When Jesus dies as "the King of the Jews," his Son of David messiahship is terminated, and by his resurrection from the dead the door to a new relationship is opened that establishes him as the "Son of Man" and draws his followers into a communion of sisters and brothers.

RESPONSIVE READING

PSALM 72:1-7, 18-19 (RCL);
PSALM 72 or 72:1-8 (BCP);
PSALM 72:1-2, 7-8, 12-13, 17 (RC)

Psalm 72, as though inspired by Isaiah 11, expresses a prayer of multiple petitions that appeals to God to raise up the ideal king. As in the Lord's Prayer, virtually every petition is spoken in the third person imperative—instead of the second person imperative—and is to be translated as a mild command: "May he judge the poor of the people and save the children of the needy" (v. 4). "May the mountains bear peace to the people" (v. 3). What God does for the king will hopefully be translated by the king into commensurate deeds for the people. When that kind of exchange takes place, mountains, as representative of the land of Israel, are entreated to be bearers of the peace that this king establishes.

The first and indeed the consummate plea is that he be endowed with God's justice. For, if Israel's covenant with Yahweh is to be fulfilled, the one who rules Israel on God's behalf must be like God in the administration of justice. That qualification above all will guarantee political stability and economic prosperity and insure "shalom" for every member of society: "In his days let righteousness flourish and peace grow until the moon is no more" (v. 7).

The decisive character that is ascribed to this anticipated king is "saving the children of the needy and crushing the oppressor" (v. 4). This is repeated in vv. 12-14, but now as deeds that are being fulfilled and no longer as petitions or imperatives. Because of the justice and peace that he constitutes, the psalmist prays, "May he have dominion from sea to sea and from the River to the ends of the earth" (v. 8). The river is the Euphrates, and to the Israelites it is the eastern boundary of their world. The petition of vv. 10-11 extends his rule all the way to Spain, "May the kings of Tarshish and of the islands render tribute; may the kings of Sheba and Seba offer their gifts; may all kings prostrate themselves before him (and) all nations serve him." Accordingly, the territory of this king's rule includes the entire then-known world: from the Euphrates to Spain, and from Sheba in Arabia to Seba in Ethiopia.

The doxology of vv. 18 and 19, the praise of God that is appended to each "book" of the Psalms, concludes this psalm of Book 2 and directs attention to the one who has been entreated by the preceding petitions. By acknowledging that it is God "who alone does wondrous things" (v. 18), this prayerful messianic psalm blesses God in anticipation of its forthcoming fulfillment.

SECOND READING
ROMANS 15:4-13 (RCL, BCP);
ROMANS 15:4-9 (RC)

With vv. 4-13 the apostle Paul concludes the third major section of his letter to the Romans. (What follows in 15:14-33 conveys personal matters addressed to his anticipated readers.) It is a consummate ending of the lengthy theological discourse that moved from an analysis of the human condition (1:18—3:20) to an explication of its resolution (3:21—8:39), continuing on to a dialectical interpretation of salvation history that includes both Jews and Gentiles, and finally culminating with an exposition of Christian ethics. This remarkable summation of the theology that he worked out in his relationship to the congregations he established in the eastern half of the Mediterranean world leads him to the hermeneutical observation, "For whatever was written in former days was written for our instruction, so that by steadfastness and by the encouragement of the scriptures we might have hope" (v. 4). Paul is enunciating the hermeneutical principle of interpreting the scriptures first and foremost in relation to our own context, a principle that is dialectically related to our employment of the historical-critical method to recover the original context of the biblical texts. In other words, the history of Israel is our history! The messianically oriented prophecies of Isaiah and the prayers of the psalms for the ideal king were also spoken to us and for us. Isaiah 11 has been fulfilled! The root of Jesse has come in the person of Jesus of Nazareth. He inaugurated the reign of God, and his resurrection from the dead established that reign in our continued historical existence. As is obvious, that fulfillment is not complete. Wolves still eat lambs; the lion does not yet eat straw like an ox. The weak are still exploited and dominated by the strong, and injustice abounds everywhere. If the reality of this fulfillment in terms of the empirical presence of God's reign is to be manifested to the world, at least in part, it depends on the extent to which Christians everywhere manifest its truth by their ethical conduct and lifestyle. Our endurance, our steadfastness, as we are

THE ROOT OF JESSE HAS COME IN THE PERSON OF JESUS OF NAZARETH. HE INAUGURATED THE REIGN OF GOD, AND HIS RESURRECTION FROM THE DEAD ESTABLISHED THAT REIGN IN OUR CONTINUED HISTORICAL EXISTENCE.

en-courage-ed by the scriptures, and as we live in harmony with each other, glorify God because the reality of scriptural fulfillment is represented by our embodiment of God's rule in our historical existence.

For a more persuasive witness of the reality of this fulfillment before the world, Paul urges his readers to accept each other into the circle of Christ's fellowship. Earlier in v. 5 he voiced the prayer that God would grant the readers of his letter "to live in harmony with one another." That is the translation of the NRSV. The Greek text literally says, "The God of endurance and en-courage-ment give you to think the same thing among each other in accordance with Christ Jesus." The history of the Christian church demonstrates that it is very difficult for Christians to think the same thing. Moreover, v. 5 (like 1 Cor. 1:10) is often interpreted to signify intellectual conformity. But "to think the same thing" means to have the same consciousness that is open to the fullness of life: at least to all those who claim to be Christians, if not also to all the human beings that are encountered along life's way. For Christians are exhorted to accept each other into the circle of Christ's fellowship even as they were accepted into that same fellowship by Christ. That kind of unity of the one and the many, Christ and the members of his body, is a manifestation of the glory of God.

In v. 8 Paul pronounces the fulfillment of the prophetic promises, "For I say [that] Christ has become a servant of circumcision on behalf of the truth of God in order to confirm the promises of the fathers and in order that the nations (or Gentiles) might glorify God for [his] mercy." To support his pronouncement of fulfillment, he proceeds to cite four Old Testament texts, all of them quotations that distinguish the fulfillment that pertains specifically to the nations: Ps. 18:50; Deut. 32:43; Ps. 116:1 (all from the Septuagint). Like the previous texts, the fourth and last in v. 12 is also drawn from the Septuagint, but it is a composite of Isa. 11:1; Gen. 49:10; and finally Isa. 11:10.

The apostle ends with a benediction (v. 13) that is most appropriate for his concluding words of scriptural fulfillment and in our context for this Second Sunday of Advent.

The Gospel
MATTHEW 3:1-12 (RCL, BCP, RC)

Unanticipated and unannounced, a new personality emerges in Matthew's story of "the origin of Jesus Christ." John the Baptizer intrudes into this narrative world as a stranger. Nothing is said of his origin. He is simply there "in the wilderness of Judea" (v. 1). He is calling the people to repentance, "for the rule of the heavens has drawn near" (v. 2). (The author of Matthew's Gospel prefers to substitute the modifying phrase "of the heavens" in place of the one that is consistently used throughout Mark's Gospel, "of God." "The heavens," in Hebrew *hashamaim*, served as a circumlocution for the divine name.) John's significance and the import of his message are established by the quotation of Isa. 40:3 in v. 3. He is the voice of the last times calling for the repentance of Israel. Repentance is imperative because God is coming: "Prepare the way of the Lord, make his paths straight." The crisis of the moment, God's imminent coming, is signaled not only by the announced fulfillment of Isa. 40:3 but also the fulfillment of Mal. 4:5. For John, who is wearing a garment of camel's hair and a leather belt around his waist, is none other than the prophet Elijah, the great representative of the prophets who has returned for a second career as God's forerunner. The clause of v. 4a "clothing of camel's hair with a leather belt around his waist") is almost a literal rendition of 2 Kings 1:8. His appearance, therefore,

ON THIS SECOND SUNDAY OF ADVENT, CHRISTIANS ARE CHALLENGED BY JOHN TO GET READY FOR THE ESCHATOLOGICAL EVENT OF CHRISTMAS, THE COMING OF GOD IN AND THROUGH THE BIRTH OF JESUS THE CHRIST, THE FULFILLMENT OF ISAIAH 11.

foreshadows the end of the old moral order that is dominated by the human disease of alienation and the resulting perpetration of evil. God is coming—at last! Through the repentance that is expressed in baptism, Israel can prepare for this eschatological event. On this Second Sunday of Advent, Christians are challenged by John to get ready for the eschatological event of Christmas, the coming of God in and through the birth of Jesus the Christ, the fulfillment of Isaiah 11.

John's success is impressive: "Then the people of Jerusalem and all Judea were going out to him, and all the region around the Jordan, and they were baptized by him in the river Jordan, confessing their sins" (vv. 5-6). The religious leaders are among them. They specifically—not the masses as in Luke 3:7—are singled out for denunciation. Like all the others, they have been baptized, confessing their sins. But the oral act of confessing sins is not enough. A genuine change of consciousness that is authenticated by corresponding deeds is what God requires. Ethnic or national identity as sons of Abraham is no guarantee for security in the impending crisis. Judgment is imminent: "already the ax is being laid to the root of the tree" (v. 10) where the fruit of repentance is not in evidence. To avoid an anti-Judaism bias, it is necessary to remember that Matthew's Gospel was written in the early 80s of the first century when Judaism was in crisis because of its loss of the temple. After Jochanan ben Zakkai, who by an arrangement with the Romans had been secretly taken out of Jerusalem before its destruction in 70 C.E., had begun the reconstitution of Judaism on the basis of the Pharisaic ideology, Gamaliel II pursued a more rigorous program of imposing that ideology on the Jewish people. The evangelist Matthew is addressing a community of Jewish Christians who are caught up in that conflict.

Matthew 3:11-12 should not be separated from vv. 7-10. There is no indication in the text that these words are directed at another group or the crowds in general. These verses continue John's address to the Pharisees and Sadducees and emphasize the preparatory character of his baptism. It is "for repentance!" They, the Jewish religious leaders, are to know that there is another baptism that will be administered by the one who comes after him, "the one who is stronger than I, whose sandals I am not worthy to carry" (v. 11). John does not say who this is, but the evangelist intimates the identification by quoting Isa. 40:3 in v. 3. It must be Yahweh! Moreover, John as the personification of Elijah reinforces that identification, for according to Mal. 3:1 and 4:5, Elijah is God's forerunner. In accordance with the expectation of Jewish apocalypticism, God is coming to render judgment, and in the great separation that takes place, the grain will be gathered into the barn and the chaff will be burned with inextinguishable fire (v. 12).

All too often Jesus is identified as the one whom John is serving as forerunner. But his characterization of the one who "is coming after me and who is stronger than I, whose sandals I am not worthy to carry" cannot refer to Jesus. In the Jewish expectation of that era, Elijah was always and only the forerunner of God, not the Messiah. Moreover, in the narrative world of Matthew's Gospel, Jesus does not baptize with the Holy Spirit. It is God who does that, and Jesus is the one who is baptized, as v. 16 indicates. Finally, as will become evident in Matt. 11:2-11, Jesus does not practice separation. He will not engage in thoroughly cleansing the threshing floor, gathering the grain into the barn and burning the chaff with unquenchable fire.

Yet it is not the Lord God who appears but Jesus. That is the irony of that moment. However, when Jesus comes up out of the Jordan River, God does come, as John predicted; and Jesus is baptized by the Holy Spirit. Although, as v. 11 indicates, John had made that promise to everyone coming to his baptism, only Jesus experiences its fulfillment. The text for the First Sunday after the Epiphany, Matt. 3:13-17, will elucidate this startling and unexpected development.

THIRD SUNDAY OF ADVENT

DECEMBER 12, 2004

REVISED COMMON	EPISCOPAL (BCP)	ROMAN CATHOLIC
Isa. 35:1-10	Isa. 35:1-10	Isa. 35:1-6a, 10
Ps. 146:5-10	Psalm 146	Ps. 146:6-7, 8-9, 9-10
or Luke 1:47-55	or 146:4-9	
James 5:7-10	James 5:7-10	James 5:7-10
Matt. 11:2-11	Matt. 11:2-11	Matt. 11:2-11

FIRST READING

ISAIAH 35:1-10 (RCL, BCP);
ISAIAH 35:1-6a, 10 (RC)

Here is another window that Isaiah opens to Israel's future! As in 2:1-5 and 11:1-10, the prophet offers a glimpse of a comprehensive restoration that will affect both the realm of nature and the physical conditions of God's people. Above all, those who have been afflicted with physiological defects and psychological disabilities will be healed: the blind, the deaf, the mute, and the lame. Controversial in the interpretation of this passage is the problem of the original context of this text. What is its location in the history of Israel? Was it spoken by Isaiah during his forty-year career (740–700 B.C.E.) or by his anonymous successor who prophesied during the Babylonian exile?

The vibrant description of this forthcoming restoration, especially the disclosure of a highway, "The Way of Holiness," linked to the promise of return (v. 10), might have been spoken originally by the anonymous prophet of Second Isaiah. It is noteworthy that the very words of v. 10 are repeated in 51:11, "And the ransomed of the LORD shall return and come to Zion with singing; everlasting joy shall be upon their heads; they shall obtain joy and gladness, and sorrow and sighing shall flee away." The placement of chapter 35, therefore, could be attributed to the final redactor of the book of Isaiah in order to prepare the reader for the oracles of Second Isaiah, chapters 40–55, by which the prophet had assured the exiled people of God in Babylon of a glorious restoration to their homeland. Isaiah's pronouncement of judgment on the sons of Hezekiah, who will be carried off into

Babylon (39:5-7), indicates that the final editor of the sixty-six chapters of Isaiah attempted to put such transitions into place in order to promote a sense of unity within the book as a whole. If, then, 35:1-10 was addressed originally to Israel in the Babylonian captivity, its historical context would have to be located sometime between 587 and 538 B.C.E.

On the other hand, 35:1-10 stands between an oracle blistering with the fury of God's wrath that is addressed to all the nations in general and to Edom in particular (34:1-17) and an account of Sennacherib's campaigns in Judea, his siege of Jerusalem, Hezekiah's prayer, and the miraculous destruction of the Assyrian army. This location would tend to place 35:1-10 in the context of 701 B.C.E. Sennacherib's doom has already been predicted in chapter 33, and his demise, his "being spoiled when he has ceased to spoil" (33:1), is representative of the retribution that God will exact from all the nations of the world. In stark contrast, Judea, devastated by the Assyrian army and deserted like a wilderness, will be transformed into a blossoming and fertile land: "The glory of Lebanon shall be given to it, the excellency of Carmel and Sharon; and they shall see the glory of the LORD" (35:2).

Homiletically at least, the problem of the original context of 35:1-10 should have little or no effect in relating this text to the Third Sunday of Advent. The meaning in front of the text corresponds to the prophecies of 2:1-5 and 11:1-10. God is coming! God is coming to save! That is also the meaning of Advent. The restoration that God is inaugurating will be accompanied by wonderful reversals (vv. 5 and 6). The eyes of the blind will be opened, the eyes of both the spiritually and the physically blind. The ears of those who hear but really do not hear and therefore do

> GOD IS COMING! GOD IS COMING TO SAVE! THAT IS ALSO THE MEANING OF ADVENT. THE RESTORATION THAT GOD IS INAUGURATING WILL BE ACCOMPANIED BY WONDERFUL REVERSALS.

not understand, to cite the words of Jesus in Mark 4:12, will be unstopped. The psychologically crippled as well as the physically lame will leap into freedom like gazelles; and the tongue of the mute will be loosened to sing. These are the realities that Christmas anticipates. These are the very conditions that Jesus will begin to fulfill in his ministry. Opened eyes, hearing ears, and people in communication with each other will constitute a society of free people who in community and communion will collaborate to achieve justice and equality for all its members. Human beings will become fully human again, as they recover the glory, honor, autonomy, and self-determination that the Creator originally willed to them, according to Psalm 8 and its reflections on the creation story of Genesis 1. The exile—whether after Sennacherib's defeat or after the Babylonian captivity—will end. The endemic alienation that separates and divides human beings from each other will cease. As an echo of Isaiah 11, "No lion will be there, nor any ravenous beast!" (35:9), regardless of whether that animal nature is incarnated in nations or individual tyrants. The redeemed shall walk in safety and in peace.

RESPONSIVE READING

PSALM 146:5-10 or LUKE 1:47-55 (RCL); PSALM 146 or 146:4-9 (BCP); PSALM 146:6-7, 8-9, 9-10 (RC)

As Christmas draws nearer, the responsive reading of Psalm 146 reinforces the vision of Isaiah. God alone can actualize the future that the prophet previewed. Kings and princes are unscrupulous! They will not beat their swords into plowshares. Even if the "shoot from the stump of Jesse" will inaugurate the wonderful conditions of paradise, as Isaiah 11 anticipates, it will only happen because the royal Son of David will serve as God's surrogate.

Psalm 146, however, prefers to look to the ultimate trustworthy and reliable ruler, the Creator "who made heaven and earth, the sea, and all that is in them" (v. 6)—Yet it is not power alone but the "truth"—the Hebrew word *emeth* means "truth," not "faith"—that the Creator "keeps forever" that is the foundation of the trust to which Israel is summoned. God alone, therefore, is the unfailing source of the restoration and renewal that humanity hopes for, as specifically vv. 7-9 affirm. The beatitude of v. 5 enunciates the well-being of those who put their trust in the God of Zion. God will reign forever, as v. 10 states, because "his" dependability and integrity are manifested in the activity of "his" divine offspring, the Son, who will begin to fulfill the expectations of vv. 7-9 that the psalmist ascribes to God. The appropriate response, therefore, is "Hallelujah," the opening summons of Psalm 146.

LUKE 1:47-55 (RCL alt.)

Mary's hymn, the *Magnificat*, conveys the social, economic, and political realities of God's activity in history and more specifically in the lives of her people, Israel. Surprisingly, however, she enunciates these realities of salvation in the aorist tense as though they have already occurred. Very likely these verbs are to be interpreted as ingressive aorists, verbs whose action has already begun in view of the reality that Mary's fetus represents. Elizabeth, her cousin, has blessed her twice. In the future, all generations will bless her, for her present shamelessness—in her honor-shame society—will be transformed into worldwide benediction.

The *Magnificat* appears to have two strophes. The first, vv. 46-50, states the basis of Mary's exultation and confidence. Her spirit can begin to exult in God because

Elizabeth's benediction is an affirmation that God has looked upon the lowliness of "his" "slave-woman." Her confidence is founded on "the Mighty One who began to do great things for me" and on "his mercy (that extends) to generations and generations of those who fear him." It is God's power and mercy that will accomplish the anticipated revolution that Mary sings about in the second strophe of vv. 51-55. As certain as she is of bearing "the Son of the Most High" in her pregnancy, so equally is she certain of the forthcoming transformation of the social construction of reality.

SECOND READING
JAMES 5:7-10 (RCL, BCP, RC)

The parousia is near! As James approaches the end of his letter, he poses the eschatological reality of what today is generally referred to as "the second coming." It is intended as a warning, perhaps especially to the rich who, in the agricultural society of that age, gained their wealth by exploiting the labor of the peasants who worked their land (v. 4).

However, it is also directed to the general addressees of his letter who, because of their social status—and perhaps also because of their Christian faith—are sojourners, *kathoikoi*, people without citizenship who have no rights and privileges in the society of the Roman Empire. They are exhorted to wait patiently for "the coming of the Lord" (v. 1), like the farmer who waits for the early and latter rains in order to gain an abundant crop. Like other authors of New Testament writings, James admonishes his addressees to wait patiently but at the same time to let this forthcoming fulfillment determine their lifestyle and ethical conduct. Their daily behavior is to mirror the anticipated consummation of history.

> LIKE OTHER AUTHORS OF NEW TESTAMENT WRITINGS, JAMES ADMONISHES HIS ADDRESSEES TO WAIT PATIENTLY BUT AT THE SAME TIME TO LET THIS FORTHCOMING FULFILLMENT DETERMINE THEIR LIFESTYLE AND ETHICAL CONDUCT.

Although James is focused on "the second coming," Advent is an anticipation of "the first coming." The word "parousia" simply means "coming" and therefore can be drawn into the season of Advent as an expression of the anticipation of God's coming in Jesus Christ. Accordingly, the exhortations of vv. 7-10 are also applicable in this season of Advent as Christians around the world await "the coming of the Lord" and the inauguration of the revolution Mary voiced in her *Magnificat*, which was previewed by Isaiah and Psalm 146.

THE GOSPEL

MATTHEW 11:2-11 (RCL, BCP, RC)

Jesus' messianic works have begun to elicit different reactions. At the conclusion of the narrative of Book Two, the crowds marveled at the healing of the mute demoniac (9:33). The Pharisees, on the other hand, attributed the deed to the agency of "the chief of the demons" (9:34). The narrator continues to recount Jesus' career by introducing the response of the imprisoned John the Baptizer at the beginning of Book Three, "Having heard about . . . the works of the Messiah, John, sending through his disciples, said to him, 'Are you the coming one or do we await another?'" (11:2). "The works of the Messiah" are the basis for evaluating Jesus' person and identity. The masses wonder, the Pharisees malevolently associate Jesus with the forces of evil, and John the Baptizer has misgivings: "Are you the Messiah?" His uncertainty must be understood in the light of his original expectation, "The coming one . . . will thoroughly sweep his threshing floor. He will gather his grain into the barn, but the chaff he will burn with inextinguishable fire" (3:11-12). John anticipated his successor to be the great separator and assumed that his mission consisted essentially in exercising judgment. Evidently he was interpreting the person and work of the Messiah in terms of the traditional categories of apocalyptic eschatology, and therefore it is no wonder that he was troubled by the inconsistency between his prediction of 3:11-12 and the subsequent "works of the Messiah."

Jesus himself acknowledged this kind of activity in 10:34, "Do not think that I came to cast peace on the earth. I came not to cast peace but a sword. For I came to separate a man against his father and a daughter against her mother and a bride against her mother-in-law, and a human being's enemies [will be] the members of her/his household." Jesus does separate! His activity divides people into opposed groups and communities. The alienation that results induces controversy and conflict that generate hostility and end in separation.

But here Jesus responds to John's christological inquiry by referring to the works of healing and restoration that he has performed. He recites a list of the mighty works that are recorded in chapters 8–9: "The blind see again and the lame walk, the lepers are cleansed and the deaf hear and the dead are raised and the poor are evangelized" (v. 5). Although separation and division belong to his messianic activity, they are not his primary objective. They are necessary results of his works of reunion and restoration.

Lest the reader should denigrate John on the basis of his misgivings about Jesus, the narrator proceeds to present Jesus' evaluation of the Baptizer's person and work. John is not an ordinary prophet. He is the fulfillment of Mal. 3:1; he is the personification of Elijah, who precedes the coming of God and is therefore the last prophet of the old moral order. As such John belongs to the time of the law and the prophets. But he also stands—with one foot at least!—in the new order God has initiated by the wonderful birth of Jesus. His ambiguous identity and position is conveyed in Jesus' asseveration, "Amen I say to you, he has not been born . . . who is greater than John; but the least in the reign of God is greater than he" (v. 11).

John is a transitional figure in Christian eschatology. His appearance marks the end of exile, of alienation, of separation. At the same time, it also bears witness to the beginning of the long-awaited fulfillment of the prophetic visions of Isaiah and other Old Testament prophets, the inauguration of the divinely promised restoration and reunion. Separation occurs, and Jesus takes responsibility for it. But it is a separation that is generated by "the coming of the Lord" among those who insist on continuity and correspondence with revered ancient patterns and precedents, as well as those who resist change and transformation and prefer to cling to the old moral order and its hierarchical realities of power, wealth, and privilege. Advent is the time of anticipating this revolution that Mary, the mother of Jesus, believed had already begun because she was pregnant with the Christ child.

> JOHN IS A TRANSITIONAL FIGURE IN CHRISTIAN ESCHATOLOGY. HIS APPEARANCE MARKS THE END OF EXILE, OF ALIENATION, OF SEPARATION.

FOURTH SUNDAY OF ADVENT

DECEMBER 19, 2004

REVISED COMMON	EPISCOPAL (BCP)	ROMAN CATHOLIC
Isa. 7:10-16	Isa. 7:10-17	Isa. 7:10-14
Ps. 80:1-7, 17-19	Psalm 24 or 24:1-7	Ps. 24:1-2, 3-4, 5-6
Rom. 1:1-7	Rom.1:1-7	Rom.1:1-7
Matt. 1:18-25	Matt. 1:18-25	Matt. 1:18-24

FIRST READING

ISAIAH 7:10-16 (RCL);
ISAIAH 7:10-17 (BCP);
ISAIAH 7:10-14 (RC)

It must have been a dramatic encounter between the king and the prophet "at the end of the conduit of the upper pool on the road to the Fuller's Field" (7:3). Certainly it was an unusual context for King Ahaz to be confronted by Isaiah with a message of assurance and warning at a place outside the city of Jerusalem where lower-class workers were engaged in their craft of bleaching cloth. It was a time of crisis, for in 734 B.C.E. Rezin of Syria and Pekah of the northern kingdom of Israel had formed a coalition in the face of the threat of the Assyrian Empire, and they had "come up to Jerusalem to war against it" (7:1) in order to intimidate Ahaz into joining them in this alliance. Commanded to take his son Shear-jashub with him, Isaiah counseled Ahaz to "keep calm and be quiet" (7:4) for the Syro-Ephraimite coalition "will not stand" (7:7). "Within sixty-five years Ephraim will be broken and not be a people" (7:8). In 721 B.C.E., less than thirteen years later, Assyria destroyed Samaria and forever terminated the kingdom of Israel. (Dates and periods of time remain problematic, especially in an attempt to correlate Isaiah 7–8 with 2 Kings 15:30-37.)

In this crisis Ahaz is urged by Isaiah to ask for a sign that will legitimate the prophecy the latter has spoken. But he refuses, "I will not ask, neither will I test Yahweh" (7:12). It is a response that seems valiant and stalwart. Why should God be put to a test? Why does God's Word have to be legitimated? However, before

Isaiah pressed the king to request a sign, he had delineated the consequences of unbelief, "If you will not believe, you will not stand" (7:9). To believe, therefore, requires asking God for a sign so that Ahaz can be reassured and therefore act in accordance with the prophecy. But he does not believe! Nevertheless, to prove that God's Word will be fulfilled, God gives him a sign anyway: "The young woman (*almah*) will conceive and bear a son and she will call his name Immanuel" (7:14). The Hebrew word *almah* means "young woman." It may also mean "maiden," but Hebrew has a technical term for "virgin" (*bethulah*), which Jeremiah and Lamentations applied to "the Daughter of Zion." The Septuagint translated *almah* as *parthenos*, the Greek term for "virgin," perhaps identifying *almah* in the light of the prophetic tradition as "the Daughter of Zion." It is the Septuagint text of Isa. 7:14 that is quoted in Matt. 1:23.

Interpreted in the context of the sign that Isaiah gave Ahaz, the woman who would give birth to a boy and name him Immanuel could be the wife of Ahaz or the wife of Isaiah. Historical scholarship generally chooses between these two possibilities. If she is the wife of Ahaz, the boy most likely would be her son Hezekiah, who succeeded his father as king of Judah and of whom 2 Kings 18:5 says, "He trusted in Yahweh the God of Israel, so that there was no one like him among all the kings of Judah after him, or among those who were before him." But according to Isaiah, before Immanuel reaches the age of moral discrimination, the land will have been devastated by the invading armies of Assyria. Agriculture will cease, and those who survive will depend on wild honey and the milk products of sheep and goats.

Although Isaiah pronounces judgment on Ahaz, he endorses the royal house of David. The original Immanuel may have been Hezekiah, but he did not, and very likely could not, fulfill the vision of Isaiah 11. Consequently, the sign of Immanuel became an eschatological vision for subsequent generations, a vision that the post-Easter Christian community claimed to have been fulfilled by the son that Mary gave birth to, and Joseph, the son of David, named Jesus. It is noteworthy that the shepherds, according to Luke 2:12, were given a sign by the angel of the Lord so that there would be a necessary correlation between the divine announcement of a savior and the unusual circumstances of stable and manger in which they would find the one designated as "Christ, Lord" (with no definite article).

> THE SIGN OF IMMANUEL BECAME AN ESCHATOLOGICAL VISION FOR SUBSEQUENT GENERATIONS, A VISION THAT THE POST-EASTER CHRISTIAN COMMUNITY CLAIMED TO HAVE BEEN FULFILLED BY THE SON THAT MARY GAVE BIRTH TO, AND JOSEPH, THE SON OF DAVID, NAMED JESUS.

RESPONSIVE READING
PSALM 80:1-7, 17-19 (RCL)

HERMAN C.
WAETJEN

Psalm 80 is a heart-rending cry invoking God, as the Shepherd of Israel, "Stir up your might and come to save us!" (v. 2). As the one whose throne is in the midst of Israel, represented by the Ark of the Covenant that is bolstered by the cherubim, God is petitioned as "God of hosts" to "shine forth" and "restore us" (vv. 2, 3), the people of Israel. According to v. 4, God has been angry for a long time and therefore has turned his face away from the "vine brought out of Egypt" (v. 8) and planted in the land of Canaan. The summons to "shine forth" (v. 7) that echoes the Aaronic benediction of Num. 6:24-26 implies a re-turning of God's face toward the people so that they will experience the radiance and power of divine grace in order to be delivered from the ravaging beast-like nations (v. 13) and restored to their former sovereignty and independence. In their desperate circumstances they plead the entreaty of v. 3 in a chorus-like refrain in vv. 7 and 19: "Restore us, O God; let your face shine, that we may be saved." If God's hand rests upon the one at God's own right hand, that is, if God empowers Israel, "Then we will never turn back from you" (v. 18). In the context of the Fourth Sunday of Advent, Psalm 80 conveys an agonizing plea for deliverance. May God's face soon, very soon, begin to shine upon us!

IN THE CONTEXT OF THE FOURTH SUNDAY OF ADVENT, PSALM 80 CONVEYS AN AGONIZING PLEA FOR DELIVERANCE. MAY GOD'S FACE SOON, VERY SOON, BEGIN TO SHINE UPON US!

PSALM 24 or 24:1-7 (BCP);
PSALM 24:1-2, 3-4, 5-6 (RC)

Psalm 24 poses a dramatic representation of the God of the universe entering the sanctuary of "his" dwelling place on earth. The poet begins with the affirmation that this sovereign is the owner of the earth and all that inhabits it. Moreover, this owner is the one who "founded" the earth upon the seas and the floods, recalling the creation myth of Gen. 1:1-2; and therefore the owner is also the ruler who orders the realm of chaos, the seas and the floods, and constitutes a creation of enduring stability.

PSALM 24 COMMUNICATES A JOYFUL ANTICIPATION OF THIS "KING OF GLORY" WHO COMES AS THE WORD MADE FLESH IN ORDER TO PITCH HIS TENT AMONG US.

Who, then, may approach this sovereign owner and ruler of the universe as "he" enters "his" dwelling place on the Temple Mount? Only those who have "clean hands," because they have not done harm of any kind to others and, at the same time, who have "pure hearts" because their wills, seated in their hearts, are committed to ethical integrity (v. 4). They will be vindicated as they approach the owner and ruler of the universe, as "he" enters the sanctuary of the temple to sit enthroned on the Ark of the Covenant as "the Lord of hosts" and Israel's "King of glory" (v. 7). Psalm 24 communicates a joyful anticipation of this "King of glory" who comes as the Word made flesh in order to pitch his tent among us.

SECOND READING
ROMANS 1:1-7 (RCL, BCP, RC)

The opening seven verses of Paul's ambassadorial letter to the Romans, which form its prescript and salutation, include a liturgical fragment of a christological confession of faith (vv. 3, 4). It is a creedal statement in a "nutshell" that is intended to convey to the Christians at Rome the essence of Paul's understanding of the good news of God to which he is committed as "a slave of Christ Jesus" and as "a called apostle" (v. 1).

This is an appropriate text for the Fourth Sunday of Advent, first of all because it stresses the anticipatory prophecies of the Christ event, which the Old Testament lessons of the four Sundays of Advent distinguish. Additionally, the creedal statement in a "nutshell" is preparatory for the forthcoming arrival of Christmas that celebrates the birth of God's Son from the seed of David.

> THIS IS AN APPROPRIATE TEXT FOR THE FOURTH SUNDAY OF ADVENT, FIRST OF ALL BECAUSE IT STRESSES THE ANTICIPATORY PROPHECIES OF THE CHRIST EVENT.

This christological fragment of vv. 3 and 4 is pre-Pauline, but it appears to be a formulation by Jewish Christians who, like Paul, belonged to the world of Hellenistic Judaism and therefore spoke Greek, in contrast to those Jewish Christians who were at home in Palestine and whose native language was Aramaic. As a confession of faith, this fragmentary creed was structured as an antithetical parallelism:

"Concerning his Son who is from the seed of David with respect to the flesh" (v. 3)

"Appointed Son of God in power with respect to the Spirit of holiness from the resurrection of the dead" (v. 4)

By quoting this creedal statement, Paul acknowledges the flesh and blood reality of God's Son as a descendant of King David. With respect to the Spirit, he avows that he is Son of God in power on the basis of the creative act of the resurrection. The phrase "Spirit of holiness" (*pneuma hagiosynē*) is somewhat ambiguous. It could refer to the human spirit or to God's Spirit. The NRSV translates the phrase in terms of the human spirit but in a footnote acknowledges that it may also designate the Holy Spirit. On the basis of its use in the *Testament of Levi* 18:11 and elsewhere, it may be more correct to consider it to be a reference to God's Spirit.

"Resurrection from the dead" is God's creative act by God's Spirit, and in Paul's Christology it establishes "the Son who is from the seed of David" as the "Son of God in power" (v. 4) and also, according to other texts of Paul's letters, as the New Adam (Rom. 5:17-19; 1 Cor. 15:22, 45). From the event of his resurrection, the New Adam, and therefore also the founder of a new humanity, has entered into the exalted state of coenthronement with God and therefore also into active rule in the world on God's behalf (1 Cor. 15:25). It is only at the end of this christological confession that Paul identifies this Son of God from the seed of David, who is also the Son of God in power, as "Jesus Christ our Lord" (v. 4). The title "Lord" has been conferred on him, as the christological hymn in Phil. 2:9-11 declares, by God "super-exalting" him and gracing to him the name that is above every name, "*Lord* Jesus Christ."

The antithetical parallelism of this creedal statement could be divided between Christmas and Easter. The former celebrates the coming of God's Son who, with respect to the flesh, is from the seed of David. The latter, Easter, celebrates Jesus' resurrection from the dead, his exaltation as "Son of God in power" and his active rule in the world. That might be the differentiation that the apostle Paul would make, in as far as his theology is focused on Jesus' death and resurrection. But in the narrative worlds of the four Gospels, Jesus bears the title "Lord" already prior to his crucifixion. Because he is the bearer of God's Spirit, he is already "the Son of God in power." According to Luke 2:11, the angel of the Lord announces the birth of the Savior who is "Christ Lord."

THE GOSPEL

MATTHEW 1:18-25 (RCL, BCP);
MATTHEW 1:18-24 (RC)

The Evangelist has ended the genealogy of Jesus in an ambiguity. Matthew 1:16 reads, "Jacob generated Joseph, the husband of Mary, from whom [feminine singular] was born Jesus, the one called Christ." What is the relationship between Jesus and Joseph? The formula, so and so generated so and so, has been employed thirty-nine times, right up to "Jacob generated Joseph." But instead of a fortieth, "Joseph generated Jesus," the pattern breaks down and Joseph is described instead as "the husband of Mary" (v. 16). If Joseph did not generate Jesus, why begin the Gospel with a family tree of Jesus the Christ? And if Joseph did not generate Jesus, how can Jesus be "the son of David and the son of Abraham"?

After offering a numerical structure of the genealogy, the narrator of Matthew's Gospel proceeds to resolve the ambiguity of v. 16: "Now the origin of Jesus Christ was thus. While his mother Mary was engaged to Joseph, before they came together, she was found pregnant by the Holy Spirit" (v. 18). Jesus has no connection to the genealogy that has introduced the Gospel. He is a New Adam, generated by God's Spirit. The christological designation that he will bear within the narrative world on the basis of his generation by God's Spirit is both "the Son of God" and "the Son of the Human Being." The title "Lord," as in 12:8, belongs to him on the basis of this origin.

Although the maternity of Mary is accentuated in the ambiguity of v. 16 and its elucidation in v. 18b, the narrative of 1:18-25 is told from the point of view of Joseph. This has been noted often but, unfortunately, it has been interpreted as an apologetic motive. The shift back to Joseph is based on his decisive position in the genealogy. For if Jesus is the climax of the history of Israel, at least in terms of his identity as the Son of David, he is that by reason of his relationship to Joseph and not to Mary. Although Joseph is not physically involved in the generation of Jesus, he is betrothed to Mary, and the irregularity of her pregnancy must be explained to him. For as a "righteous" Jew, as he is characterized in v. 19, and therefore as one who is obedient to the law, he is obliged to dissolve this betrothal in view of Mary's apparent unfaithfulness. While contemplating a quiet divorce, he is approached by the angel of the Lord, addressed as "son of David" (v. 20), and commanded to make Mary's child his own.

Matthew's Joseph is unique in Gospel literature. Nowhere is he sketched more concretely; nowhere does he play a more active role in relation to the birth of Jesus. Only Matthew characterizes him as "righteous" (v. 19) and then proceeds to show how this basic trait is manifested in his conduct toward Mary and Jesus. While he wants no part in Mary's seeming unchastity, he has no desire to shame her publicly. Making Mary his wife will involve him in adopting her child and relating to the child as a father. In obedience to the divine summons, he not only takes Mary to himself as his wife, but he also assumes the prerogative that usually belongs to the mother; "he called his name Jesus" (v. 25). By naming Mary's child, Joseph performs the official act of adoption, and it is on this basis that Jesus is incorporated into the genealogy of Joseph. Because of Joseph's obedience, Jesus is linked to the history of Israel; because of his obedience, Jesus becomes "the son of David and

> BY NAMING MARY'S CHILD, JOSEPH PERFORMS THE OFFICIAL ACT OF ADOPTION, AND IT IS ON THIS BASIS THAT JESUS IS INCORPORATED INTO THE GENEALOGY OF JOSEPH.

the son of Abraham" (1:1). And that is the other christological trajectory that arises out of 1:18-25: Jesus as the Son of David and therefore the Messiah of Israel.

The child that Mary gave birth to will be called "Emmanuel, that is, God with us" (v. 23). At the conclusion of Matthew's Gospel, the risen Jesus, who is "Emmanuel, God with us" declares, "*I* with you *AM* all the days even to the consummation of the age" (28:20). Jesus had appropriated the divine self-identification of the Septuagint version of Exod. 3:14, *I AM*, as he walked on the Sea of Galilee (Matt. 14:27). After his resurrection from the dead, he establishes a New Israel, a new people of God, and embraces them in his divine *I AM*. The relationship that formerly was hierarchical is now horizontal. Christians are drawn into the divinity of Jesus, as Matt. 13:43 and 17:2 already intimate.

How can Christians relate to the virgin birth of the one who is called Emmanuel, God with us? On the basis of intellectual assent? There are many who acknowledge it simply as an article of faith. By dismissing it altogether as a myth?

THE THEOLOGICAL INTENTION OF THE VIRGIN BIRTH IS TO MARK THE END OF THE OLD HUMANITY AND TO ESTABLISH THE INAUGURATION OF A NEW HUMANITY.

There are also many who consider it to be a meaningless aspect of the Christmas story. Since many kings and divine heroes in antiquity claimed a virgin birth for their origin, how can the virgin birth make Jesus distinctive, singular, unique? But the virgin birth is not simply an objective fact of Jesus' origin; it is a myth! But a true myth, and therefore a story that builds or constructs reality for those who embrace it. The theological intention of the virgin birth is to mark the end of the old humanity and to establish the inauguration of a new humanity. Consequently Jesus' virgin birth is intended to draw all those who follow him as the Christ into the New Creation that he has constituted. His virgin birth is the virgin birth of all Christians! Every year all those who engage in a genuine celebration of Christmas should renew their participation in the virgin birth of Jesus. Old things have passed away; all things have become new! God is the "Father" and "Mother" of all those who are "in Christ." Physical parents incorporate their offspring as "living souls" into their genealogies and give them a past history that extends back to the beginning of human history. God, by the agency of the Holy Spirit, incorporates those "living souls" into the new humanity of "life-giving spirits" (1 Cor. 15:45).

THE SEASON
OF CHRISTMAS

HERMAN C. WAETJEN

Introduction

Christmas, the mass or the service that celebrates the birth of Jesus Christ, "the Son of Man" and "the Son of God," is the beginning of the "good news of a great joy that will come to all the people." For, as the angelic messenger announced to the shepherds, "to you is born this day in the city of David a Savior, who is Christ, Lord" (Luke 2:10-11).

But neither the Gospels nor any of the other New Testament writings state the date of Jesus' birth. Our celebration of Christmas on December 25 was unknown to Christians of the first three centuries. During that early period of the Christian church the birth of Jesus remained unacknowledged and uncelebrated. Efforts were expended to determine that date, but without success. Jesus' birth date could not be verified. At the end of the second century, Clement of Alexandria ridiculed efforts to ascertain it. Origen protested against it because he considered it to be pagan.

Luke's reference to the shepherds in the field suggests a time between March and November when Palestinian shepherds remain with their flocks in the field, in other words, in spring, summer, or autumn. One text from the year 243 C.E. designates March 25 as the birthday of Jesus. In the Roman calendar the vernal equinox was set for March 25, the day that spring begins to triumph over winter, and new life bursts forth in the realm of nature. Many Christians appropriated this cultural perspective but interpreted it according to Gen. 1:4 as the first day of creation, the day that God separated the light from the darkness. Malachi 4:2

> OUR CELEBRATION OF CHRISTMAS ON DECEMBER 25 WAS UNKNOWN TO CHRISTIANS OF THE FIRST THREE CENTURIES. DURING THAT EARLY PERIOD OF THE CHRISTIAN CHURCH, THE BIRTH OF JESUS REMAINED UNACKNOWLEDGED AND UNCELEBRATED.

reinforced this perspective with its metaphorical identification of the Messiah as "the sun of righteousness" who "shall rise with healing in his wings." To many, a spring birthday was preferable, and April 19, May 20, and April 2 are a few of the dates that were proposed for the birth of Jesus.

Some Christians favored spring as the time of Mary's conception. January 6 was sanctioned as Jesus' birth date because it was believed that Mary had conceived Jesus on April 6. But March 25, the Roman dating of the vernal equinox, linked by Christians to the first day of creation, became the preferred date of Mary's conception. That advanced the birthday of Jesus by nine months to December 25, the winter solstice, the time when the sun would begin to climb into the sky, and daylight would gradually conquer the night. December 25 may have been celebrated as the birthday of Jesus in Rome already during the reign of Constantine the Great (d. 337). In fact, it may have been Constantine himself who united the birth of Jesus with Mithraism's celebration of the sun god on December 25 and therefore ordained that date as the birthday of a new sun god, Jesus, "the Light of the world." John Chrysostom, in a famous Christmas sermon on December 20, 386, attempted to convince Christians that the birth of Jesus must be celebrated on December 25 because Jesus was actually born on that day.

But December 25 is not the correct day of Jesus' birth. The actual day remains indeterminable. Nevertheless, the theological reflection that related Gen. 1:4 to the vernal equinox as the first day of creation and therefore also as the day of Mary's virginal conception of Jesus as the New Adam who inaugurates a new humanity (1 Cor. 15:45) is intensely meaningful. Although the calendar date of the winter solstice was subsequently moved up to December 21, the celebration of Jesus' birthday on December 25, as the light begins to overcome the darkness, corresponds perfectly to the witness of John 1:5, "And the light shines in the darkness, and the darkness has not begun to overtake it." (Some of this material has been drawn from Hermann Usener, *Das Weihnachtsfest*, 3rd ed. [Bonn: Bouvier Verlag, 1969; originally published in 1888], and some from Oscar Cullmann, *Der Ursprung des Weihnachtsfestes* (Zürich/Stuttgart: Zwingli Verlag, 1960).

THE NATIVITY OF OUR LORD / CHRISTMAS EVE

DECEMBER 24, 2004

REVISED COMMON	EPISCOPAL (BCP)	ROMAN CATHOLIC MASS AT MIDNIGHT
Isa. 9:2-7	Isa. 9:2-4, 6-7	Isa. 9:1-6
Psalm 96	Psalm 96 or 96:1-4, 11-12	Ps. 96:1-2, 2-3, 11-12,13
Titus 2:11-14	Titus 2:11-14	Titus 2:11-14
Luke 2:1-14 (15-20)	Luke 2:1-14 (15-20)	Luke 2:1-14

FIRST READING
ISAIAH 9:2-7 (RCL);
ISAIAH 9:2-4, 6-7 (BCP);
ISAIAH 9:1-6 (RC)

Deliverance has been realized and "the rod of the oppressor has been broken." Consequently the darkness that the threat of invasion imposed on the people of Jerusalem and Judah has been lifted. It is a new day! Its dawning ushers in the great light of sunshine and with it a new age in which to actualize the new possibilities of freedom. But it is not clear whether the ending of the night is to be identified with the military defeat of the Syro-Ephraimite coalition or with the failure of the Assyrian siege of Jerusalem. A resolution of this ambiguity may not be possible, but for the celebration of the new day that Christmas inaugurates, it is unnecessary.

The principle objective of Isaiah's oracle is the celebration of the birth of a new king, most likely Hezekiah, son of Ahaz. According to the prophetic preview, "The government will be on his shoulders" (v. 6). The sign that God gave Ahaz in 7:14 has been fulfilled. Immanuel, who is "God with us," has been born. In this context, however, the crown prince is given another name or series of names: "Wonderful in counsel is God the Mighty, the Everlasting Father, the Prince of Peace" (v. 6b). These are "throne names" that will signify to the people the kind of rule that he will exercise during his kingship on the throne of David. His kingship, therefore, will be directed toward the perpetuation of the Davidic kingdom, but by conducting his rule in loyalty to God and in dedication to justice.

The birth of a royal child is linked to the dawn of a new day that marks the shattering of the yoke of oppression. Together they constitute the beginning of a new time in Israel's history that will include the disposal of military clothing and footwear (v. 4) and, if 2:4 may be drawn in, the widespread activity of beating swords into plowshares and spears into pruning hooks. It is "the zeal of the LORD of hosts" (v. 7) that will insure its actualization. The new day, inaugurated by the birth of a king and the concurrent defeat of the enemy and its resulting liberation necessitate a celebration that is as joyful and festive as the merrymaking at harvest time.

In spite of the assessment of Hezekiah's kingship that is offered in 2 Kings 18:5, the son of Ahaz never fulfilled the promise of a glorious rule that Isaiah had previewed. In both 2 Kings 20:16-18 and Isa. 39:5-7, judgment is pronounced upon Hezekiah for joining with the Babylonian revolutionary, Merodach-baladan, in a plot against Assyria that precipitated the Assyrian attack of 701 B.C.E. Hezekiah did not and could not fulfill his ascribed role, either as Immanuel, "God with us," or as the one who bore the throne names, "Wonderful in counsel is God the Mighty, the Everlasting Father, the Prince of Peace." Like the earlier Advent texts of Isa. 7:14 and 11:1-10, Isa. 9:1-7 was transmitted into Israel's future as the vision of a king yet to come, whose birth would terminate the night of oppression, marginalization, and dehumanization and usher in a new day of light and with it a time of healing and restoration.

> THE BIRTH OF A ROYAL CHILD IS LINKED TO THE DAWN OF A NEW DAY THAT MARKS THE SHATTERING OF THE YOKE OF OPPRESSION.

RESPONSIVE READING

PSALM 96 (RCL);
PSALM 96 or 96:1-4, 11-12 (BCP);
PSALM 96:1-2, 2-3, 11-12, 13 (RC)

The psalmist issues a call to all the peoples of the earth to worship Yahweh. But conventional praise and thanksgiving on this occasion are inadequate. This summons to worship is to be expressed by singing "a new song" (v. 1). If the original context of this psalm was postexilic, perhaps the decree of the Persian king Cyrus to set the Jewish captives free and its mandate to the returning exiles would have been profoundly apposite. But Psalm 96 is reproduced verbatim in 1 Chron. 16:23-33 and placed in the preexilic context of David bringing the Ark of the Covenant to Jerusalem in order to constitute it as the center of God's rule.

In either case a new song is warranted that includes the nations of the world and invites them to join God's people in entering God's courts for worship, honor, and praise. In the postexilic temple there were two courts, one for the priests and one for the Israelites. Here the Gentiles are bidden to enter God's court with the Israelites. It is imperative that the former are present for, as v. 13 states, God has come to judge the earth. God will judge the world with justice and with truth.

Psalm 96 is a matchless psalm for the Christmas Eve service of worship, particularly if the service of worship extends beyond midnight into the dawning of a new day that has been inaugurated by the birth of Jesus the Christ, who is Immanuel, "God with us," and "Wonderful in counsel is God the Mighty, the Everlasting Father, the Prince of Peace."

> PSALM 96 IS A MATCHLESS PSALM FOR THE CHRISTMAS EVE SERVICE OF WORSHIP, PARTICULARLY IF THE SERVICE OF WORSHIP EXTENDS BEYOND MIDNIGHT INTO THE DAWNING OF A NEW DAY THAT HAS BEEN INAUGURATED BY THE BIRTH OF JESUS THE CHRIST.

SECOND READING

TITUS 2:11-14 (RCL, BCP, RC)

The dawning of a new day that necessitates the singing of a new song requires ethical conduct that harmonizes with the newness of life that has been constituted. If the new creation that the new day has brought into being is to be manifested as a present reality, it must be validated by moral behavior that is tantamount to its value and effect. That is the compelling meaning of this text.

Its keynote is its opening phrase, "the salvation-bringing grace of God" (v. 11), for it is the realities of grace and salvation that the new day that dawns with the birth of Jesus, "our great God and Savior" (v. 13) brings forth. "The salvation-bringing grace of God" is, of course, the freely given unmerited favor and love of God. It was manifested again and again in the history of Israel, above all in the exodus. Salvation in that context constituted deliverance from the oppression and exploitation of enslavement, but it did not resolve its underlying reality. It did not restore the image and likeness of God in the lives of the Israelites.

> IF THE NEW CREATION THAT THE NEW DAY HAS BROUGHT INTO BEING IS TO BE MANIFESTED AS A PRESENT REALITY, IT MUST BE VALIDATED BY MORAL BEHAVIOR THAT IS TANTAMOUNT TO ITS VALUE AND EFFECT.

The salvation-bringing grace of God through Jesus the Christ redeems or liberates human beings from the condition of being disposed to lawlessness. In the words of John the Baptizer in John 1:29, Jesus is "the lamb of God who removes the sin of the world." This is not simply the grace of God's forgiveness. It is more radical than that. This salvation-bringing grace of God initiates the healing of the human infection of sin. The powerful disease that induces men and women to abuse and degrade each other has been terminated by "our great God and Savior Jesus Christ." That too is the reality of this new day that requires the singing of a new song and with it a lifestyle of "being zealous for good deeds" (v. 14) that mirrors the reality of this paradigm shift.

THE GOSPEL
LUKE 2:1-14 (15-20) (RCL, BCP);
LUKE 2:1-14 (RC)

For Christmas Eve the focus of Luke's account of the Christmas story is the birth of Jesus—but the birth of Jesus as it may be viewed and interpreted in the light of the prophecies of First Isaiah. Mary has placed her virginity in God's service in order to give birth to a new ruler over Israel, whom God will give "the throne of his father David" (1:30-38). But how can David be designated as "his father" in view of the virgin-birth origin of Jesus? The Lukan genealogy of 3:23-38, like Matthew's genealogy of 1:1-16, disconnects Jesus from Joseph (3:23) and therefore also from David, Abraham, and Adam. God's coming in the Christ event of Christmas is embodied by God's Son (1:35), who has been generated within Mary's womb by the creative act of the Holy Spirit. Jesus, therefore, is a New Adam, and like the first Adam, he inaugurates a new humanity. To convey the eschatological character of this identity in the narrative world of Luke-Acts, he will bear the title "the Son of the Human Being" or, to translate it more intelligibly, "the New Human Being." Jesus will employ this christological identity twenty-three times in Luke's Gospel.

BOTH EPITHETS, "CHRIST, LORD," ARE APPLICABLE TO THE RULE THAT HE WILL EXERCISE AS THE INCARNATION OF THE LORD GOD WHOM HIS MOTHER HAS EXTOLLED IN THE MAGNIFICAT.

Luke also, like the evangelist Matthew, has adopted the Christology of the messianic Son of David. This is the prophetic orientation of First Isaiah, as it has become apparent in Isa. 7:14; 9:6-7; and 11:1-9. Although the basis of that identity is ambiguous, it is supported by Jesus' birth in Bethlehem and perhaps also by his being swathed by his mother to signify his royalty. It is noteworthy, however, that the title "Christ" is used only nine times in Luke's Gospel. The angelic announcement to the shepherds identifies this newborn Savior, this new Adam, by juxtaposing the two epithets by which he will be addressed, "Christ, Lord" (without a definite article between them) and, at the same time, distinguishing him as "being swathed" as a mark of identification (vv. 11 and 12).

Both epithets, "Christ, Lord," are applicable to the rule that he will exercise as the incarnation of the Lord God whom his mother has extolled in the *Magnificat*. As the "Christ," Jesus will rule from the cross, and by the utter weakness of his crucifixion he will overcome the enemies of humankind, sin and death. The title "Lord" is linked to Jesus' identity as "the Son of the Human Being." As the lordly "Son of Man" he will depose the mighty from their thrones and exalt the humble, the nobodies of the world (see 6:5; 22:69).

Very likely that is why Luke has placed the birth of Jesus in the political context of Augustus Caesar's decree to register the inhabited world. (Matthew has located the birth of Jesus prior to the death of Herod the Great in 4 B.C.E.). But there is no historical record of such a census. However, a registration of the inhabitants of Judea occurred in 6 C.E. during the time Quirinius was governor of Syria. Its objective was to determine the taxes that the Jews of Judea would have to pay to the crown after Archelaus was deprived of his ethnarchy and Judea became an imperial province governed by procurators who represented the emperor. As a result of Augustus's decree, Joseph, who was "from the house and family of David" (v. 4) but who resided in Nazareth, is required to journey to Bethlehem in order to be enrolled. Mary, his betrothed who is pregnant by the Holy Spirit, travels with him and, while they are in Bethlehem, gives birth to Jesus in a stable. An immense contrast appears to be implied here! While Caesar is enthroned at the top of the socioeconomic pyramid of the Roman Empire, Jesus the "Christ Lord" who is divinely destined to overthrow the powers and principalities of the world, is born in a stable and bedded in a feeding trough for animals. In the light of Mary's *Magnificat* and the angelic proclamation to the lowly shepherds, there will be reversals that the narrative world of Luke-Acts will disclose. Jesus will die as "the King of the Jews," terminating his christological identity as "Christ," and he will be resurrected as "the new human being" in accordance with the identity that is based on his virgin birth, the identity that he referred to when he predicted his forthcoming death and resurrection in Luke 9:22; 18:31-33; and Acts 7:56.

The third annunciation in Luke's Gospel is made to the shepherds at night while they were living out of doors and engaged in the vocation of guarding their flocks. Shepherds, of course, evoke the memory of King David's youth as a shepherd, and therefore it is logical that they should be the first to be informed of the good news. On the other hand, they may be intended as unexpected recipients of the epiphany they witness. Shepherds were stereotyped as unclean because they were regarded as thieves who stole, slaughtered, and sold the newborn lambs of the flock that had been entrusted to them. Contrary to expectations, therefore, they are the first to hear the good news of Jesus' birth. They receive a sign from the angel of the Lord, even as Ahaz had been granted a sign by God at the crisis of the threatened invasion of the Syro-Ephraimite invasion of Judah. By the tokens of "being swathed" and "lying in a feeding trough" (vv. 7 and 12), they would be able to identify the newborn Savior.

The annunciation of the divine messenger is followed by another epiphany of a multitude of the heavenly armies. These are "the hosts" (v. 13) whom "the Lord of hosts" commands, and they sing a new song that essentially conveys the visions of Isaiah: "Glory to God in the highest (of the heavens) and *on earth peace* among human beings of good will" (v. 14). The peace they sing of is the promised salvation of God that engenders peace between God and human beings and reconciliation in human relationships.

LUKE 2:15-20 (RCL, BCP)

For Christmas Eve this is a secondary text. It focuses on the shepherds' hurried visit to Bethlehem "to see the matter that has happened which the Lord made known to them" (v. 15). They experience the fulfillment of the sign that was given them, and, as the first witnesses of this divine fulfillment, they broadcast the good news of their epiphany, both the angelic annunciation followed by the song of the heavenly chorus and their personal encounter with Jesus, the "Christ Lord," in the Bethlehem stable. Mary holds on to all the things she has heard and ponders them in her heart.

THE NATIVITY OF OUR LORD / CHRISTMAS DAWN

DECEMBER 25, 2004

REVISED COMMON	EPISCOPAL (BCP)	ROMAN CATHOLIC
Isa. 62:6-12	Isa. 62:6-7, 10-12	Isa. 62:11-12
Psalm 97	Psalm 97	Ps. 97:1, 6, 11-12
	or 97:1-4, 11-12	
Titus 3:4-7	Titus 3:4-7	Titus 3:4-7
Luke 2:(1-7) 8-20	Luke 2:(1-14) 15-20	Luke 2:15-20

FIRST READING

ISAIAH 62:6-12 (RCL);
ISAIAH 62:6-7, 10-12 (BCP);
ISAIAH 62:11-12 (RC)

Isaiah 62 moves the celebration of Christmas into a new orientation, indeed, a more radical orientation. Embedded in the prophecy of Third Isaiah (chapters 56–66), it is directed toward a fundamental transformation of the old moral order that has dominated the historical existence of God's people from the time of the fall of Adam and Eve to the beginning of the postexilic period of Israel's history. First Isaiah (chapters 1–39) foresees the coming of a "shoot from the stump of Jesse," a messianic Son of David who will return Israel to the conditions of paradise. Second Isaiah (chapters 40–55) speaks from the context of the Babylonian captivity promising a return to the Holy Land, but at the same time urging the people of God to adopt the nomadic heritage of Abraham and Sarah during their exile and, for the time being, accept their circumstances wherever they happen to be. Third Isaiah marks the beginnings of Jewish apocalypticism, a perspective that rejects the possibility of reform in the present moral order and anticipates the inauguration of a new creation. For the first time in Israel's history, a prophet in the tradition of Isaiah voices the expectation of God's direct intervention in history in order to make a new beginning, to constitute a new moral order. In 65:17 God responds to the plight of Third Isaiah's community by declaring, "For behold, I create new heavens and a new earth, and the former things shall not be remembered nor come into mind." The same words are repeated in 66:22.

In that early postexilic period of Third Isaiah's career, the exiled Zadokite priests have returned from Babylon and have reclaimed their place as the rightful priests of the temple cult. Solomon, according to 1 Kings 2:26-27, 35, had expelled Abiathar from the high priesthood and appointed Zadok in his place, and his descendants continued to dominate the priesthood to the time of the Babylonian captivity. When the Zadokites were carried off into exile, their role was taken over by the Levitical descendants of Abiathar in the administration of the temple cult. They were the eschatological visionaries, egalitarian, universalistic, and therefore inclusive in their ideology. They were the representatives of the vision of restoration that Second Isaiah had previewed in Babylonian exile. As 56:3-7 indicates, they were ready to welcome unclean foreigners and eunuchs. Noteworthy in this respect is God's declaration in 56:7d, "For my house shall be called a house of prayer for all peoples"—a text that Jesus cites in Luke 19:46. God's direct intervention would transform the entire nation into "priests of Yahweh" who would minister on behalf of God, and those who had been their oppressors would bow at their feet, repair their cities, feed their flocks, and serve as their plowmen and vinedressers (Isaiah 61 and 62).

The returning Zadokite priests, however, brought with them the vision of restoration that Ezekiel had formulated for them during the exile and recorded at the culmination of his prophecy in chapters 40–48. It is a vision that favors the Zadokites, safeguards their holiness, and secures their authority to lay down for the people the ordinances and judgments of God (44:10-14). Pragmatic and administratively oriented, its goal is to reestablish the cultic life of the community by building the new temple according to the specifications that Ezekiel had laid down. Ideologically, this community was hierarchical, separatist, and exclusive.

According to the communal lament of 63:16-19, the Levitical priests were excluded from their functions in the temple cult. Trodden down by their adversaries and no longer called by God's name, they call upon God to "rend the heavens and come down" in order to reconstitute the world by bringing about the promised transformation. It is noteworthy that the name "Israel" is used only twice in the eleven chapters of Third Isaiah, in 56:8 and 63:16. Evidently, in the light of 63:16, the name is claimed exclusively by those who refuse to recognize the legitimacy of the Levitical priesthood. To this community of disinherited Levites God announces the giving of a new name that denotes a new status: "You shall be called Hephzibah and your land Beulah" (62:4b). Hephzibah is the feminine name that may be divinely ordained to replace the masculine name Israel (which had been given to Jacob), and it means, "My delight is in her." Beulah is also a feminine name meaning "Married" and may be intended to replace "Judah." "And as the bridegroom rejoices over the bride, so shall your God rejoice over you" (62:5). (It is noteworthy that Nathaniel Hawthorne appropriated the name "Hephzibah" as the main character of his novel, *The House of the Seven Gables*, a story that captures the reversals of Third Isaiah.)

In the light of this renaming and its change in status that the Levitical priests will experience, Yahweh will station watchmen on the walls of Jerusalem. Most likely they are prophets who will remind Yahweh "and give him no rest until he establishes Jerusalem and makes it a praise on earth." This is the injunction of vv. 6 and 7.

With an oath, God then promises an end to the exploitation and expropriation that the people of Judah have been experiencing economically: "I will not again give your grain to be food for your enemies . . . for which you have labored" v. 8). Verses 10-12 conclude with a call to preparation for the radical reversal that is coming: "Enter through the gates!" Begin to act by clearing the highway of stones. It is an echo of Second Isaiah's summons to "prepare the way of the Lord, make straight in the desert a highway for our God." God's people, renamed Hephzibah, are addressed as "the daughter of Zion" and told the good news, "Your salvation is coming!" As redeemed people, they will also be called Derusha, another feminine name meaning "Sought Out." Jerusalem will become the city that all the nations of the world will seek out for the salvation that it has obtained and therefore has to offer to others.

According to the Gospels, Jerusalem is replaced as the center of the world by the new humanity that God has pioneered through Jesus Christ. In John 1:51, the heavenly ladder that unites heaven and earth will no longer rest on Jerusalem and its temple but on "the Son of the Human Being," a corporate reality according to Dan. 7:13-14, 27. On Christmas Day, therefore, Christians can appropriate these divine injunctions and promises: "Go through the gates!" Enter into this new heaven and new earth that God has begun to bring into existence with the birth of Jesus! At the same time, clear the highway of its stones so that nothing hinders or prevents the fullness of God's coming in Jesus Christ at Christmas. Those who are ready to receive this gift will be called "The Holy People" (v. 12)—as the apostle Paul does when he greets his addressees as "saints" or "the holy ones." The salvation that Christmas inaugurates is the beginning of a new moral order. Enter into it! And work with others to clear out the stones from the road into this New Age so that the rest of the world will be able to come and seek out the New Jerusalem, the people of God, the body of Christ.

> THE SALVATION THAT CHRISTMAS INAUGURATES IS THE BEGINNING OF A NEW MORAL ORDER.

RESPONSIVE READING

PSALM 97 (RCL);
PSALM 97 or 97:1-4, 11-12 (BCP);
PSALM 97:1, 6, 11-12 (RC)

In some respects Psalm 97 is a continuation of Psalm 96. If God has come, then God reigns. God is king! That is the reality that is actualized by the birth of Jesus the Christ. In God's incarnation of Jesus of Nazareth, God's rule has gained a foothold in the world of human beings and their affairs. Therefore, "Let the earth rejoice!" (v. 1) because its consequences are universal.

The first part of this psalm, vv. 1-5, conveys a powerful impression of God's power and majesty, as nature responds to God's kingship. God comes out of the concealment of "clouds and darkness" (v. 2), and nature responds with lightnings that light up the world and mountains that melt like wax. Because "righteousness and justice are the foundation of his throne" (v. 2b), the wicked, God's adversaries, should tremble.

> IF GOD HAS COME, THEN GOD REIGNS. GOD IS KING! THAT IS THE REALITY THAT IS ACTUALIZED BY THE BIRTH OF JESUS THE CHRIST.

The second part, vv. 6-9, presents the response of the people of the earth as they perceive the glory of God. Idolaters are struck with shame because the gods they worship are reduced to nothing. But Zion, the Temple Mount that represents God's presence, rejoices because of the reports of God's victorious rule.

Part three, vv. 10-12, is the application of the psalm. All those who love God are summoned to hate evil. For God not only preserves and delivers them from the wicked; God is a farmer who sows light that in the course of time will sprout and grow into the bright sunshine of truth.

SECOND READING

TITUS 3:4-7 (RCL, BCP, RC)

Here is a creedal formulation that may have been used in the early church's rite of baptism. It has been inserted into a context that prescribes ethical conduct in order to remind Titus, the addressee of this letter, that the reality that he experienced in his baptism is the foundation of the lifestyle that belongs to his calling as a Christian. "When the goodness and loving kindness of God our Savior appeared, he saved us" (vv. 4, 5a). The verb, *epephanê*, which is all too often translated "appeared," conveys the force of sense experience. In other words, the goodness and loving kindness of God were manifested empirically and therefore is discernible to the human senses. That manifestation is Jesus Christ, the physical expression of God's goodness and loving kindness by which salvation was actualized. It is reconciliation and health; it is participation in a new moral order, a new creation.

Moral conduct does not generate salvation; good works cannot inaugurate this new age. It was simply and entirely God's mercy manifested concretely in the life, death, and resurrection of Jesus Christ and working through baptism. On the one hand, baptism is characterized as a "washing away of sins" (v. 5). At the same time, it is a regeneration that presupposes a death experience—an eschatological drowning, so to speak—followed by a re-creation, or being made new, that is effected by the Holy Spirit. Beyond this regeneration, the goodness and loving kindness of God are expressed by the continued indwelling of God's Spirit: "which he poured out upon us richly through Jesus Christ our Savior" (v. 6).

Verse 7 concludes the baptismal formula with two clauses that are characteristic of the theology of the apostle Paul: "justified by his grace" and "heirs in hope of eternal life." Those who participate in the body of Christ are justified by God's grace, as Paul had stated in Rom. 5:17. At the same time, they have a share in eternal life through Jesus Christ.

THE GOSPEL
LUKE 2:(1-7) 8-20 (RCL);
LUKE 2:(1-14) 15-20 (BCP);
LUKE 2:15-20 (RC)

Both Luke 2:1-7 and 2:1-14 are secondary texts for Christmas Dawn. They recount the birth of Jesus but with intimations of earth-shaking reversals. Augustus Caesar exercises the power of his rule to decree a census that will determine the tax payments of his subjects and therefore continue the sovereignty of his rule. But as Mary has predicted in her *Magnificat*, the mighty will be deposed from their thrones, as the new moral order, the reign of God that Jesus inaugurates, will act like a fistful of yeast that leavens fifty pounds of flour (Matt. 13:33). Jesus, who, as a result of the census, is born in a stable, will act as God's surrogate to reverse the structures of power in the world and establish God's justice and peace that will exalt the nobodies of the world and fill the hungry with good things.

LUKE 2:8-20 and 15-20

The lectionary emphasis of Christmas Dawn is placed on Luke 2:8-20. That brings the shepherds into sharper focus in all the readings of the Gospel lesson for this Christmas morning. The scene has changed from the Bethlehem stable to the fields of a nearby region. It is night and the shepherds are carrying out their vocation of guarding their flocks of sheep. Suddenly and unexpectedly an angel of the Lord "stood by them" (v. 9), and they are surrounded by a dazzling display of God's glory. Their fear, aroused by this epiphany, is immediately mitigated by the angel's charge, "Stop being afraid!" (v. 10).

This is the third annunciation in Luke's Gospel, and it is difficult to determine whether its recipients, the shepherds, are to be regarded as an expected or unexpected audience to hear the good news. Shepherds, of course, evoke the memory of King David's youth as a shepherd, and therefore it seems logical that they should be the first to be informed of the good news. Moreover, their lowly status would correspond to Mary's declaration that God would exalt the humble while deposing the mighty from their thrones. But their lowly status is also suspect, for their vocation has been stereotyped as unclean in as far as they are viewed with a lingering mistrust of stealing, slaughtering, and selling the newborn lambs of the flock that had been entrusted to them. On the one hand, therefore, in view of 1:52b, they appear to be the logical recipients of the angelic annunciation. But perhaps also contrary to expectations, they are the first to hear the good news of Jesus' birth.

> THIS IS THE THIRD ANNUNCIATION IN LUKE'S GOSPEL, AND IT IS DIFFICULT TO DETERMINE WHETHER ITS RECIPIENTS, THE SHEPHERDS, ARE TO BE REGARDED AS AN EXPECTED OR UNEXPECTED AUDIENCE TO HEAR THE GOOD NEWS.

They receive a sign from the angel of the Lord, even as Ahaz had been granted a sign by God at the crisis of the threatened invasion of the Syro-Ephraimite invasion of Judah. By the tokens of "being swathed" and "lying in a manger" (vv. 7, 12) they would be able to identify the newborn Savior.

Another epiphany follows the angelic annunciation. In response to the good news that the angel of the Lord has made known, a multitude of the heavenly armies appears vocalizing a doxology in praise to God. These are "the hosts" (v. 13) whom "the Lord of hosts" commands, and they sing a new song that essentially conveys the visions of Isaiah: "Glory to God in the highest (of the heavens) and *on earth peace* among human beings of good will." The peace they sing of is the salvation of God that Third Isaiah was charged to proclaim to the daughter of Zion. It is the peace between God and human beings and between human beings themselves that is divinely willed to motivate the beating of swords into plowshares and spears into pruning hooks. It is the beginning of a new moral order in which all will be called "the holy people." For it is the entrance into a new creation in which the eyes of the blind will be opened, the ears of the deaf unstopped, the mute will sing for joy, and the lame and crippled will walk and be treated as fully human again.

Their song, however, is reversed by the crowds when Jesus rides triumphantly into Jerusalem after a long inverted exodus journey (9:51—19:48) and is welcomed with their song of adulation: "Blessed is the King, the one coming in the name of the Lord. *Peace in heaven* and glory in the highest." At this moment at least, the peace on earth that the angels sang in praise to God at Jesus' birth has not yet been realized. There is only peace in heaven and glory in the highest of heavenly realms.

The shepherds experience the fulfillment of the sign that was given them, and, after visiting this child and sharing with his parents the epiphanies they had witnessed, they become the first witnesses of this divine revelation. They broadcast the good news of the angelic annunciation followed by the song of the heavenly chorus and their personal engagement with Jesus, the "Christ Lord," in the Bethlehem stable. Mary holds on to all the things she has heard, and, as she ponders them in her heart, she wonders, and in her wondering she struggles to interpret their significance.

THE NATIVITY OF OUR LORD / CHRISTMAS DAY

DECEMBER 25, 2004

REVISED COMMON	EPISCOPAL (BCP)	ROMAN CATHOLIC
Isa. 52:7-10	Isa. 52:7-10	Isa. 52:7-10
Psalm 98	Psalm 98 or 98:1-6	Ps. 98:1, 2-3, 3-4, 5-6
Heb. 1:1-4 (5-12)	Heb. 1:1-12	Heb. 1:1-6
John 1:1-14	John 1:1-4	John 1:1-18 or 1:1-5, 9-14

FIRST READING
ISAIAH 52:7-10 (RCL, BCP, RC)

In the lectionary text Isa. 62:6, prescribed for Christmas Dawn, God announced that watchmen had been set on the walls of Jerusalem who would never hold their peace day and night, who would never take their rest, and who would never give God rest until salvation comes. What Third Isaiah expected imminently, Second Isaiah saw fulfilled from the distance of the Babylonian captivity. It is this preview of Second Isaiah to which the lectionary turns for the celebration of Jesus' birth on Christmas Day.

The watchmen on the walls of Jerusalem are the first to see and report that Yahweh is returning to Zion (62:8). Returning with Yahweh are the exiles who have been held captive in Babylon, for God and God's people have been in captivity together. This is a momentous insight that all too often is unknown or forgotten. God is always in solidarity with women and men who are in covenant with God and therefore are committed to the fulfillment of God's will in all areas of human life, regardless of what their circumstances and conditions may be.

In such a covenantal relationship with God there will always be an expectation of deliverance from any and every disinheritance that diminishes the image and likeness of God in which human beings have been created. From the context of captivity, therefore, Second Isaiah foresees that redemption and celebrates it as though it has already occurred. He previews the messenger who is carrying the good news across the mountains to Zion and in exultation exclaims, "How beautiful are the feet of the messenger of good tidings!" (v. 7).

The apostle Paul repeats this very outcry in Rom. 10:15 in which he acknowledges the necessity of messengers to announce the good news of God's salvation: "For everyone who calls on the name of the Lord will be saved. How then will they call upon the one into whom they did not believe? And how will they believe in the one of whom they have not heard? And how will they hear without a proclaimer? And how will they proclaim unless they are sent?" (vv. 13-15). The good news must be heard, and that requires ministers of the word who will preach it so that those who hear will call upon the name of the Lord and be saved.

The watchmen, who "eye to eye" (v. 8b) have viewed God's return to Zion, burst into song because God has established the kingdom. God reigns! Jerusalem has been redeemed, and therefore the waste places of the city can join in the joyful song, for their restoration is a sign that God has comforted his people.

> THE GOOD NEWS MUST BE HEARD, AND THAT REQUIRES MINISTERS OF THE WORD WHO WILL PREACH IT SO THAT THOSE WHO HEAR WILL CALL UPON THE NAME OF THE LORD AND BE SAVED.

The reality of God's reign is a show of strength to the nations of the world: "The LORD has made bare his holy arm in the eyes of all the nations" (v. 10a). But this is not to be interpreted as a threat or an intimidation. The objective of God's kingship is a demonstration of power that will manifest "the salvation of our God" that will become visible to "all the ends of the earth" (v. 10b).

Albert Camus, in his novel *The Plague*, utilizes the bubonic plague metaphorically in order to characterize the separation and alienation that produces the condition of "exile" among the people of the Algerian city of Oran.

> Thus, the first thing that plague brought to our town was exile. . . . It was undoubtedly the feeling of exile—that sensation of a void within which never left us, that irrational longing to hark back to the past or else to speed up the march of time, and those keen shafts of memory that stung like fire. . . . In short we returned to our prison-house, we had nothing left us but the past, and even if some were tempted to live in the future, they had speedily to abandon the idea.

Christians, unlike the Jews of Second Isaiah's time, have not been carried off into a Babylonian exile. Nevertheless, they, like all human beings, experience the exile of separation and alienation that the infection of sin engenders in human relationships. The text of Isa. 52:7-10 speaks to this existential reality on this day of the nativity of the Lord. Ministers of the word are the watchmen on the walls who have been commissioned by God to proclaim the glad tidings of Christmas: God reigns! With the birth of Jesus, God's incarnate Son, the kingship of God has begun. Salvation is here now, and the process of redemption and healing will commence. Christmas is the moment in history when God bares his holy arm before the eyes of all the nations in order to manifest the salvation that will end the exile of all human beings by inaugurating world reconciliation.

RESPONSIVE READING

PSALM 98 (RCL);
PSALM 98 or 98:1-6 (BCP);
PSALM 98:1, 2-3, 3-4, 5-6 (RC)

This psalm, like Isa. 52:7-10, previews the expected victory of God over all the forms and forces of death that diminish the image and likeness of God, which all human beings bear by right of God's creation. Here is the ideal poetry for the celebration of the manifestation of God's salvation. As in Isa. 52:10, God has bared "his right hand and his holy arm" and "has wrought deliverance [*hoshiya*, from *yasha*, the verb from which Jesus' name is drawn] for him." That deliverance, that salvation, is manifest in the birth of the Christ child.

Moreover, as the psalmist says, "The Lord has made known his salvation; his righteousness he has disclosed to the eyes of the nations" (v. 2). This also has occurred at the birth of the Christ child. In an epiphany, the angelic messenger has announced the good news to the shepherds and the heavenly armies have sung the Lord's song, "Glory to God in the highest (of heavens) and on earth peace among human beings of good will."

God has kept the promises made in the past, although the exiles had complained in Isa. 49:14, "Yahweh has forsaken me; Yahweh has forgotten me." God has intervened so publicly that all the ends of the earth will see God's salvation. Therefore, the world is summoned to acclaim God by making music with harps, trumpets and horns, and nature is exhorted to respond with the crashing of waves on the shore and with the trees of the forest clapping their hands.

SECOND READING

HEBREWS 1:1-4 (5-12) (RCL);
HEBREWS 1:1-12 (BCP);
HEBREWS 1:1-6 (RC)

Christology, the interpretation of the person and work of Jesus Christ, rises to a momentous climax in this second reading for Christmas Day. The opening verses of the treatise addressed to the Hebrews (Christian Jews) unfold a cosmic Christology that relates Jesus Christ to creation and to the rule of the universe—yet surprisingly without naming Jesus in the entire first chapter. An ethnic or nationalistic interpretation of Jesus emphasizes his work as the Messiah, the Son of David. A Christology that is universally oriented accentuates Jesus' lordship as "the Son of the Human Being" or "the New Human Being." Hebrews, in order to stress the superiority of Jesus as God's Son over prophets, priests, and angels, presents an interpretation of Jesus that is multifaceted in as far as it combines various figures that in one way or another serve as God's agents. In its cosmic orientation, Heb. 1:1-12 is similar to the christological hymn of Col. 1:15-20, particularly vv. 16 and 17.

First, Jesus as God's Son is connected to the tradition of "the eschatological prophet," the prophet at the end of history who speaks the last Word of God. God spoke through Moses and Elijah, as well as other prophets. But the final Word that God speaks is through God's own offspring; it is his participation in God's deity that makes him the ultimate mouthpiece of God in history.

CHRISTOLOGY, THE INTERPRETATION OF THE PERSON AND WORK OF JESUS CHRIST, RISES TO A MOMENTOUS CLIMAX IN THIS SECOND READING FOR CHRISTMAS DAY.

The Son has been predestined to inherit the entire creation, for the Son is also God's agent in the creation of the world. Here the author seems to have drawn upon the philosophical tradition of the Logos that Philo, the Jewish philosopher of Alexandria, had adapted from Middle Platonism's concept of the Logos. The Logos is the Word, God's speech activity by which the creation is brought into being, as Genesis 1 narrates. All the words that God spoke at creation are unifiable into one being or person as the plan and meaning of the universe. And that one being has been enfleshed in Jesus of Nazareth. This too is the meaning of the incarnation that is celebrated at Christmas.

The author of Hebrews is also conversant with the Wisdom of Solomon and in v. 3 adapts an attribute that is ascribed to Sophia, Wisdom, in 7:26. "She is a reflection of eternal light, a spotless mirror of the working of God and an image of his goodness." Like Sophia, the Son is "the fashioner of all things" (7:22). Sophia "in every generation passes into holy souls and makes them friends of God and prophets" (7:27). But the Son, in contrast, made human beings friends of God by establishing reconciliation through the purification of sins. After effecting at-one-ment between God and humankind, the Son "sat down at the right hand of the majesty on high" (Heb. 1:3b). Begotten by God and co-enthroned with God, the Son is exercising power on behalf of God and gradually drawing all things to himself in order to actualize his divine inheritance.

"The Son" naturally appears to be a masculine being, but that is unfortunately determined by the androcentrism of the Greek language. In view of the Son's relationship to the Logos, God's creative speech activity, and also to Sophia, God's agent of unification, the Son should be interpreted and viewed as an androgynous being uniting both genders, male and female. The divine person that became incarnate in Jesus of Nazareth was Logos-Sophia.

THE GOSPEL

JOHN 1:1-14 (RCL, BCP);
JOHN 1:1-18 or 1:1-5, 9-14 (RC)

The prologue of the Fourth Gospel presents a summary account of the activity of the preexistent Logos (Word) in its vocational fulfillment as the divine agent of creation, communication, and redemption. Originating from God, the Logos is both independent of God and dependent on God. That is, the Logos enjoys a horizontal relationship of interdependence with God. Primordially the Logos is directed toward union with God: "and the Word was *toward the God*" (v. 1). The Greek preposition *pros*, which is employed here, should be translated with an English equivalent that conveys movement when, as here, it governs the accusative case. The Logos is actively engaged in a dynamic relationship with God that oscillates between differentiation and union.

As God's speech activity, the Logos serves as the divine agent of creation: "All things happened through him and without him there happened nothing that has happened" (v. 3). The Word, by naming things, differentiates and in the process produces a world. Words build world! Originated by God, the Logos is the bearer of God's life and God's light. When, therefore, the Logos becomes incarnate in Jesus of Nazareth, Jesus becomes the bearer of God's life and light.

The Logos here, as in Hebrews 1, is also related to Sophia, God's Wisdom. Even as Sophia "passes into holy souls in every generation and makes them friends of God" (Wisd. of Sol. 7:27), the Logos in the role and activity of Sophia is always coming into the world in order to unite with human beings and draw them into union with God. It is noteworthy that in John 15:14, Jesus says to his disciples, "You are my friends." But in the history that the Old Testament recounts, the world did not know the Logos. The Logos in the role and activity of Sophia also came to its "own possessions," namely, Israel as the people of God, but "his own" did not receive the Logos-Sophia (v. 11). Some did, however, and the Logos gave them authority to become God's children, who were born not from the mixing of female and male bloods, nor by the flesh and blood power of the human will, nor by the design and intention of the male, but *from God* (v. 13).

Verse 14, as C. H. Dodd has observed, "takes us beyond the range of Jewish ideas. . . ." "The Logos happened flesh!"[1] The momentous event of the incarnation requires the reintroduction of the name Logos for the first time since v. 1. Now the Logos has become a historical actuality by uniting itself with a flesh and blood human being named Jesus. In this union it will continue to serve as God's agent and fulfill its function by drawing Jesus into the same relationship that it enjoys with God, and eventually by drawing humanity into that relationship as well. By pitching its tent in its enfleshment in Jesus of Nazareth, the Logos will manifest its glory, but in a manner that has never before been disclosed. This is the "grace in place of grace" (v. 16). God's relationship with Israel in the Old Testament was grace, but this incarnation of the Word is a grace that supersedes the grace that preceded it.

John the witness, who has already testified about the Logos in v. 8, reappears to bear witness to the Logos incarnate: "The one who comes after me has happened before me because he was my First" (v. 15). Generally *protos* in v. 15 is translated as a preposition, as in "he was *before* me." But *protos* is an adjective meaning "first," and it is an echo of the Septuagint translation of

> THE LOGOS HAS BECOME A HISTORICAL ACTUALITY BY UNITING ITSELF WITH A FLESH AND BLOOD HUMAN BEING NAMED JESUS.

Isa. 48:12, where Yahweh declares, "I AM First." The predication of "First" that God claims in Isa. 48:12 must also belong to the Logos and to the Logos incarnate. Accordingly, Jesus can declare in John 8:58, "Before Abraham was, I AM." Even as the Logos has been in "the bosom of the Father" (v. 18b), so now Jesus, the enfleshed Logos, is so intimately united with the Father that he will interpret God in the forthcoming narrative of the Fourth Gospel. Subsequently when Philip asks Jesus during his farewell speech, "Show us the Father!" Jesus will respond, "Whoever has seen me has seen the Father" (John 14:8). As in the second reading of Christmas Day, the prologue of the Fourth Gospel reaches the zenith of New Testament Christology and its interpretation of the person and work of Jesus Christ.

Note

1. C. H. Dodd, *The Interpretation of the Fourth Gospel* (Cambridge: Cambridge University Press, 1960), 271.

ST. STEPHEN, DEACON AND MARTYR

DECEMBER 26, 2004

REVISED COMMON
2 Chron. 24:17-22
Ps. 17:1-9,15
Acts 6:8—7:2a, 51-60
Matt. 23:34-39

FIRST READING
2 CHRONICLES 24:17-22

There is no account of this event in the earlier Old Testament record of the reign of Joash, namely, 2 Kings 11-12. Zechariah's martyrdom, however, gains a new significance by its placement at the end of a long history of martyrdom in Luke 11:45-52 and Matt. 23:34-39. Jesus condemns lawyers and Pharisees for building the tombs of the prophets whom their ancestors had killed, "from the blood of Abel to the blood of Zechariah who perished between the altar and the sanctuary."

Ironically, it was Joash, the son of Ahaziah, who directed a conspiracy against Zechariah that led to his death by stoning. Joash had been rescued from the murderous crusade of Athaliah, his grandmother, as she undertook the destruction of the entire royal family of the house of Judah. When she was slain after six years of rule, Joash, her grandson, was placed on the throne at the age of seven by the high priest Jehoiada, and he reigned in Jerusalem for forty years. According to the judgment of the chronicler (24:4) and 2 Kings 12:2, "Joash did what was right in the eyes of the LORD all the days of Jehoiada the priest." After the latter's death, however, he began to be adversely influenced by the nobles of Judah, most likely prebendal lords who, as powerful clan leaders, had received grants of large tracts of agricultural land, probably from Joash's father, Ahaziah, and eventually had been drawn into the fertility cult of the Asherim.

ZECHARIAH'S MARTYRDOM, HOWEVER, GAINS A NEW SIGNIFICANCE BY ITS PLACEMENT AT THE END OF A LONG HISTORY OF MARTYRDOM IN LUKE 11:45-52 AND MATT. 23:34-39.

Zechariah, the son of the high priest Jehoiada who had placed Joash on the throne, was among the prophets raised up by God: "Then the Spirit of God took possession of Zechariah, the son of Jehoiada the priest" (v. 20). In typical prophetic style he began to censure the king and his nobles for their idolatry: "Why do you transgress the commandments of the LORD so that you cannot prosper? Because you have forsaken the LORD, he has forsaken you" (v. 20b).

By the command of Joash, Zechariah was stoned to death "in the court of the house of the LORD" (v. 21). His last words, as he was dying, called for God's vengeance against his enemies, "May the LORD see and avenge!" (v. 22). Eventually Joash himself was slain by his servants in retaliation for the murder of Zechariah.

RESPONSIVE READING
PSALM 17:1-9, 15

This psalm is introduced as "a prayer of David" and may possibly intimate his entreaty for deliverance from the pursuit and persecution by his predecessor to the Israelite throne, Saul. In any case, it is easily imaginable that its words could have been spoken by Zechariah as he was being stoned to death. There is a great tension in this psalm between confidence and anxiety. It is already manifested at the very beginning, as the psalmist enters into his prayer with a plea of innocence that simultaneously is also a piercing cry from "lips without deceit" (v. 1). He dares to plead for God's deliverance because he knows that God has examined him, indeed, tested his heart in the night, and has found nothing that would implicate him as a perpetrator of violence and lawlessness. He claims steadfast obedience to God's will: "My feet have not slipped" (v. 5).

Because of his divinely assured integrity, he makes his petition with great confidence in vv. 6-9, "Keep me as the apple (the pupil) of the eye. Hide me in the shadow of your wings from my deadly enemies who oppress me about."

His enemies are characterized in vv. 10-12: "They have shut their hearts to pity. . . . They have tracked [me] down. They have set their eyes to cast [me] down to the ground." Neither the personal pronoun "me" or "us" occurs in his petition, but in view of the psalm's relationship to Zechariah and Stephen on this day that is set aside for God's martyrs, it seems legitimate to insert either of the two possible pronouns.

The psalm climaxes in a prayer for deliverance (vv. 13-14): "Arise, O LORD, confront him! Cast him down. Deliver my soul from the wicked." One of his enemies, perhaps their leader, is described as a "lion eager to tear to pieces" (v. 12). His own aspiration, as v. 15 indicates, is to behold God's face in righteousness and, when he awakens, to be satisfied with God's likeness. That may refer to the prospect of seeing God that would occur in the temple, as Ps. 63:2 acknowledges. But it may also refer to the future event that Jewish apocalypticism envisions. The psalmist may be concluding with the hope of resurrection and its attendant recovery of God's image and likeness.

SECOND READING
ACTS 6:8—7:2a, 51-60

As the Christian community grew in numbers in Jerusalem, two different orientations began to emerge among them. According to Acts 6:1, they were the *Hebraioi* and the *Hellenistai*. The former were Aramaic-speaking Jewish Christians who undoubtedly worshiped God with an Aramaic liturgy. Their leaders were the Twelve, especially Peter and James, the brother of Jesus, who continued to observe the purity code of Leviticus that constituted a world of binary oppositions between the clean and the unclean and therefore between Jews and Gentiles. The *Hellenistai* were Greek-speaking Jewish Christians who worshiped God with a Greek liturgy. They appear to have been less inclined to build their ethical conduct on a pollution system that separated the Gentiles from the Jews, and consequently they were more ecumenical. They were willing to receive Gentile "God-fearers" into their synagogue community and permit them to have table fellowship with them.

According to Acts 6:1, the Hellenists were being neglected in the daily welfare distribution to the poor, particularly widows, and they began to complain about it. No reason is offered to account for this, but very likely it was due to the ideological differences that separated the two groups of Jewish Christians. The Hebrews controlled the purse and, as their prejudice against the Hellenists intensified, they began to withhold the distributions that provided the care for the widows and orphans.

To resolve the inequity seven deacons were appointed, and a separate welfare fund was set up that would support the poor among the Hellenists. This, of course, tended to exacerbate the separation between the two groups and their ideological differences. It is at this point in the Acts of the Apostles that Luke begins to prepare the reader for the forthcoming separation of these ideological orientations and ultimately the rift between Christianity and Judaism. Acts 6:40-42 indicates that the Twelve continued to worship in the temple, and, since the temple was the guardian of the pollution system, they also continued to conduct their daily life according to the purity code.

The Hellenists were moving in the opposite direction, away from the temple and therefore in contradiction to the purity code. Stephen, "full of grace and power, who did great wonders and signs among the people" (v. 8) was their spokesperson. He engaged in a dispute with the synagogue communities of Hellenistic Jews over the issue of the temple and the law and was brought before the supreme council and accused of using the teaching of Jesus to speak against the temple and the law.

In his defense speech, Stephen recites the history of Israel from Abraham to Moses, including the Joseph story and the exodus under Moses. His discourse reaches its climax in his rejection of the view that God dwells in "houses made with hands" (7:48) and ends with a characterization of Israel as a rebellious people of God. "Which of the prophets did your fathers not persecute? And they killed those foretelling the coming of the Righteous One whom you now betrayed and murdered, you who received the Law by directions of angels, and you did not keep it" (v. 52).

His critical perspective of Israel's history infuriated his adversaries, and while they raged, "he gazed up into heaven and saw the glory of God and Jesus standing on the right hand of God and said, 'I see the heavens opened and the Son of the Human Being standing on the right hand of God'" (vv. 55, 56). In his confession before the Sanhedrin in Luke 22:69, Jesus had declared that he was seated "at the right hand of the power of God." Stephen, however, sees him standing, perhaps because he is ready to welcome and receive him. Like Zechariah, Stephen was stoned to death without a verdict and, like Zechariah, his stoning appears to have been an act of popular enmity. However, instead of calling upon God to avenge his death, as Zechariah had done, he prayed, in an imitation of Jesus in Luke 23:34, 46, committing his spirit to God and pleading that the sin of his murder not be ascribed to his enemies.

> LIKE ZECHARIAH, STEPHEN WAS STONED TO DEATH WITHOUT A VERDICT AND, LIKE ZECHARIAH, HIS STONING APPEARS TO HAVE BEEN AN ACT OF POPULAR ENMITY.

THE GOSPEL
MATTHEW 23:34-39

Matthew's Gospel was written after the destruction of Jerusalem and therefore also soon after the initial efforts of the Pharisees under the leadership of Jochanan ben Zakkai to reconstitute Judaism on the basis of the Pharisaic heritage of the two traditions of the law, the written and the oral Torahs. Matthew 23 in its entirety should be interpreted in the light of this post–70 C.E. context, and therefore Jesus' diatribe against the scribes and Pharisees is to be treated as a composition of the evangelist who, in the name of Jesus, is condemning these religious leaders for persecuting and ostracizing Jewish Christians who refuse to submit to their separatist ideology.

Accordingly, Jesus is presented in a prophetic role issuing six indictments. The first two, vv. 13 and 15, are judgments against the kind of ministry and mission that they are conducting. The next two, vv. 16 and 23, condemn their distorted and absurd casuistry that diverts them from the original intention of the law. The last pair, vv. 25 and 27, exposes their schizophrenic condition in their pursuit of holiness. The seventh and last stands by itself and serves as a point of departure for the conclusion of his discourse:

> Woe to you, scribes and Pharisees, hypocrites! For you build the graves of the prophets and you adorn the tombs of the righteous. And you say, "if we had been (alive) in the days of our fathers, we would not have been partners in the (spilling of the) blood of the prophets." So you testify against yourselves that you are the sons of those who murdered the prophets. (23:29-31)

All of the persecution and martyrdom of the past and all that will continue to occur in the future belongs to the filling up of "the measure of your fathers" (v. 32). All of it will be avenged, "from the blood of Abel the righteous to the blood of Zechariah the son of Barachiah whom you killed between the Temple and the altar" (v. 35). The phrase, "son of Barachiah," has been inserted into this Q tradition for a more precise identification. Because it creates more problems than it solves and because some manuscript authorities, notably the Sinaiticus and Eusebius, do not include it, it is tempting to dismiss it as a later scribal interpolation.

JESUS' DIATRIBE AGAINST THE SCRIBES AND PHARISEES IS TO BE TREATED AS A COMPOSITION OF THE EVANGELIST WHO, IN THE NAME OF JESUS, IS CONDEMNING THESE RELIGIOUS LEADERS FOR PERSECUTING AND OSTRACIZING JEWISH CHRISTIANS WHO REFUSE TO SUBMIT TO THEIR SEPARATIST IDEOLOGY.

"The son of Barachiah" could refer to the prophet Zechariah of Zech. 1:1, or one of the reliable witnesses Isaiah obtained in Isa. 8:2. Due to an error of one kind or another, it may also denote Zechariah, son of Jehoiada, of 2 Chron. 24:20ff., or the man of "pronounced hatred of wrong and love of liberty" described by Josephus in *The Jewish War* 4.5.4. Zechariah, the son of Baris, was unjustly tried and executed "in the middle of the temple" prior to the destruction of Jerusalem. Perhaps the prophet Zechariah of Zech. 1:1 should be eliminated first, for although he identifies himself as "the son of Barachiah," there is no record of his martyrdom that has survived in tradition. The Zechariah of Isa. 8:2 is also an unlikely candidate for the same reason. Zechariah, the son of Baris, is suitable as the terminal point of the history of martyrdom. All the blood unjustly shed from the beginning of the Old Testament to the time of the destruction of Jerusalem will be requited. But there is no way to reconcile Matthew's "son of Barachiah" with Josephus's "son of Baris." The most logical prospect fitting the description of 23:35 is the Zechariah of 2 Chron. 24:20ff., who in fact was stoned "in the court-yard of the house of the LORD" and who, as he was dying, exclaimed, "May the LORD see and avenge!" In as far as his murder is cited in the last book of the Jew-ish canon, he would be the last of the martyrs of the Jewish Old Testament canon.

FIRST SUNDAY AFTER CHRISTMAS/HOLY FAMILY

DECEMBER 26, 2004

REVISED COMMON	EPISCOPAL (BCP)	ROMAN CATHOLIC
Isa. 63:7-9	Isa. 61:10—62:3	Sir. 3:2-6, 12-14
Psalm 148	Psalm 147 or 147:13-21	Ps. 128:1-2, 3, 4-5
Heb. 2:10-18	Gal. 3:23-25; 4:4-7	Col. 3:12-21
Matt. 2:13-23	John 1:1-18	Matt. 2:13-15, 19-23

FIRST READING
ISAIAH 63:7-9 (RCL)

These three verses introduce a liturgy of lament that encompasses 63:7—64:11. Before the community's complaint is voiced, however, there is an acknowledgment in vv. 7-9 of God's acts of deliverance in the past. As bitter as the present conditions are, as 63:16-19 testifies, the memory of God's mercy and goodness in former times inspires confidence and hope that God will act on behalf of God's people again. In their exploration of the past, they are reminded of the exodus (63:11), and therefore they unhesitatingly address their question to God:

> Where is he who brought up out of the sea the shepherds of his flock? Where is he who put in the midst of them his holy spirit, who caused his glorious arm to go at the right hand of Moses, who divided the waters between them, to make for himself an everlasting name, who led them through the depths? (vv. 11-12)

In this prayer of intercession the community desperately clings to its self-understanding as God's people, based on God's own words in the past: "For he said, 'Surely they are my people'" (v. 8). At the same time, they remind God in v. 8 that "he became their Savior" and that "in all their affliction, he was afflicted."

As the first reading for the First Sunday after Christmas, this text can be used in two ways at least. On the one hand, it acknowledges the deliverance that God has inaugurated through God's incarnation in Jesus Christ. Verse 7 celebrates God's "great goodness" and "the abundance of his steadfast love" for, as v. 8 reminds us, God has become our Savior. Culminating this text is the attendant reality that all too often is forgotten and that could be given special emphasis on this particular Sunday: in our affliction God was afflicted! God suffered with us whatever misfortune, misery, or wretchedness we may have experienced.

Since the First Sunday after Christmas is also the last Sunday of the calendar year, this text can also be used to reflect on the misfortunes and misery of the present or recent past—not only to remind the people of God that God continues to be afflicted with us in our journey through life, but to reaffirm that Christmas is only the beginning of the New Exodus. The birth of Jesus is also the anticipation of Easter when the New Exodus will be culminated by Jesus' resurrection from the dead, and the New Creation that Christmas introduced will be established forever.

SINCE THE FIRST SUNDAY AFTER CHRISTMAS IS ALSO THE LAST SUNDAY OF THE CALENDAR YEAR, THIS TEXT CAN ALSO BE USED TO REFLECT ON THE MISFORTUNES AND MISERY OF THE PRESENT OR RECENT PAST—NOT ONLY TO REMIND THE PEOPLE OF GOD THAT GOD CONTINUES TO BE AFFLICTED WITH US IN OUR JOURNEY THROUGH LIFE, BUT TO REAFFIRM THAT CHRISTMAS IS ONLY THE BEGINNING OF THE NEW EXODUS.

ISAIAH 61:10-62:3 (BCP)

Third Isaiah presents his vision of Israel's restoration in chapters 60–62, and much of it corresponds to Second Isaiah's vision, especially 52:7-10, the first reading for Christmas Day. This text for the First Sunday after Christmas offers new language to communicate the significance of Christmas and the salvation that the birth of Jesus inaugurates. It is the metaphor of marriage!

Christmas, therefore, may be interpreted as the beginning of the kind of new creation that marriage initiates. A union is established in which there is a dynamic movement between the two-ness of separate identities: both the groom and the bride retain their individuality without the identity of the one being absorbed into the other. At the same time, the two become one, and, if their love is genuine, their one-ness will constitute a horizontal relationship. God and God's people, as bridegroom and bride, will enjoy a profound union in an egalitarian relationship.

CHRISTMAS, THEREFORE, MAY BE INTERPRETED AS THE BEGINNING OF THE KIND OF NEW CREATION THAT MARRIAGE INITIATES.

God, as the groom, will adorn his people, as the bride, with new clothing, "the garments of salvation" (v. 10). The outer garment, which will be visible to others, is "the robe of righteousness." It is noteworthy in this context that the apostle Paul in Gal. 3:27 speaks of putting on Jesus Christ as a new garment. If the outer garment is Jesus Christ, "the robe of righteousness," it must be empirically evident to the world.

Moreover, a new status will be acquired by the people of God in their marriage union with God as their groom. They will be elevated to royalty by being "a royal diadem in the hand of your God" (62:3). Metaphorical language like this is rarely heard within Christian communities at Christmas, perhaps because the Augustinian misinterpretation of Rom. 5:12 continues to dominate much of the theologizing of the church. To be clothed with the new garments of salvation and to be elevated to a participation in God's royalty implies a new creation in which human brokenness can begin to be healed and human alienation can begin to be eliminated from human existence. Is it possible to exaggerate the good news of Christmas?

SIRACH 3:2-6, 12-14 (RC)

The *Wisdom of Sirach*, it must be remembered, belongs to the canon of Scripture according to the Fourth Decree of the Council of Trent. Written around 190 B.C.E. by Joshua ben Sira, a Jewish scribe, it presents itself as a guide in ethical and religious matters. These particular verses are intended to remind children of their indebtedness to their parents; they are summons to sons and daughters to honor their parents in words and in deeds. Many benefits are promised to those who glorify their fathers and refresh their mothers: "Whoever honors his father atones for sins and whoever glorifies his mother is like one who lays up treasure."

HONORING PARENTS IS A SIGN OF OBEDIENCE TO GOD
AND EVIDENCE OF BEING AT-ONE-MENT WITH GOD.

Obedience to the Fourth Commandment bears vital consequences. Kindness to parents will not be forgotten "and against your sins it will be credited to you" (v. 14). No other commandment offers such a promise. Honoring parents is a sign of obedience to God and evidence of being at-one-ment with God. Accordingly, whoever honors his or her father (and mother) in spite of the stark reality of the Hebrew proverb, "The fathers (and mothers) have eaten sour grapes and set their children's teeth on edge" (Jer. 29:30), atones for sins in as far as the children do not pay back in kind the sins the parents committed in raising their children. Human beings can atone for the sins of others by not engaging in any kind of retaliation, but promoting reconciliation and peace.

Most likely this text is the first reading for the First Sunday after Christmas, because the Gospel lesson for this same Sunday narrates the story of Joseph's obedience to the divine command to deliver Jesus and his mother from the murderous designs of Herod the Great by fleeing into Egypt for safety. Parents, like Joseph, who are faithful to God in raising their children according to God's will, should be honored, no matter to what extent they may have eaten sour grapes and set their children's teeth on edge.

PSALM 148 (RCL)

The birth of Jesus Christ is an event of significance for the whole world. It inaugurates the triumph of God, which has meaning for the entire universe. What psalm could be more appropriate for Christmas and the First Sunday after Christmas than one that invites everything in heaven and on earth to join together in a chorus of praise?

Verses 1-6 summon praise from heaven, beginning with angels and God's hosts, the armies of God. Sun, moon, and stars are urged to join in the thanksgiving. Even "the heavens of heavens," whatever regions or levels that may be, and the rain clouds, "the waters above the heavens," are bidden to add their voices.

> WHAT PSALM COULD BE MORE APPROPRIATE FOR CHRISTMAS AND THE FIRST SUNDAY AFTER CHRISTMAS THAN ONE THAT INVITES EVERYTHING IN HEAVEN AND ON EARTH TO JOIN TOGETHER IN A CHORUS OF PRAISE?

Verses 7-13 exhort praise from the earth. Mountains, hills, trees, beasts, cattle, birds, and creeping things—all are called upon to join in the hymn of praise. But above all, kings, princes, judges, people young and old are charged to participate in this universal chorus.

The reason, according to v. 14, is the event of deliverance: God "has lifted up a horn for his people." A horn is symbolic of strength. It is analogous to the biblical references to God's arm and God's right hand. God has manifested power in God's incarnation in Jesus Christ. "Hallelujah," therefore, is the appropriate climax of this hymn of praise.

PSALM 147 or 147:13-21 (BCP)

According to this psalm, there are four reasons for praising God. One, the restoration is the evidence of God's continuing love and concern for God's people: "who heals the broken of heart and binds up their wounds" (v. 3). Two, God continues to provide the sustenance needed by human beings and animals: "who prepares rain for the earth and gives food to the beasts" (vv. 8, 9). Three, the power by which God acts on behalf of Israel: "For he has made strong the bars of your (Jerusalem's) gates" (v. 13). Four, God's revelation to God's people: "He declares his word to Jacob, his statutes and ordinances to Israel" (v. 19). No other people have experienced God in this way. To no other people has God disclosed his word. All four reasons may be included in the celebration of Christ's birth, as the narratives of the four Gospels demonstrate.

PSALM 128:1-2, 3, 4-5 (RC)

THE SEASON
OF CHRISTMAS

HERMAN C.
WAETJEN

In its focus on the family, the six verses of this psalm are a fitting continuation of the wisdom that Sirach invokes children to observe. However, in contrast to Sirach 3, it is addressed to fathers, but specifically fathers who "fear the Lord and walk in his ways" (v. 1). That kind of commitment produces wonderful consequences: happiness in enjoying the fruits of one's labor; a wife who, like a fruitful vine, bears many children; and children like olive plants around the table producing the oil of gladness. The welfare of a nation

THE WELFARE OF A NATION DEPENDS UPON THAT
KIND OF FAMILY LIFE THAT IS PROMOTED BY PARENTS
AND CHILDREN WHO "WALK IN GOD'S WAYS."

depends upon that kind of family life that is promoted by parents and children who "walk in God's ways." The promise is "the prosperity of Jerusalem" (v. 5) or the well-being of the society in which God-fearing families pursue their lives, and "peace upon Israel" (v. 6) or the wholeness that is enjoyed by all who are members of such a community.

SECOND READING
HEBREWS 2:10-18 (RCL)

Jesus, in his prayer of John 17:14-16, acknowledges that he and his disciples have the same origin: "they are not from the world even as I am not from the world." In a similar manner Heb. 2:10-11 affirms that Jesus, the pioneer of our salvation, and the many sons and daughters who are brought to glory by his death and resurrection have one origin: "The one who sanctifies [namely, Jesus Christ] and those who are sanctified [his followers] have all one origin" (v. 11). Both Jesus and those who follow him into death and resurrection have been generated by God. "That is why," as v. 11 continues, "he is not ashamed to call them brothers and sisters." This is a cardinal feature of the good news of Christmas and Easter. Jesus and his disciples belong to one great family of God's offspring. Together they constitute God's family, and they are horizontally related to each other and to God. There is no hierarchy here. Christians are heirs of Christ, and Christ is God's heir. Verses 12-13 reinforce this relationship by citing texts from Ps. 22:22 and Isa. 8:17-18 that support this sister-brother relationship between Jesus and his community of followers.

To establish this equality, the one who, according to Heb. 1:1-3, is the ultimate spokesperson for God and who is both the Logos (Word) and Sophia (Wisdom) of God, "partook of the same nature" (v. 14) of flesh and blood. Moreover, as a flesh and blood human being, he, the Son whom God appointed the heir of all things, died so that "through death he might destroy the one who has the power of death, the devil" (v. 14).

The humanity of Jesus the Christ was the same as ours: "He had to be made like his brothers and sisters in every respect" (v. 17). Only in that identical humanity could he become "a merciful and faithful high priest to make expiation for the sins of the people." The testings and sufferings he endured enable him to help those who are being tested.

This too and perhaps this especially belongs to the good news of Christmas. It is vital that Christians, who tend to subordinate themselves to Jesus Christ, learn to understand that Jesus' kingship ended at his death on the cross. In his resurrection he is engaged in a second career constituting God's family of sisters and brothers, as he himself declared to Mary Magdalene in John 20:17.

> THE TESTINGS AND SUFFERINGS HE ENDURED ENABLE HIM TO HELP THOSE WHO ARE BEING TESTED.

GALATIANS 3:23-25; 4:4-7 (BCP)

God established a covenant with Abraham (3:15-16) that functions like a "last will and testament." It is inviolable, and therefore it cannot be annulled nor can a codicil be added to it. Yet a codicil, the law, was added to this covenant "because of transgressions" (3:19) in order to serve as a mirror and make human beings conscious of their infection of sin.

If a last will and testament is inviolable, how could the codicil of the law have been added? It could not have been ordained by God—at least directly—because God was one of the two parties who had to consent to the addition of this codicil to the last will and testament. As Paul says in 3:19-20, "the law was ordained by angels." The other party would have been Abraham's descendants, Israel, and Moses was the negotiator between them: "Now an intermediary implies more than one, but God is one" (3:20). A negotiator arbitrates an issue between two parties, and God was one of the two.

The codicil was added. Indeed, it was necessary to make human beings aware of their sinful condition. That codicil of the law, then, functioned as a truant officer leading children to school and turning them over to their teacher, namely, Jesus Christ, who fulfilled the conditions of the last will and testament and thereby made its benefits universally available to all of Abraham's offspring, Jews and Gentiles who live by faith.

"Faith" in this context, however, should be rendered as "trust" because it is used and it functions in this context in terms of the Roman juridical principle of *fidei commissum*, the laws governing inheritance under last wills and testaments. So, as Paul states in 3:25-27, "Now when the trust came, we are no longer under the truant officer. For you all are sons and daughters of God through the trust of Jesus Christ, for as many of you as are baptized into Christ, you have put on Christ."

It was in "the fullness of time that God sent forth his son" (4:4) so that we would receive adoption. Adoption into God's family includes receiving the gift of the Holy Spirit by which we have the privilege of addressing God as *Abba*, an Aramaic colloquialism that is still used in Israel today and means "Papa" or "Daddy." Surely this is a horizontal relationship, and it includes the status of being fellow heirs with Christ and therefore heirs through God. This too belongs to the good news of Christmas! Additional exegesis is offered in the second reading for the observance of the Holy Name of Jesus/Mary, Mother of God on January 1, 2005.

COLOSSIANS 3:12-21 (RC)

This reading consists of two parts. Verses 12-17 unfold an ethical lifestyle that is in keeping with the baptismal experience of "putting off the old human being" and being reclothed with the new human being or the new nature. The apostle Paul had characterized this new humanity in 1 Cor. 15:45 as the "last Adam [who is] a life-giving spirit." Participation in this new humanity involves a continuous renewal in knowledge in order to move toward the recovery of the image and likeness of God that God willed at creation. Love especially is featured as the mark of maturity and completeness (3:14).

Christian identity begins with the self-understanding implied in the exhortation of 3:12, "God's holy and beloved elect." This identity is manifested by the attributes of character that are highlighted in vv. 13-17.

The second part of this text, vv. 18-21, introduces a christianized version of a non-Christian household code that is directed at the Christian family. To what extent it is a betrayal of the attributes of character that mark the Christian identity of God's new humanity, each reader will have to decide individually. Wives are summoned to be subordinate to their husbands, as is fitting in the Lord. Husbands are charged to love their wives and not be exasperated toward them. Children are commanded to obey their parents, for this is pleasing to God. Clearly the patriarchal structures of Mediterranean honor-shame culture have replaced the horizontal configuration of God's family in Christ Jesus.

The Gospel

MATTHEW 2:13-23 (RCL); MATTHEW 2:13-15, 19-23 (RC)

When the magi do not return to inform Herod about the young king, he sends out his soldiers to slaughter "*all* the boys in Bethlehem and in *all* its surrounding regions from two years and under" (v. 16). The phrase "two years and under" suggests the possible age of Jesus at this time, as discerned by Herod from the testimony of the magi. But it may also indicate the fact that the boys who were killed had not yet been enrolled among the men of Israel by genealogy because they were not yet three years old (2 Chron. 31:16). Jesus is the only survivor of a lost generation!

The story of the flight into Egypt is told from Joseph's point of view, but at the same time it is fixed on the necessity of Jesus' withdrawal. It is incongruous for the Messiah to be dispossessed of his rule and to be forced to find asylum in Egypt by his own people. Matthew, however, estab-

JESUS IS THE ONLY SURVIVOR OF A LOST GENERATION!

lishes this anomaly by noting the fulfillment of Hos. 11:1, "Out of Egypt I called my son" (v. 15).

The tragedy of the boys' massacre is also incompatible with the beginning of the messianic age. For the evangelist, it is nevertheless confirmed by the prophecy of Jer. 31:15. The fulfillment formula begins with a favorite adverbial particle, *tote*, "then" (v. 17). Only one other quotation is introduced in this manner, 27:9-10, Judas's betrayal of Jesus. By using it and simultaneously omitting the phrase, "by the Lord," Matthew avoids attributing these events to the intention of God. Both occurrences, Herod's slaughter of the innocents and Judas's betrayal of Jesus, are initiated by the will of human beings. The adverbial particle "then" serves as the immediate connecting link between these actions and the terrible fulfillment that they bring about. Israel's rejection of Jesus the Messiah already at the beginning of his life, as signified by the persecution of Herod, leads to self-inflicted judgment. Coincidental with the eschatological joy of the magi there is the bitter lamentation of Mother Israel weeping for her murdered children, the fulfillment of Jer. 31:15.

The flight into Egypt and the massacre of the boys are concomitant eschatological realities that, like the Old Testament events of the exodus and the Babylonian deportation, signal an end and concurrently a new beginning. On the one hand, Jesus' expulsion from "the land of Israel" (vv. 20, 21) is an exile that is terminated by his repatriation after Herod's death. But on the other hand, his flight into Egypt is a reversal of the exodus typology. Judea is the new land of bondage, and the persecution of Jesus is analogous to that which Moses experienced as an infant. As the sole survivor of the children of Rachel and therefore the only link between the past and the future, Jesus, like Moses, will launch a new exodus and a new history of Israel. The explicit verbal reproduction of parts of the Septuagint text of Exod. 4:18-20 in Matt. 2:19-21 hint at this implicit exodus model. The similarity between the command given to Joseph, "Arise, take the young child and his mother and return to the land of Israel for those seeking the life of the young child have died" (v. 20) and that spoken to Moses in Exod. 4:19 intimates a Moses typology and suggests the substitution of the "land of Israel" in place of Egypt.

After Herod's death Jesus is returned to the land of Israel; it is his legacy as the Son of David. However, in view of the rule of Archelaus, Herod's son, and the threat that it imposes on the life of the young Messiah, Joseph is compelled to transfer him from Judea once more. This time he takes up residence in Nazareth and that, according to Matthew, is how Jesus the Messiah came to be called "the Nazarene" (v. 23).

Throughout these events, as also in Matt. 1:18-25, Joseph is the heroic "father" who collaborates with God by adopting Jesus, by rescuing him from Herod's murdering soldiers and delivering him into the safety of the Old Testament land of bondage, and finally by finding a safe place for him to grow into adulthood in the village of Nazareth. Joseph, therefore, upholds the continuity of Israel's history and the fulfillment of the Davidic promise.

JOHN 1:1-18 (BCP)

See the comments on the Gospel for The Nativity of the Lord (Christmas Day).

HOLY NAME OF JESUS / MARY, MOTHER OF GOD

JANUARY 1, 2005

REVISED COMMON	EPISCOPAL (BCP)	ROMAN CATHOLIC
Num. 6:22-27	Exod. 34:1-8	Num. 6:22-27
Psalm 8	Psalm 8	Ps. 67:2-3, 5, 6, 8
Gal. 4:4-7	Rom. 1:1-7	Gal. 4:4-7
or Phil. 2:5-11	or Phil. 2:9-13	
Luke 2:15-21	Luke 2:15-21	Luke 2:16-21

The Roman Catholic lectionary also appoints these lessons, designated for the celebration of the Holy Name of Jesus and Mary, Mother of God, for the Second Sunday after Christmas, January 2, 2005.

FIRST READING

NUMBERS 6:22-27 (RCL, RC)

The Aaronic benediction is a very appropriate text for the beginning of a new year. It is the blessing that Moses, under God's instruction, commanded Aaron, his sons, and their descendants to pronounce upon the people of Israel; and down through the centuries it was used in the temple services at Jerusalem. It is noteworthy that the Septuagint translation of this text adds a parenthetical sentence that elucidates the momentousness or magnitude of enunciating this benediction. Between the charge to bless Israel and the words of the benediction, God interposes a reminder of what is actually happening as these words are spoken: "And they will place my name upon the sons and daughters of Israel, and I [the] LORD will bless them" (v. 27). The power of the blessing and the effect that it will have are not to be attributed to the priests who enunciate these words. God, whose name is being placed or laid upon the people, is the source of every endowment that the benediction is commanded to bestow.

All the benefits that the benediction conveys are essential for the New Year. The priests or the pastors who speak these words are representing God by uniting God with the imperative mood in order to give expression to God's will. In that capacity as God's representatives, they [priests and pastors] are charging God to bestow favor upon God's people, and by that favor to guard and protect them. Moreover, they are directing God's face toward God's people so that they will bask in the radiance that emanates from it and consequently reflect it in their own faces. When God's face shines upon human beings, they become aware that they are experiencing God's favor, and accordingly they know that God will act on their behalf. As the psalmist prays in Ps. 80:3, "Let your face shine that we may be saved." Similarly in Ps. 31:16, "Let your face shine on your servant; save me in your steadfast love."

Although the same Hebrew noun, *panah*, is employed in vv. 25 and 26, God's face and God's countenance appear to have different connotations. Both are analogous to the sun, but God's face (*panah*) reflects God's glory and splendor, as the apostle Paul implies in his interpretation of Moses' reflection of God's brightness in his own face in 2 Cor. 3:7-13. When God "lifts up his countenance" (*panah*) upon human beings, light shimmers and radiates forth to illuminate the existence of those who experience it. Psalm 89:15 declares, "Blessed are the people . . . who walk, O LORD, in the light of your countenance." The light of God's countenance enables God's people to find their way into the future. In any and every exposure to God's countenance a sense of affirmation or judgment is also perceivable. If there is approval, the resulting benefit is *shalom*, a relationship of wholeness between God and the person who is experiencing God's acceptance. In this blessed condition it can be assumed with confidence that God is disposed to hearing the petitions that will be spoken in prayer. On the other hand, if God's countenance reveals reproof and displeasure, there can be no peace and therefore no wholesome relationship until repentance has taken place.

> IN THAT CAPACITY AS GOD'S REPRESENTATIVES, THEY [PRIESTS AND PASTORS] ARE CHARGING GOD TO BESTOW FAVOR UPON GOD'S PEOPLE, AND BY THAT FAVOR TO GUARD AND PROTECT THEM.

EXODUS 34:1-8 (BCP)

This text offers another perspective for the entry into the New Year; that is, undertaking a self-examination by reviewing the events, the deeds, and the actions of the past year in order to evaluate the integrity of Christian discipleship. Exodus 34 presupposes the events of Exodus 32. Israel has committed idolatry by following Aaron into the worship of a golden bull while Moses was communing with Yahweh on Mount Sinai for forty days and forty nights. Upon his descent from the mountain Moses learns of Israel's sacrilege and smashes the two tablets of the commandments that Yahweh had written into stone for Israel. In the name of Yahweh, Moses responds by sending the sons of Levi through the camps of Israel with the charge to slaughter all those who had participated in this idolatry;

"and there fell of the people that day about three thousand men" (32:28). The result is the abolition of the covenant between God and Israel.

Subsequently Moses is commanded to cut new stones, and God once again will inscribe them with the same commandments in order to renew the covenant. Yahweh, after descending in a cloud, stands with Moses and proclaims "the name of Yahweh" (34:5). In this new theophany Yahweh discloses the paradoxical identity that is to be associated with the meaning of "his" earlier self-identification to Moses in Exod. 3:14 as "*Ehyeh asher Ehyeh*" or "I will be who I will be." God is a God of love and faithfulness and forgiveness. But God is also a God of anger "who will by no means clear the guilty, visiting the iniquity of the fathers upon the children and the children's children to the third and fourth generation" (v. 7). The consequences of an individual's wrongdoing can extend into the lives of the grandchildren and great-grandchildren.

THIS TEXT OFFERS ANOTHER PERSPECTIVE FOR THE ENTRY INTO THE NEW YEAR; THAT IS, UNDERTAKING A SELF-EXAMINATION BY REVIEWING THE EVENTS, THE DEEDS, AND THE ACTIONS OF THE PAST YEAR IN ORDER TO EVALUATE THE INTEGRITY OF CHRISTIAN DISCIPLESHIP.

Moses responds by interceding for his people and begging God to forgive "our iniquity and our sin and take us for your inheritance" (v. 9). He does not hesitate to identify himself with the transgressions that Israel has committed.

The first day of the New Year is a suitable opportunity to look back into the previous year and participate in devout self-reflection. Whatever failures, weaknesses, derelictions, and mistakes have been evoked, the text of Exodus 34 serves as a reminder of God's renewal of the covenant, above all the new covenant through Jesus Christ.

RESPONSIVE READING
PSALM 8 (RCL, BCP)

This psalm is a hymn of praise inspired within the wisdom tradition of Israel in its reflection on the creation myth of Genesis 1. According to the heading, it is sung "upon the Gittith," a name that may have been derived from the Hebrew *gath*, meaning "winepress," and may designate a tune associated with vintage songs. It is a hymn addressed to "Yahweh, *our* LORD" (v. 1) instead of "*my*" Lord, and it celebrates God's majesty in the name of the people. Yahweh's *name* is glorious in all the earth because Yahweh's name denotes all that is connected with Yahweh, above all, the creation. God's glory is extolled by angels in heaven, and the prattle of infants on earth is evidence of God's creative power by which God's enemies are silenced.

Verses 3 and 4 contrast the glory and greatness of God, as manifested by the creation of the heavens and especially by the nighttime appearance of the moon and the stars, with the implied frailty and mortality of human beings. Why should God be concerned about such insignificant creatures? The same question is asked in Ps. 144:3.

The answer is given in vv. 5-8, and it is based on Gen. 1:26. Because God created both men and women in God's own image and likeness, the psalmist has concluded, "Yet you made them little less than God" (v. 5a). It is the Septuagint translation that substitutes "angels" in place of God, and it is this rendition that was taken over in Heb. 2:7. Unfortunately it places human beings in an even lower status in their relationship to the Creator. But the following sentence cancels such a diminishment, for the psalmist continues, "You crowned them with glory and honor" (5b). Since these attributes of "glory and honor" are ascribed to God in Ps. 29:1; 104:1; 145:5, human beings, who have been created in God's image and likeness, have been endowed with them at creation. Moreover, they have been entrusted with the guardianship of the creation by being granted sovereignty over God's creation, "You have given them dominion [lordship] over the works of your hands" (v. 6). Verses 6-8 are based on Gen. 1:28. Daniel 7:14 anticipates a recovery of this sovereignty in the future and, according to the eschatology of the apostle Paul as expressed in 1 Cor. 15:25, human beings who are living under the new covenant of God in Christ Jesus are beginning to regain it. This too can be a pivotal theme for the entry into a new year, for it is a Christian hope that is to be realized in historical existence.

PSALM 67:2-3, 5, 6, 8 (RC)

This psalm, to be sung with stringed instruments, is equally appropriate for New Year's Day insofar as it is a hymn of thanksgiving for a good harvest or, in the present context, for the year that has passed and all the benefits and blessings that have been received throughout that time. Verse 1 echoes the opening words of the Aaronic benediction, but it is oriented toward Israel reflecting the radiance of God so that God's way and God's salvation will be known

THE NATIONS ARE TO BE GLAD AND SING FOR JOY, FOR GOD'S SALVATION INCLUDES AGRICULTURAL ABUNDANCE.

among all nations. If Christians are the light of God's face, the world cannot remain in darkness. See 2 Cor. 3:18 and 4:6.

The divine objective is expressed in vv. 5 and 8. The nations are to be glad and sing for joy, for God's salvation includes agricultural abundance. When God's rule is embraced throughout the world and God's justice and equality have been established, "the earth will have yielded her increase" (v. 6). Under God's covenant with Israel the actualization of God's justice is linked to agricultural productivity.

GALATIANS 4:4-7 (RCL, RC)

This text in the Episcopal lectionary is the second lesson for the First Sunday after Christmas. But more needs to be said here, particularly in relation to New Year's Day and both the "Holy Name of Jesus" and "Mary, the Mother of God."

In Gal. 3:15-29 the apostle Paul has confronted the Galatian Christians with the covenant of a last will and testament that God established with Abraham in order to determine when, for whom, and on what basis the inheritance that God has authorized is to be granted. The Roman juridical principle of *fidei commissum*, which sets forth the laws regarding inheritance, is used to determine the answer to these issues. A fundamental reality of a last will and testament, as 3:15 indicates, is its inviolability; it cannot be annulled nor can a codicil be added to it. Yet Moses negotiated an agreement between God and Abraham's descendants to incorporate the law into this last will and testament in order to raise to consciousness the human infection of sin (3:19-22). "By the law is the recognition of sin" (Rom. 3:20). Israel, therefore, would be aware of the conditions that had to be fulfilled by Abraham's lineal descendant in order to make the benefits of the inheritance available to all of Abraham's offspring in faith, both Jews and Gentiles.

According to Paul, a time was fixed, but until it arrived, we were heirs apparent, children subject to guardians waiting to come of age in order to receive the inheritance. "In the fullness of time God sent forth his Son, born from a woman, born under the law in order to redeem those under the law" (v. 4, 5). Jesus Christ, Abraham's descendant, having fulfilled the terms of the covenant by eliminating the infection of sin and its consequence of death, opened the trust and made both Jews

ALTHOUGH PAUL NEVER ALLUDES TO A VIRGIN BIRTH, HE ACKNOWLEDGES THE INDISPENSABLE ROLE THAT MARY PLAYED IN GIVING BIRTH TO GOD'S SON WHO WOULD FULFILL THE TERMS OF GOD'S LAST WILL AND TESTAMENT AND MAKE GOD'S INHERITANCE AVAILABLE TO ALL HUMAN BEINGS.

and Gentiles beneficiaries of God's last will and testament. Those who are "in Christ," those who have "put on Christ" have been adopted into God's family as fellow heirs with Christ, and they have the status of being God's offspring and may address God most intimately as "Papa" or "Daddy" (v. 6). To become an heir of God with Jesus Christ requires adoption into God's family; and adoption brings with it the gift of the Holy Spirit. In turn the gift of the Holy Spirit initiates a process of transfiguration, as Paul states in 2 Cor. 3:18.

This too is an applicable text for the New Year, drawing the congregation into a greater awareness of the inheritance that God has willed for all human beings in and through Jesus Christ. Mary, the mother of Jesus, can be brought into focus in relation to 4:4. God's Son was born of a woman! Although Paul never alludes to a virgin birth, he acknowledges the indispensable role that Mary played in giving birth to God's Son who would fulfill the terms of God's last will and testament and make God's inheritance available to all human beings.

PHILIPPIANS 2:5-11 (RCL alt.)

In order to reinforce the ethical exhortations he has prescribed in 2:1-4, the apostle Paul adds a christological hymn that he has appropriated from a Hellenistic Jewish-Christian source. Verse 5 serves as the introduction to this poem of two stanzas: "Be conscious among yourselves that which is also in Christ Jesus." Although the hymn focuses on the humiliation and exaltation of Jesus as the Christ, its function in this context is to serve as a model that is to be emulated in the ethical sphere of historical existence.

The first stanza (vv. 6-8) conveys the downward movement of the Christ from "being in the *form* of God" to "taking the *form* of a slave." This is essentially an emptying of the state of being equal with God. Christ, who was in the essence of God, did not regard equality with God as booty, as a prize, as something to be exploited for self-aggrandizement. Emptying himself, he took the essence of a slave.

Christian women and men, who "in Christ Jesus" are daughters and sons of God, are confronted with this model. What will they do with their identity and status as God's offspring?

Christ's emptying of himself and taking the form of a slave was a historical event, an event of incarnation: "Being in the likeness of human beings and being found with respect to outward appearance as a human being, he humbled himself being obedient unto death, but death of a cross" (vv. 7b-8). The humanity of the Christ who emptied himself by entering completely into historical existence was authentic and culminated in death by crucifixion.

The second stanza (vv. 9-11) expresses Christ's subsequent exaltation: "God super-exalted him and graced to him the title that transcends every name" and therefore evokes the worship of all beings in the three-storied universe of antiquity: heaven, earth, and under the earth, confessing "Lord Jesus Christ to the glory of God." Jesus Christ is the glory of God because he renounced what he possessed by exchanging equality with God for genuine historical existence even to the extent of death on the cross. To emulate this model, however, it is necessary for Christians to begin with their identity as sons and daughters of God and then in that sovereignty to determine to what extent servanthood is to be expressed in daily life. First and foremost Christians are God's

IT IS NECESSARY FOR CHRISTIANS TO BEGIN WITH THEIR IDENTITY AS SONS AND DAUGHTERS OF GOD AND THEN IN THAT SOVEREIGNTY TO DETERMINE TO WHAT EXTENT SERVANTHOOD IS TO BE EXPRESSED IN DAILY LIFE.

offspring! They assume the role of servant by right of their divine autonomy and authority.

PHILIPPIANS 2:9-13 (BCP alt.)

Verses 9-11 present the upward movement of the exaltation of the Christ. The divine title Lord, which is the name above every name, supersedes the state of being that is its opposite, the ignominious status of slave. The universal confession that the last line eschatologically foresees is "Lord Jesus Christ" (v. 11). Even as the enthronement of the Israelite king was reenacted at the beginning of a new year, so it is also fitting that the enthronement of Jesus Christ as Lord is celebrated on this New Year's Day.

Verses 12 and 13 offer another kind of application of this christological hymn. In the light of the introductory mandate of v. 5, "Be conscious among yourselves that which is in Christ Jesus," the Philippian Christians are charged to work out their own salvation. Each individual, proceeding from her or his participation in Christ's sovereignty, must determine how to live the Christian life in authentic historical existence, how to go about serving God and following Jesus Christ into death and resurrection. They are urged to do it with "fear and trembling" (v. 12), because at the same time they are engaged in their Christian response-ability, God is at work in them "to will and to work God's good pleasure" (v. 13).

ROMANS 1:1-7 (BCP)

See the comments on the second reading for the Fourth Sunday of Advent.

THE GOSPEL
LUKE 2:15-21 (RCL, BCP);
LUKE 2:16-21 (RC)

For exegesis on the adoration of the shepherds in 2:15-20, see the comments for the Gospel lection for both Christmas Eve and Christmas Dawn. Verse 21, however, is not included there, because it is reserved by the Revised Common and Episcopal lectionary traditions for the naming of Jesus that is to be celebrated on New Year's Day, 2005. If the eighth day, the day of Jesus' circumcision and naming, is to be counted from the day of his birth, December 25, it would then be celebrated on January 1. But if these two events are to be counted from the day after his birth, their celebration would fall on January 2, the Second Sunday after Christmas.

In either case, Mary's son was circumcised on the eighth day and given the name Jesus according to the instruction of the angel Gabriel. In contrast to Matt. 1:21, the meaning that his name bears is not offered. Instead, the focus is on his naming in conjunction with his circumcision. From the very beginning of his life, Jesus' parents are fulfilling the Jewish religious tradition of circumcision that is the mark of the covenant between God and Israel.

Ironically, the eighth day is the mark of the new covenant that God has established through Jesus the Christ. It is identified with Sunday, the day of resurrection and the beginning of a new week that symbolizes and celebrates the inauguration of the new creation. It is noteworthy how the raising of Jairus's daughter that is foreshadowed as the seventh mighty work of Jesus in Matt. 9:18-19 becomes his eighth in 9:23-26. The church fathers of the second and third centuries made much of the eschatological significance of the number eight. See also Thornton Wilder's novel *The Eighth Day*.

THE EIGHTH DAY IS THE MARK OF THE NEW COVENANT
THAT GOD HAS ESTABLISHED THROUGH JESUS THE CHRIST.

SECOND SUNDAY AFTER CHRISTMAS

JANUARY 2, 2005

REVISED COMMON	EPISCOPAL (BCP)	ROMAN CATHOLIC
Jer. 31:7-14	Jer. 31:7-14	
or Sirach 24:1-12		
Ps. 147:12-20	Psalm 84 or 84:1-8	
or Wisd. of Sol. 10:15-21		
Eph.1:3-14	Eph.1:3-6, 15-19a	
John 1:(1-9) 10-18	Matt. 2:13-15, 19-23	
	or Luke 2:41-52	
	or Matt. 2:1-12	

The Roman Catholic lectionary tradition appoints the lessons, designated for the celebration of the Holy Name of Jesus and Mary, Mother of God, also for the Second Sunday after Christmas on January 2, 2005.

FIRST READING

JEREMIAH 31:7-14 (RCL, BCP)

Jeremiah lived and prophesied through the final catastrophic decades of the little kingdom of Judah. He survived the Babylonian destruction of Jerusalem in 587 B.C.E. and subsequently was taken to Egypt by exile-seeking refugees. It is there that he lived out his last years.

His call, as God informed him, was "to pluck up and to pull down, to destroy and to overthrow, to build and to plant" (1:10). He expresses it by announcing the imminent prospect that confronts Judah: the destruction of Jerusalem and captivity and exile in Babylon. Divine judgment, however, will be followed by deliverance because of God's "everlasting love" (31:3). Although Jeremiah belongs to the kingdom of Judah, his prophecies of a future restoration are inclusive and encompass "all the families of Israel" (31:1).

The promise of a new covenant in 31:31-34 is set in the literary context of an anticipated homecoming that is addressed to "virgin Israel" (v. 4): "Again you shall plant vineyards on the mountains of Samaria; the planters shall plant and shall enjoy the fruit. For there shall be a day when sentinels will call. . . . 'Come, let us go up to Zion, to Yahweh our God'" (vv. 5–6). Judah and Israel will be reunited! For that time in the future he pledged,

> They shall come and sing aloud on the height of Zion, and they shall be radiant over the goodness of Yahweh, over the grain, the wine, and the oil, and over the young of the flock and the herd; their life shall be like a watered garden, and they shall never languish again. (v. 12)

Jeremiah endorsed this propitious forecast with the purchase of a family plot in Anathoth to symbolize the eventual repossession of the land: "Houses and fields and vineyards shall again be bought in this land" (32:15). Chapters 31–32 are linked by the same hope of deliverance and restoration, so their juxtaposition seems intentional.

The return from exile, the repossession of the land, and the reunion of Judah and Israel will inaugurate a new age in the history of God's people. The old Sinai covenant will no longer be adequate. The history of the past 500 years has obviated its limitations. This new time will be marked by a paradigm shift that Jer. 31:22 characterizes dramatically as "a female presses around a (heroic) male." The NRSV reads, "A woman encompasses a man." But the translation of Smith-Goodspeed may be more accurate than the more recently produced versions, "The woman woos the man." In view of the people of God addressed as "O virgin Israel" in v. 21 and God's self-designation as Israel's husband in v. 32, it may imply that Israel as "the virgin" will finally take the initiative to seek union with Yahweh.

THIS NEW TIME WILL NECESSITATE THE CUTTING OF A NEW COVENANT AND, LIKE THE CHANGE IN THE STATUS OF WOMEN, IT WILL BE ANOTHER SIGN OF THE TRANSFORMATION THAT THIS PARADIGM SHIFT WILL INAUGURATE.

This new time will necessitate the cutting of a new covenant and, like the change in the status of women, it will be another sign of the transformation that this paradigm shift will inaugurate. In fact, the new covenant will be the foundation of the paradigm shift because, as v. 34 indicates, it will constitute a new relationship with God: "No longer shall they teach one another, or say to each other, 'Know Yahweh!' for they shall all know me from the least of them to the greatest." Jeremiah can make this resolute promise because the new covenant will be unlike the old. It will not be imposed on God's people externally from above by authorities and teachers who represent the law. It will be inscribed on the fleshly tablets of their hearts: "I will put my law within them, and I will write it on their hearts" (v. 33). As a result, the people of a reconstituted Israel will fulfill God's will naturally by being motivated in freedom from the very center of their being.

This startling shift from one covenantal relationship to another implies a movement from childhood to adulthood. Such is the interpretation of the apostle Paul in Gal. 4:1-7. Israel, as God's first household of faith, consisted of a family of children. Although they were heirs and a divine inheritance awaited them, they were no better than slaves. They had not yet come of age. The old covenant to which they subordinated themselves included purity codes that established discrete boundaries between the realms of the clean and the unclean for protection against contamination and transgression. Their process of redemption, as the book of Deuteronomy attests, was based on reciprocity in order to guarantee their well-being and security by binding God's family into a relationship of indebtedness and obligation. These ideological codes ensured their allegiance to God and guaranteed stability for a secure and prosperous future. But as Jeremiah appears to have realized, the rules and regulations of the law, as imposed from above, proved to be ineffective in constituting a society of justice and peace.

Jesus' death, according to Paul, marked the end of the old moral order of the Mosaic covenant. His resurrection, therefore, established the new moral order of God's kingdom. It is a kingdom or rule, however, that God had conferred on Jesus, and Jesus in turn has conferred on his disciples. But, as disciples, they are no longer children in God's household; they are adults. They have come of age. "Old things have passed; new things have happened," as Paul declares in 2 Cor. 5:19.

Among those "new things" is the fulfillment of Jeremiah's expectation of the enactment of a new covenant: "not of letter but of spirit" (2 Cor. 3:6). The covenant that God had established with the first family of faith "came in glory," but it was "chiseled in letters on stone tablets" (2 Cor. 3:7). The new covenant is "written not with ink but with the Spirit of the living God, not on tablets of stone but on tablets of human hearts." The divine gift that makes the fulfillment of Jeremiah's prophecy possible is the long-awaited inheritance of the Holy Spirit. It is this "Spirit of his Son," as Paul tells the Galatian Christians, that "God sent forth . . . into our hearts, crying 'Abba,' Father" (Gal. 4:6). So we are no longer slaves but sons and daughters who have come of age.

Consequently, the only evidence that Jeremiah's prophecy has been fulfilled and that a new covenant has been enacted is the manifestation of the justice and righteousness God wills in the concrete deeds and activities of human beings. Proceeding from this orientation Paul can identify the Corinthian Christians as "a letter of Christ" (2 Cor. 3:3). As incarnations of God's love, their lives are like a letter or a book that bears witness to the realities of reconciliation and the defeat of death.

SIRACH 24:1-12 (RCL alt.)

Three texts in the Jewish tradition of wisdom literature distinguish Wisdom as a feminine being that emanated from God at creation. In Prov. 8:22-31, Wisdom speaks in the first person and acknowledges herself to be the first of God's acts of old in the form of God's speech activity in calling forth the creation: "I was beside him like a master coordinator" (Prov. 8:30). In Wisd. of Sol. 7:22—8:1, Wisdom, distinguished by twenty-one attributes, appears to be regarded as a preexistent divine being independent of God who "in every generation passes into holy souls and makes them friends of God and prophets."

Wisdom in the poem of Sir. 24:1-12, in contrast to the other Wisdom songs, is ethnically disposed toward Jerusalem and the Jewish people. She glorifies herself as speech emanating "from the mouth of the Most High" (v. 3); and, as she searches for a resting place, she is commanded by God to "Make your dwelling in Jacob, and in Israel receive your inheritance" (v. 8). Established in Zion, Jerusalem becomes her dominion: " So I took root in an honored people, in the portion of the Lord, who is their inheritance" (v. 12). This self-characterization of Wisdom can be related meaningfully to the Gospel lesson of John 1:1-18, especially vv. 10-18. Wisdom eventually makes her dwelling place, pitches her tent, in Jesus of Nazareth and draws Jesus into union with God so intimately that Jesus can say to his disciples in John 14:9-11, "If you have seen me, you have seen the Father."

RESPONSIVE READING
PSALM 147:12-20 (RCL)

This psalm celebrates God's gracious disposal toward Jerusalem, the architectonic center of Israel. Composed perhaps at the time of Nehemiah's completion of the city walls during his governorship over Judah between 426 and 424 B.C.E., vv. 12-20 give thanks to God for building up Jerusalem and gathering the outcasts of Israel. Jerusalem and Zion are charged to "Praise the LORD, for he strengthens the bars of your gates . . ." and "makes peace in your borders" (vv. 12-14). God's grace is manifested above all in privileging Israel by committing "his statutes and ordinances unto Israel. He has not dealt thus with any other nation; they do not know his ordinances" (vv. 19-20). Sirach 24:1-12 testifies to this grace by certifying that Wisdom, which "came forth from the mouth of God," pitched her tent in Jerusalem among God's people.

Jerusalem was God's residence or, more precisely, the place where God's name resided. According to the apostle Paul, the New Jerusalem is the "Jerusalem above" (Gal. 4:26), the transcendent Jerusalem where Christians hold their citizenship (Phil. 3:20), and this heavenly reality is empirically and indeed physically manifested wherever the church or the body of Christ is present. God's Word and God's Wisdom reside in this sacred communion. As Jesus informed his disciples in Matt. 18:20, "For where two or three are gathered in my name, there am I in the midst of them."

WISDOM OF SOLOMON 10:15-21 (RCL alt.)

For a brief period of time, according to the Muratorian Fragment (the earliest record of the church's efforts in the second half of the second century to constitute a second testament alongside the first), the Wisdom of Solomon was included in the canon of the New Testament. Today, of course, it is found among the Apocrypha of the Old Testament.

Verses 15-21 continue the recitation of Wisdom's acts of deliverance, preservation, and restoration. Here the focus is the exodus, the rescue of the Israelites from "a nation of oppressors" under the leadership of a "servant of the LORD" (vv. 15-16), namely, Moses, into whose soul Wisdom had entered. Wisdom also serves as God's surrogate bringing God's people through the Red Sea, drowning their enemies, and guiding and sheltering them along the way to the Promised Land. Wisdom, as God's speech activity, is especially solicitous toward those who are unable to communicate. She opens the mouth of the mute and enables the tongues of infants to speak clearly.

This RCL lection is perfectly suited for the BCP Gospel, Matt. 2:13-15, 19-23, the story of Joseph taking Mary and the child Jesus and fleeing into Egypt to find safety from Herod the Great's intention to kill Jesus. Ironically it is an exodus, but an exodus in reverse.

PSALM 84 or 84:1-8 (BCP)

Here again, as in Ps. 8:1, this psalm is to be sung "upon the Gittith," a tune that was associated with vintage songs. Like Ps. 42, it is a Korahite psalm, and it is appropriately so. For 2 Chron. 20:19 bears witness that there were Korahites among the Levitical choristers in the temple. But the former, Psalm 42, laments that circumstances have denied the poet the privilege of participating in the temple service, while Psalm 84 expresses the intensity of yearning for communion with God that is being fulfilled in the sanctuary. The tone is very personal but at the same time universal in its reverberation of the sentiments of human spirituality. Verse 3 is generally mistranslated in most of the English versions. In Hebrew the sentence presupposes the completion of the psalm by the reader after the phrase "my God" at the end of the verse. Employing the metaphor of the sparrow building a nest for itself and the young, the Korahite poet desires to find a resting place at God's altar; for "Happy are they who dwell in your house" (v. 4).

In the human heart there are highways into God's presence. Among them there is the road that passes through the valley of Baca, a waterless valley. But for the pilgrim journeying to the temple to experience God's presence, it becomes a place of springs because of the early rains that clothe the valley with blessings.

The psalm ends with a prayer in the temple that acknowledges the Lord God who has been experienced along the way to the sanctuary as "a sun and a shield" who "gives grace and glory and who withholds no good thing from those who walk uprightly" (v. 11).

Second Reading

EPHESIANS 1:3-14 (RCL);
EPHESIANS 1:3-6, 15-19a (BCP)

Ephesians 1:3-14 is a thanksgiving formulated in a lengthy sentence of multiple clauses that introduces a letter that was written in the name of Paul but probably is to be attributed to one of his disciples of the generation following the apostle's death.

The Jerusalem of Psalms 147 and 84 has been replaced by "the heavenly places in Christ Jesus" (v. 3) or, according to Gal. 4:26, "the Jerusalem above, that is free, who is our mother." Ephesians introduces the concept of Jesus Christ as "the head" of the body, the church (1:22-23), a metaphor that is not found in the seven letters of Paul that scholarship generally acknowledges as genuinely Pauline. God raised Jesus from the dead and enthroned him at his right hand in the heavenly regions far above all the powers and principalities that impose living death upon human beings.

THE SPIRITUAL BLESSINGS THAT ARE RECITED IN THIS THANKSGIVING ARE NUMEROUS. CHRISTIANS MAY REGARD THEMSELVES AS THOSE WHO WERE CHOSEN IN CHRIST, THE PROTOTYPICAL HUMAN BEING, AND UNDERSTAND THEMSELVES AS PARTICIPANTS IN THIS DIVINE HUMANITY PAR EXCELLENCE.

Christians, who constitute the body of Christ, are joined to Christ as the head. As they continue their historical existence, serving God in and by their living and working, they are "blessed with every spiritual blessing in the heavenly regions in Christ" (v. 3). They are seated with Christ in the heavenly regions (2:6); they are co-enthroned with the head.

The spiritual blessings that are recited in this thanksgiving are numerous. Christians may regard themselves as those who were chosen in Christ, the prototypical human being, and understand themselves as participants in this divine humanity par excellence. They are holy and blameless before God, bearing the identity of God's daughters and sons who have been drawn into God's purpose in Christ to unite heaven and earth. "Redemption through his blood" (v. 7) is also a blessing,

but it is vital to a correct understanding of the atonement that no magical significance is attached to the blood of Jesus Christ. Redemption through his blood is
redemption through his death "for the blood is the life," as Deut. 12:23 states.
When blood is shed for the forgiveness of sins and therefore for reconciliation to
God, the principle that is implied is the sacrifice of a life for a life.

Still another blessing is the disclosure of the mystery of God's will for the
fullness of time, that is, to sum up, or literally "to bring to a head all things in
Christ." The eschatological perspective that is expressed here is derived from the
Jewish tradition of Wisdom, namely, to unify the entire creation in Christ; and it
stands in contrast to the Jewish apocalyptic tradition that culminates in cosmic
separation.

THE GOSPEL

JOHN 1:(1-9) 10-18 (RCL)

In part or in whole, this reading corresponds to the Gospel lection prescribed for the Nativity of the Lord (Christmas Day) and also the BCP lection for
the First Sunday after Christmas. See the comments on this text offered for Christmas Day.

MATTHEW 2:13-15, 19-23 (BCP)

See the comments on the Gospel for the First Sunday after Christmas.

LUKE 2:41-52 (BCP alt.)

Jesus has been born into a Jewish family that fulfills the requirements of
the law. He is circumcised on the eighth day and named Jesus. After thirty-three
days of purification (Lev. 12:4), his parents take him to the temple in Jerusalem in
order "to present him to the Lord" and to enable Mary to offer a sacrifice for her
cleansing (2:22-24). Since Jesus is a first-born son, "a male who opened the
womb," he like all first-born males has to be sacrificed to the Lord. As Exod.
13:13-15 states, "All the males that first open the womb shall be sacrificed to the
Lord. For when Pharaoh refused to let us go, the Lord slew all the first-born in
the land of Egypt." Joseph and Mary, therefore, were confronted with two alter-
natives: to redeem or ransom Jesus or to allow him to be sacrificed to God. They
chose not to redeem him but "to present him to the Lord" (2:22). By being dedicated to God, Jesus remains God's property.

Joseph and Mary also fulfill the requirements of the law by journeying to Jerusalem to observe the Jewish feasts (Exod. 21:14-17). When Jesus is twelve years old, nearing the age of his bar mitzva, his parents take him with them "to keep the feast of unleavened bread" (2:41-42). Perhaps Mary accompanies the two males, because Hillel had prescribed that women should participate in the festival of the Passover.

At the end of the feast, Joseph and Mary join their caravan of relatives to return to Nazareth, but unknown to them Jesus remains behind. When they discover his absence among their kinsfolk, they return to Jerusalem in order to search for him. After three days they find him in the temple, seated in the middle of the teachers, hearing and interrogating them; "and all who heard him were amazed at his understanding and his answers" (v. 47). Already at the age of twelve, before his bar mitzva, Jesus is a person of unusual discernment. His parents are astonished but also indignant, "Why did you treat us like this? Your father and I have been searching for you anxiously" (v. 48).

Since Jesus had been dedicated to God, it should have been no surprise to his parents—and to the reader!—that he should be found in the temple. Yet it is startling that in response to his mother's reprimand, "Your father and I have been searching for you anxiously," Jesus differentiates another father, "Don't you know that it is necessary for me to be in the things of my Father?" (v. 49). Gabriel had informed Mary that her son would be called "Son of the Most High" and "Son of God." Now, already in his youth, Jesus begins to claim that filial relationship with the Most High by referring to him as "my Father." That filial relationship will be presupposed throughout the Gospel. It will be the form of address that Jesus will teach his disciples in the Lord's Prayer (11:2).

AS A BOY HE IS IN THE TEMPLE INVOLVED IN HIS FATHER'S BUSINESS. AT THE CLIMAX OF HIS CAREER, HE WILL CLEANSE THE TEMPLE BUT SOON AFTERWARDS ENUNCIATE ITS IMMINENT DESTRUCTION.

Jesus' relationship to the temple will be reoriented when he returns to Jerusalem for a second time in the narrative world of Luke's Gospel. As a boy he is in the temple involved in his Father's business. At the climax of his career, he will cleanse the temple but soon afterwards enunciate its imminent destruction (19:45-48; 21:5-6). The temple, like the law, is worthy of the highest respect, but it cannot impart salvation to Israel. Stephen, in Acts 7:44-49, will reject the temple because "the Most High does not dwell in houses made with hands." And in Acts 13:38-39, the apostle Paul will declare: "Let it be known to you, therefore, brothers and sisters, that through this man forgiveness of sins is proclaimed to you, and by him everyone that believes is freed from everything from which you could not be freed by the Law of Moses."

Joseph and Mary did not comprehend Jesus' response. But then to what extent will the reader? The narrator concludes this episode by stating that Jesus returned to Nazareth with his parents and was subordinate to them. He may identify himself with God as his Father, but at the same time he acknowledges and submits himself to the authority of his earthly father and mother.

Mary stores up all these things in her heart as treasures. But what a paradox must confront her at this point! Gabriel's annunciation has portrayed a glorious future for her son: "He will be great and be called Son of the Most High, and the Lord God will give him the throne of his father David, and he will rule over the house of Jacob forever, and of his rule there will be no end."

Simeon, on the other hand, has told Mary: "This child is destined for the fall and rising of many in Israel and for a sign to be opposed—and a sword will pierce your own soul—so that the reasonings of many hearts are exposed." The narrator's reference to Mary's storehouse of memories will, of course, be directed at the reader at this junction in the narrative world of the Gospel. Before the careers of John and Jesus are narrated, the reader is lured into reflection on the contradictory projections of Jesus' forthcoming ministry. What kind of future is to be anticipated for him?

More immediately, however, the narrator sums up the so-called unknown years that precede the commencement of Jesus' ministry: "Jesus advanced in wisdom and stature and in grace with God and human beings" (v. 52). The remarkable parallel to this verse in 1 Sam. 2:21 and especially v. 26 may be intended to remind the reader of the experience of the young Samuel in the tabernacle of God before he entered into his career as judge and prophet of Israel.

MATTHEW 2:1-12 (BCP alt.)

See the comments on the Gospel for the Sunday that celebrates the Epiphany of the Lord.

THE SEASON OF EPIPHANY

JACK DEAN KINGSBURY

Introduction

Epiphany is the great season of light and overwhelming joy. The light is Jesus, who is the Christ, the king, and the Son of God. The church celebrates Epiphany by focusing on the person of Jesus. Jesus is the light of God's grace that shines upon Gentiles and therefore also upon us Christians. In the lectionary texts, preachers find three time-honored themes that enable the proclamation of the gospel. All three turn on metaphors associated with light, such as enlightenment, revelation, and insight or perception.

The first theme surfaces in Isa. 60:1-6. Isaiah promises that the day would come wherein the glory of the Lord would arise upon Israel. Israel would become God's light to the Gentile nations, who live in spiritual darkness. The nations would stream to Israel's light to be enlightened by it and to acknowledge Israel's God as Lord. During Epiphany, the church rejoices because Isaiah's promise has at last been fulfilled. The "new Israel" has appeared, Jesus Christ, and it is he who draws the Gentiles to his light and dispels their spiritual darkness.

The second theme dwells on the profound mystery God has disclosed (Eph. 3:1-12). Although God fashioned this mystery already in eternity, he has kept it hidden throughout the ages. Now, however, God has revealed it to the church and to Paul. This mystery, proclaimed by Paul, is that in Christ Jesus, the Gentiles, too, have become partakers of God's promise of salvation.

A third theme typical of the Epiphany season addresses the foolishness of the wise of this world and the wisdom of the foolish (1 Cor. 1:18-31). On the one hand, the wise of the world, whether Jews or Gentiles, perceive the gospel about Christ crucified to be foolishness. On the other hand, the foolish of this world, whether Jews or Gentiles, perceive the gospel about Christ crucified to be the power and wisdom of God unto salvation.

The temptation the preacher faces is to think that these themes are either too familiar within the world of the church or too foreign within the world of glass and steel to capture the interest of the hearers. The key to freshness is to appreciate the intrinsic power that lies in the coherence, both homiletical and theological, of these themes. All three have the goal of leading the hearers, through the appearance of God's light that is Jesus Christ, to renewed trust and confidence in God, their great Savior. Although the hearers have already been enlightened by God through the light of Christ, they nonetheless find themselves conflicted. They encounter enticements to veer away from the light, to reenter the spiritual darkness, and to become lost in it. To combat this, they are summoned to look to the Christ who shines so radiantly in our Epiphany texts. His light enables them to resist the enticements of spiritual darkness, to walk with steady feet through arduous situations, and in renewed trust and confidence to hold firmly to God, their great Savior.

Accompanying this intense focus on the person of Jesus Christ is an apparent difficulty: Within our American pluralistic society, what is one to make of Christianity's absolute claim that Jesus is God's light to the world? Or what is one to make of the merely relative claim, to which the virtue of tolerance is ascribed, that those in other religions who approximate Jesus are equally God's light to the world? Many Christians appear to be so fearful that anyone could in any sense think of them as intolerant that they readily surrender Christianity's absolute claim on behalf of Jesus.

> UNLESS CHRISTIANITY IS TO LOSE ITS VERY SOUL, IT HAS NEVER BEEN, AND CAN NEVER BECOME, A RELIGION THAT SURRENDERS ITS ABSOLUTE CLAIM THAT JESUS CHRIST IS GOD'S LIGHT TO THE WORLD.

Others, while calling for dialogue with world religions, denounce the claim as imperialistic. Still others argue that Jesus is indeed God's light but exclusively for us Christians; the church, therefore, should prescind from engaging in any mission to make of nations disciples of Jesus.

Christianity has encountered such difficulty from the beginning. In the first century, its absolute claim that Jesus Christ is God's light to the world prevented it from making common cause with Judaism. In the second and third centuries especially, this claim prevented Christianity from making common cause with any of the Greek philosophies. The place to which Christianity's focus on Jesus Christ led it is to its trinitarian understanding of God: God is one in essence (nature, substance) but three in persons, God the Father, God the Son, and God the Holy Spirit.

What we find in these developments is that unless Christianity is to lose its very soul, it has never been, and can never become, a religion that surrenders its absolute claim that Jesus Christ is God's light to the world. From of old, the church has reserved the season of Epiphany to acknowledge, confess, and celebrate this absolute claim. As the lectionary texts indicate, the spirit in which the church announces this claim is by no means that of arrogance, intolerance, or imperialism. On the contrary, this claim is preached in the power of the Holy Spirit: Because it constitutes the gospel of God's grace to humankind, it is part and parcel of the very best that the church has to share with the world.

EPIPHANY OF OUR LORD

JANUARY 2/6, 2005

REVISED COMMON	EPISCOPAL (BCP)	ROMAN CATHOLIC
Isa. 60:1-6	Isa. 60:1-6, 9	Isa. 60:1-6
Ps. 72:1-7, 10-14	Psalm 72 or 72:1-2, 10-17	Ps. 72:1-2, 7-8, 10-11, 12-13
Eph. 3:1-12	Eph. 3:1-12	Eph. 3:2-3a, 5-6
Matt. 2:1-12	Matt. 2:1-12	Matt. 2:1-12

These texts paint a fulsome picture of Jesus Christ whom the church celebrates during the season of Epiphany as God's gracious light. In the Old Testament oracle, the church hears Isaiah's prophecy wherein Israel is typed as God's light to which the Gentile nations stream. The antitype to Israel is Jesus Christ, to whose light we Gentile Christians flock. Psalm 72 elaborates on Isaiah's oracle by telling of the "person" and "work" of Jesus. In his person, Jesus is king; in his work, he establishes righteousness and peace, vindicates the poor and oppressed, and reigns over earth, nations, and kings. The Gospel text meshes with Isaiah's oracle and Psalm 72 by characterizing Jesus as the Messiah (Christ) and the king of the Jews. The gospel is also ironical, however, for whereas the Jews (King Herod, all Jerusalem, Jewish authorities) repudiate their newborn king, the Gentile magi receive him. In Ephesians 3, all of these texts soar to their culmination in the proclamation of the gospel, to wit: That the mystery foreordained by God but kept hidden throughout the ages has now been made known and announces to us Gentiles that Christ is the wisdom and power of God unto our salvation.

FIRST LESSON
ISAIAH 60:1-6 (RCL, RC);
ISAIAH 60:1-6, 9 (BCP)

Isaiah 56-66 is generally regarded as Third Isaiah. Because historical and social indicators are sparse, scholarly speculation about its setting is rife. Perhaps those scholars are correct who theorize that the anonymous author of Third Isaiah was a disciple of the author standing behind Second Isaiah (Isaiah 40-55). On this hypothesis, Third Isaiah stems from around the time of the restoration of the temple (515 B.C.E.) following Israel's return to Palestine from Babylon.

Literarily and theologically, 60:1-6, 9 lies at the center of Third Isaiah. It is an oracle of prophetic proclamation that was at home in the temple life of worship and has an end-time (eschatological) coloring. It predicts God's final vindication of Israel in the sight of the Gentile nations. Such vindication, however, makes of Israel God's gracious light to the nations. The nations, therefore, stream to Israel from out of the darkness of their spiritual ignorance to the praise of Israel's God.

It is a mark of Israel's vindication that the Gentile nations heap vast wealth upon Israel (vv.4-6). The metaphors are replete with ancient concepts of this nature: sons and daughters, the abundance of the sea, the wealth of nations, a multitude of camels and young camels, and gifts that befit royalty, such as gold and frankincense. In v. 9, yet another gift is bestowed upon Israel: From afar, its own sons return, not as slaves or the wretched of the earth, but as elites whom the Gentiles have also ladened with silver and gold.

In a homily on Isa. 60:1-6, 9, the preacher will want to stress the eschatological element, which makes the text pregnant for Epiphany Sunday. What binds the text to Epiphany are the interpretive devices of prophecy and fulfillment and of type and antitype. Whereas Israel is the type, Christ is the antitype. Whereas the prophecy of the oracle is that one day Israel, God's light, will

THE PREACHER WILL WANT TO STRESS THE ESCHATO-
LOGICAL ELEMENT, WHICH MAKES THE TEXT PREGNANT
FOR EPIPHANY SUNDAY.

dispel the spiritual benightedness of the Gentile nations, Epiphany reveals that this prophecy has now been fulfilled in Christ: As God's end-time light, Christ is he who dispels the spiritual benightedness of the Gentiles and, on Epiphany Sunday, shines as God's gracious light upon us Gentile Christians. The additional feature that the Gentile nations will heap their plenitude upon Israel engenders in our hearts both anticipation and eagerness: We anticipate the reading of the Gospel text, for therein the Gentile magi will adore the infant Jesus by rendering to him their costly gifts and worship; this makes us eager to bestow on the infant Jesus our costly gifts and worship.

RESPONSIVE READING

PSALM 72:1-7, 10-14 (RCL);
PSALM 72 or 72:1-2, 10-17 (BCP);
PSALM 72:1-2, 7-8, 10-11, 12-13 (RC)

Psalm 72 is a royal psalm. It served as a prayer addressed to God and was uttered during the ceremony of coronation in which the prince in David's line ascended to the throne of Judah and became king. This prayer is eschatological in nature, for it calls upon God to establish an ideal kingdom over which an ideal king rules.

Again, the interpretive device of type and antitype stands out. The terms "king" and "royal son" (v. 1) are antitypical of Jesus as "the king of the Jews" and "the Son of God" (Matt. 2:2, 15; 3:17). The supplication is that God bless the king's rule with, respectively, righteous judgment (v. 2), national prosperity (v. 3), deliverance from social oppression (v. 4), longevity (v. 5), national fertility (v. 6), peace (v. 7), dominion over foes (v. 8), exaltation over the kings of the earth (vv. 10-11), and surcease from need, poverty, and destitution (vv. 12-14). Petition is further made for the king to enjoy long life (v. 15), the nation to live in superabundance (v. 16), and the king's name and fame to endure forever as a blessing to both his own land and the Gentile nations (v. 17).

Matthew is the Gospel of Year A. In it, the coming of Jesus Christ, the Messiah-King of the Jews, marks the inauguration of the kingdom of God (4:17, 23). Noteworthy is that God's kingdom is both a present and future reality (12:28; 25:31-46). Because the future kingdom already impinges upon the present, Jesus' disciples already receive a foretaste of such end-time benefactions as are cited in Psalm 72 and in the Beatitudes (Matt. 5:3-11). Under Jesus, Messiah-King, we Christian disciples live even now in the sphere of God's end-time rule. Even now we raise our joyful hearts to offer up praise and thanksgiving for all the benefactions God has poured out upon us in Jesus Christ.

> WE CHRISTIAN DISCIPLES LIVE EVEN NOW IN THE SPHERE OF GOD'S END-TIME RULE.

SECOND READING
EPHESIANS 3:1-12 (RCL, BCP);
EPHESIANS 3:2-3a, 5-6 (RC)

The shorter text of Eph. 3:2-3a, 5-6 captures in a nutshell what the longer text of 3:1-12 would also say. Both texts highlight one of the major themes of Epiphany, namely, the unveiling of God's mystery, which is Christ himself. Paul boasts that this mystery, which was kept secret from humankind in former generations and which has only now been made known by the Spirit to the church of the holy apostles and prophets, has nevertheless been revealed also to him (vv. 3, 5). In his ministry, Paul unveils this mystery to the Gentiles. It tells how God, through the gospel about Christ, has made Gentiles "fellow heirs" of the apostles and prophets, members of the same body of Christ, and partakers of the promise of salvation (v. 6). Reverberating throughout this text is the note of eschatological joy.

The rhetorical device of which the preacher will want to take advantage is the marked contrast Paul draws between his personal lowliness and the exalted nature of the mission he carries out (vv. 7-12). Paul says of himself, "I am the very least of all the saints" (v. 8). He thus picks up on v. 1 of Ephesians 3, which is not included in the text but is salient to the argument: "I Paul am a prisoner for Christ Jesus for the sake of you Gentiles." In both v. 1 and v. 8, Paul clothes himself in lowliness.

Despite this, Paul is eager not to exclude himself from the circle of the church. His argument is not, say, that he is the scum of the world. Instead, he is a "prisoner for Christ Jesus" and "the least of all the saints." Whereas Paul does place himself at the bottom of the roster, the roster is nevertheless one of supreme dignity, for it is that of the church.

Paul emphasizes his abject lowliness to pave the way for the exalted heights to which his boasting about his mission will soar. He delivers a series of powerful declarations: Just think of it! God has given grace to me so that I, Paul the lowliest, have been raised up to carry out such an exalted mission as that I preach to the Gentiles "the boundless riches of Christ" (v. 8). I make all people "see what is the plan of the mystery hidden for ages in God" (v. 9). I labor so that the church makes known Christ, "the wisdom of God in its rich variety . . . [even] to the rulers and authorities in the heavenly places" (v. 10). On Epiphany Sunday, the preacher announces God's grace to us Gentile Christians so that we, who share in Paul's lowliness, may also carry out the high mission of making known to both the lowly and the exalted of this world the mystery of the gospel of Christ.

> THE PREACHER ANNOUNCES GOD'S GRACE TO US GEN-TILE CHRISTIANS SO THAT WE, WHO SHARE IN PAUL'S LOWLINESS, MAY ALSO CARRY OUT THE HIGH MISSION OF MAKING KNOWN TO BOTH THE LOWLY AND THE EXALTED OF THIS WORLD THE MYSTERY OF THE GOSPEL OF CHRIST.

THE GOSPEL

MATTHEW 2:1-12 (RCL, BCP, RC)

In the Gospel text, Matthew tells the story of Epiphany (2:1-12), which heralds Jesus, the Christ, as the newborn king of the Jews (vv. 1-12). Shaping the story is a fundamental schema that runs through Matthew and other books of the New Testament like a red thread: Salvation is proffered first to the Jews, and then to the Gentiles. This schema entails the repudiation of Jesus by Israel and the acceptance of him by Gentiles. Nevertheless, to proclaim this schema without vitiating it does not call for condemnation either of Israel or of our Jewish neighbors today.

Contrary to much scholarly commentary, at the center of the story stands neither the magi on the one hand nor King Herod, all Jerusalem, and the religious authorities on the other. At the center is the star, which betokens God's grace to Gentiles as imparted by Jesus, the Christ and newborn king of the Jews. The sighting of the star is what first impels the Gentile magi to undertake the arduous journey from the East to Jerusalem (vv.1-2). By no means ordinary, the star is revelatory: It discloses to the magi where Jesus is to be found. The star is characterized as "his" (v. 2), referring to "Jesus." The star is thus the "Jesus star," for its reference to Jesus is its defining characteristic. Although the magi are confronted with deceit and fraud, the star never lets them down. Instead, it remains their steadfast hope and leads them to their goal. The moment the star stops over the house that is home to the infant Jesus, the magi swell with overwhelming eschatological joy. In joy, they offer Jesus both treasure and worship. Precisely as Gentiles, they have been graced by God.

Matthew presents the religious authorities in this story as masters of scripture, or God's word. Scarcely does Herod ask them where the Christ is to be born than they reply, "In Bethlehem of Judea," and quote the passage in which this is prophesied (vv.4-6). Their mastery of scripture, however, does not induce them to hear this word of God and to hasten to Bethlehem to find Jesus, Christ and king. They thus never see the "Jesus star," the star of revelation, but remain where they are, which is in darkness.

THE STAR IS THUS THE "JESUS STAR," FOR ITS REFERENCE TO JESUS IS ITS DEFINING CHARACTERISTIC.

King Herod functions in 2:1-12 as the epitome of "deceit"; his heart is dark and he is evil. No sooner does he hear the "good news" of the magi about the king's birth than he and all Jerusalem with him become seized with fear (v. 3). Herod deceives the magi: "Go and search diligently for the child; and when you have found him, bring me word so that I may also go and pay him homage [worship him]" (v. 8). To Joseph, the angel reveals Herod's real intent: "Herod is about to search for the child, to destroy him" (v. 13). The deep irony is that when the magi do not return to him, Herod must recognize that he is the one who has been "deceived" ("tricked," v. 16).

One possibility for preaching this story of Epiphany is to deliver an expository sermon on it. This would enable the preacher to hold several features in tension: to place the emphasis on the "Jesus star" that reveals God's grace to the Gentile magi and to us Gentile Christians; to keep in view both the flow of the story and the various characters; and to give attention to the schema of salvation to the Jews first and then to the Gentiles.

This last item calls for special comment. In approaching the schema, the preacher will avoid two extremes. The first extreme is to be so theologically unsophisticated as to maim the text by making no mention of the fearful heart of all Jerusalem, the deceitful heart of Herod, or the disobedient heart of the religious authorities who, after having uttered the word of God themselves, do not do it by going to Bethlehem to find Jesus. To avoid this extreme, the preacher need only observe that this story of Epiphany is a perfect model of what preachers say they are about, namely, the proclamation of God's justice and grace, God's law and gospel. Without justice or law, the proclamation of the gospel becomes a mouthing of cheap grace.

The other extreme to be avoided is also one of theological naiveté: to use the story as an occasion to launch harsh words in the direction of our Jewish neighbors whether then or now. In speaking of fearful, deceitful, and disobedient hearts, the preacher will have us Christians in mind. The story is to be applied to us. Even at this, however, the preacher will not scold the hearers as though they are rank unbe-

WITHOUT JUSTICE OR LAW, THE PROCLAMATION OF THE GOSPEL BECOMES A MOUTHING OF CHEAP GRACE.

lievers. Instead, the preacher will lead the hearers to yearn in their hearts for God's forgiving grace in Jesus, our Christ and our king. In yearning for, and receiving, forgiveness, the hearts of the hearers, just like those of the magi, will swell with the overwhelming eschatological joy of Epiphany.

THE BAPTISM OF OUR LORD / FIRST SUNDAY AFTER THE EPIPHANY

JANUARY 9, 2005

REVISED COMMON	EPISCOPAL (BCP)	ROMAN CATHOLIC
Isa. 42:1-9	Isa. 42:1-9	Isa. 42:1-4, 6-7
Psalm 29	Ps. 89:1-29 or	Ps. 29:1-2, 3-4, 5,
	89:20-29	9-10
Acts 10:34-43	Acts 10:34-38	Acts 10:34-38
Matt. 3:13-17	Matt. 3:13-17	Matt. 3:13-17

These texts feature God as elector and the Servant of God as foreshadowing Jesus, the Christ and Son of God. In the prophecy of the Old Testament texts, God chooses the Servant to be his light to the Gentile nations. In fulfillment of this prophecy, the New Testament texts depict Jesus as the one chosen by God to be the end-time light to the Gentiles.

Each of the texts from Isaiah 42 and Psalm 89 divides itself into two parts, with one part devoted primarily to God and the other to the Servant. In both texts, the relationship between God and the Servant is that of the Servant's having been chosen by God. In Isaiah 42, the two parts constitute Servant Songs. The first Song tells of the Servant whom God has chosen to bring forth justice to the nations (vv. 1-4). The second Song tells of God as the almighty Creator who has called the Servant to be a light to the nations (vv. 5-9). In Psalm 89, the two parts are a hymn and a prophetic oracle. In the hymn, God is extolled for having chosen David to be his Servant (vv. 1-18). In the prophetic oracle, the exalted reign of David, the Servant whom God has chosen to rule forever, is lauded (vv. 19-29).

The other texts for the day also focus on God or on Jesus who, in his person and work, fulfills the role of the Servant. Psalm 29 is a paean of praise to God. It is also suggestive of the Gospel story of Jesus' baptism: Just as the powerful voice of God speaks from out of a mighty storm, so the powerful Spirit of God descends upon Jesus from out of heaven (Matt. 3:16). In the narration of the baptismal story itself, the declaration God makes over Jesus, "This is my Son, the Beloved, with whom I am well pleased" (Matt. 3:17), echoes the opening verse of the first Servant Song (42:1). The great difference, however, is that Matthew heightens the dignity of the figure involved so that Isaiah's Servant of God becomes Matthew's Jesus, the Son of God. In the second reading, Acts 10:34-43, the sermon of Peter to Cornelius and those assembled with him strikes the familiar chord of Epiphany: The ministry of Jesus Christ, which began in Israel and has now been spread to the Gentiles, is truly universal, for "everyone who believes in him receives forgiveness of sins through his name" (v. 43).

In these texts, therefore, both God and Jesus are celebrated: God as the one who chooses Jesus, and Jesus as the chosen of God. Jesus is presented as the Christ and Son of God whom God endows with the Spirit in fulfillment of Old Testament prophecy that speaks of the Servant of God. The end-time ministry of Jesus, which follows the pattern of "to the Jews first and then to the Gentiles," is to grant forgiveness to all who believe in him.

FIRST READING

ISAIAH 42:1-9 (RCL, BCP);
ISAIAH 42:1-4, 6-7 (RC)

Isaiah 42 encompasses two Servant Songs. Whereas the first Song tells of the person and work of the Servant (vv. 1-4), the second Song tells of the awesome authority and power with which God endows the Servant to win over the hearts of the Gentiles (vv. 5-9). Whether the Servant is to be thought of as an individual such as a prophet or as a corporate figure such as Israel is a question that the texts themselves do not decide. In the eyes of the church during Epiphany, the Servant foreshadows Jesus, the Christ and the Son of God.

In the first Song, the declaration, "Here is my Servant" (42:1) is the equivalent of the declaration "This is my Servant!" It is a solemn formula used by God to identify the human figure in the Song. In the story of Jesus' baptism, God uses the same formula: "This is my Son!" (Matt. 3:17). The formula makes of both "the Son of God" and "the Servant" titles of majesty.

IN THE EYES OF THE CHURCH DURING EPIPHANY, THE SERVANT FORESHADOWS JESUS, THE CHRIST AND THE SON OF GOD.

As was noted, however, they cannot be used interchangeably. Whereas "the Son of God" defines the "person" of Jesus especially in his relationship to God, the Servant points to the "work" of Jesus (e.g., Matt. 12:18; Acts 3:26; 4:27, 30). Matthew understands the relationship between the two along these lines: Jesus is the Son of God who carries out a ministry of servanthood in fulfillment of Isaiah's initial Servant Song (vv. 1-4).

Isaiah and Matthew also highlight the Servant of God or Jesus, the Son of God, in terms of their chosenness. Isaiah's words, in fact, anticipate those of Matthew.

In Isaiah, God says of the Servant, "My chosen, in whom my soul delights; I have put my spirit upon him" (v. 1). At 3:16-17, Matthew relates, "Jesus saw the Spirit of God descending . . . on him. And a voice from heaven said, 'This is my Son, the Beloved, with whom I am well pleased.'" Not only is the wording of these quotations remarkably similar but it also extends to the mixture of first-person discourse ("I") and third-person discourse ("he"). Of these types of discourse, first-person discourse is the more dramatic and forceful. Isaiah begins with first-person discourse ("My chosen, in whom my soul delights") and Matthew switches to it at 3:17 ("My Son, the Beloved, with whom I am well pleased"). The weight of such discourse rests on "my chosen" and "my Beloved." These are terms of election and they call attention to the absoluteness of God's choice of Jesus to be the Savior of the world ("Jesus and no other").

As crucial as the identity and election of the Servant are, the first Song also does not neglect to tell of his work (Isa. 42:1-4). Three times within four verses one reads: The Servant will "bring forth justice" to the nations (v. 1); he will faithfully "bring forth justice" (v. 3); and, until he has "established justice" in the earth (v. 4). No mistake, the end-time ministry of the Servant is to establish justice among the Gentiles. What, however, does "justice" imply? In *Isaiah 40–66* (Philadelphia: Westminster, 1969), Claus Westermann argues that the two clauses in v. 3, "a bruised reed he will not break, and a dimly burning wick he will not quench," indicate that the Servant establishes justice not in wrathful judgment of the Gentiles but in grace that bestows life. Verse 4 seems to support this, for it pictures the Gentiles as "waiting for," or anticipating, the Servant's ministry to them.

The second Servant Song focuses on the awesome authority by which God entrusts the Servant with his end-time ministry to the Gentiles (Isa. 42:5-9). God's authority rests in his power to have created heaven, earth, and humankind (v. 5). Besides God the Creator, no other god exists but only graven images (v. 8). The Creator God, in fact, is also Lord of the future (v. 9). This God and none other has called the Servant to a ministry of enlightening the Gentiles (v. 6). As the light, the Servant opens blind Gentile eyes to see and releases Gentiles from their prison of darkness (v. 7).

Although this Servant Song proclaims the absolute sovereignty of God, God's sovereignty manifests itself in the Servant's ministry to the Gentiles not as terrible judgment but as the grace of salvation. Most of us Christians, too, are Gentiles. In this season of Epiphany, we Gentile Christians raise our songs of praise as we exult in the grace God has poured out upon us in his Servant-Son, Jesus Christ.

RESPONSIVE READING
PSALM 29 (RCL);
PSALM 29:1-2, 3-4, 5, 9-10 (RC);
PSALM 89:1-29 or 89:20-29 (BCP)

During Epiphany, Psalm 29 invites the church to identify the almighty God whose voice rings out in a fierce storm with the God who, at baptism, fills Jesus with the Spirit. Verse 4 captures well the tone and tenor of the psalm: "The voice of the LORD is powerful; the voice of the LORD is full of majesty." In this vein, the psalm calls upon all beings in heavenly places to ascribe glory to God (vv. 1-2). The Lord's voice has command of the waters of chaos (v. 3), breaks the mighty cedars of Lebanon (vv. 5-6), flashes forth in flames of fire (v. 7), makes the wilderness quake (v. 8), and uproots great oaks and strips the forest bare (v. 9). Verse 10 again sounds the theme of the psalm: "The LORD sits enthroned over the flood; the LORD sits enthroned as king forever." In speaking of God at Jesus' baptism, the preacher has opportunity to give the sermon a fresh touch by describing God in terms of this psalm.

Whereas Ps. 89:1-29 encompasses both a hymn to God (vv. 1-18) and a prophetic oracle about God's establishing the reign of "my servant David" forever (vv. 19-29), the shorter version (vv. 20-29) is confined to the oracle itself. The opening hymn to God resounds with praise for God's everlasting "faithfulness" to the covenant he has made with his servant David and his people. This note of God's faithfulness is struck twice in the opening verse of the hymn: "I will sing of your *steadfast love,* O LORD, forever; with my mouth I will proclaim your *faithfulness* to all generations" (emphasis added).

ALTHOUGH THIS SERVANT SONG PROCLAIMS THE ABSOLUTE SOVEREIGNTY OF GOD, GOD'S SOVEREIGNTY MANIFESTS ITSELF IN THE SERVANT'S MINISTRY TO THE GENTILES NOT AS TERRIBLE JUDGMENT BUT AS THE GRACE OF SALVATION.

In the prophetic oracle, God's servant David responds to God's faithfulness by himself being "faithful" to God (v. 19). God's covenant with David seals God's promise that the reign and line of David will last forever (vv. 28-29). In passages that depict the Servant as one who is "mighty," "chosen" from among Israel's people, "anointed" by God, and "strengthened" by God's arm forever (vv. 19-21), the church will see the oracle as being fulfilled in the story of the baptism of the Son of God (Matt. 3:16-17). Should the preacher base the sermon on the longer version of Psalm 89, the reciprocal features of God's "faithfulness" to the Servant and the Servant's "faithfulness" to God will combine to form a potent message. Into this message of the psalm at Epiphany, however, the preacher will incorporate the place at which the Servant's faithfulness reaches its supreme fulfillment, namely, in the perfect obedience to God of Jesus Son of God.

Second Reading
ACTS 10:34-43 (RCL);
ACTS 10:34-38 (BCP, RC)

In this text from Acts 10, both the longer and shorter versions portray Peter as delivering a sermon to Cornelius and an assembly of Gentiles in which Peter announces salvation in the name of Jesus Christ (vv. 34-35). Such salvation is proffered in accord with the familiar pattern of "to the Jews first" and "then to the Gentiles" (vv. 34-36). The shorter version of the text presents Jesus as God's Anointed whose saving ministry to Israel is also indicative of God's grace toward Gentiles (vv. 34-38). This version culminates at

> IN SPEECHES IN ACTS SUCH AS THIS ONE BY PETER, LUKE'S PROCLAMATION ENCOMPASSES ALL OF WHAT JESUS BOTH SAYS AND DOES.

the end in an expansive description of Jesus' public ministry in Israel: "How God anointed Jesus of Nazareth with the Holy Spirit and with power; how he went about doing good and healing all who were oppressed by the devil, for God was with him" (v. 38). The intention of this version is to place correspondingly more emphasis on Jesus' baptism as the seminal event in his life in which he was equipped by God for his messianic ministry to Israel.

The longer version of this text (10:34-43) depicts Peter as expanding upon his sermon by presenting a fully rounded picture of Jesus' public ministry to Israel that the disciples, authorized to be Jesus' witnesses, have now brought to Cornelius and the Gentiles, to wit:

- The twelve disciples are witnesses of Jesus' ministry in Judea and Jerusalem.
- Israel put Jesus to death, but God raised him from the dead.
- Jesus' disciples can be known to have been authorized to be his witnesses, because the risen Jesus appeared to them, God chose them to attest to Jesus' resurrection, and Jesus ate and drank with them following his resurrection.
- Jesus' disciples were commanded by him to testify to Israel that he is the one ordained by God to judge the living and the dead.
- In consequence of Jesus' anointing by God and ministry, everyone who believes in him receives the forgiveness of sins in his name (vv. 39-43).

This longer version provides the preacher with insight into Luke's understanding of what it is to preach the gospel as compared with that of other New Testament theologians. For example, Paul's proclamation of the gospel concentrates on the death and resurrection of Jesus. Mark's proclamation deals with Jesus' public ministry but in such fashion as to lay greatest stress on his death and resurrection. Matthew's proclamation also emphasizes Jesus' death and resurrection but his teaching as well. In speeches in Acts such as this one by Peter, Luke's proclamation encompasses all of what Jesus both says and does ("did and taught," Acts 1:1), including his return for judgment. For the preacher, therefore, the knack is to proclaim the gospel within the context of each author's theology.

THE GOSPEL

MATTHEW 3:13-17 (RCL, BCP, RC)

Half of Matthew's story of Jesus' baptism tells of Jesus' encounter with John the Baptist leading up to the baptism (vv. 13-15). Of all four evangelists, Matthew is the only one who gives answer to a particularly puzzling question: Why did Jesus have to be baptized at all? Matthew answers this question so as to avoid two badly mistaken notions: (a) that Jesus, like the Jewish crowds who flock to John for baptism, has need to confess his sins (vv. 5-6), and (b) that Jesus is to be thought of as a disciple of John. To dismiss the latter notion, Matthew pictures John himself as saying, "I need to be baptized by you, and do you come to me?" (v. 14). Customarily, the greater person baptizes the lesser. Since Jesus comes to John, Matthew has John declare outright that he is less than Jesus.

To dismiss both mistaken notions, Matthew draws on words of Jesus: "Let it be so now; for it is proper for us in this way to fulfill all righteousness" (v. 15). Matthew is not content that John has already acknowledged he is inferior to Jesus. John must demonstrate in deed the truth of his words. Hence, when Jesus commands John to baptize him, John obeys (v. 15). Such obedience shows that Jesus is in no sense the disciple of John.

To explain why Jesus, unlike the crowds, has no need to confess sins, Matthew describes Jesus as asserting, "It is proper" (3:15). "It is proper" is an equivalent expression of "it is necessary" (16:21). Both expressions refer to the "will of God": John baptizes Jesus because this is part of God's plan of salvation.

The other half of the story dwells on the baptism of Jesus (vv. 16-17). Key points are these. First, some translations mislead the reader into thinking that John—or also the crowds or even the Pharisees and Sadducees (v. 7)—witnesses the two revelatory events that take place immediately following the baptism. If either John, or the crowds, or the religious authorities saw "the Spirit of God" and heard God himself speak, Matthew could not possibly depict John later as doubting (11:3), or the crowds as thinking that Jesus is no more than a prophet (16:13-14), or the Pharisees as plotting to kill Jesus (12:14). What kind of a paltry deity would Matthew have if the divine Spirit and the divine voice can be seen or heard and human beings not be instantly transformed by them?

No, the clue is to observe that in the Greek, Jesus alone sees ("he saw") the descent of the Spirit upon him (v. 16). In vv. 16-17, the text notes that once Jesus had been baptized, he left John behind and stepped unattended into the presence of God. There Jesus alone sees the Spirit descend, and Jesus alone hears the voice. If Jesus alone sees and hears, then why does the voice not say to Jesus, "You are my Son," instead of, "This is my Son"? The reason is that God makes a public, not a private, declaration. God's declaration, however, is not to John, not to the crowds, and not to the religious authorities, but to us, the readers of Matthew's story. The power of the baptismal declaration is that none other than God makes known to us readers, far in advance of any other human character within the story, the deepest mystery of the person of Jesus, namely, that he is the Son of God.

Other noteworthy points are these: No conflict exists between God's pouring out of the Spirit of God upon Jesus at his baptism and the conception of Jesus in Mary by the Holy Spirit (1:18, 20). Jesus' conception by the Spirit explains that his origin is in God. Jesus' endowment with the Spirit at baptism explains the divine authority on which he speaks and acts during his end-time ministry (vv. 16-17). In Matthew's eyes, Jesus is the Son of God in at least three respects: First, Jesus has such an intimate relationship with God that it can only be compared to the "knowledge" that the "one flesh" of man and woman can be said to have (11:25-26); second, Jesus is perfectly obedient to God, even unto death; and third, God is at work in Jesus in a way in which the divine Self has been at work in no other human being in all of history.

GOD IS AT WORK IN JESUS IN A WAY IN WHICH THE DIVINE SELF HAS BEEN AT WORK IN NO OTHER HUMAN BEING IN ALL OF HISTORY.

SECOND SUNDAY AFTER THE EPIPHANY / SECOND SUNDAY IN ORDINARY TIME

JANUARY 16, 2005

REVISED COMMON	EPISCOPAL (BCP)	ROMAN CATHOLIC
Isa. 49:1–7	Isa. 49:1–7	Isa. 49:3, 5–6
Ps. 40:1–11	Ps. 40:1–10	Ps. 40:2, 4, 7–8, 9–10
1 Cor. 1:1–9	1 Cor. 1:1–9	1 Cor. 1:1–3
John 1:29–42	John 1:29–41	John 1:29–34

The texts that sound the overall theme of any given season are those of the Gospel. The theme of Epiphany is Jesus Christ himself, namely, the significance of his "person" and "work" with emphasis on his being God's light to the Gentiles. During the first three Sundays, the Gospel readings have highlighted the "person" of Jesus by ascribing titles of majesty to him: On Epiphany Sunday, the magi identify Jesus as the king of the Jews (Matt. 2:1-12); on the first Sunday, God declares Jesus to be the beloved Son of God (Matt. 3:13-17); and on this second Sunday, John the Baptist bears witness to Jesus and designates him as the Lamb of God and the Son of God (John 1:29-42).

On the third and fourth Sundays after Epiphany, the Gospel lections highlight the "work" of Jesus. On the third Sunday, Matthew provides a summary description of the whole of Jesus' public ministry to Israel and characterizes it as one of teaching, preaching, and healing (4:12-23). On the fourth Sunday, the teaching of Jesus is singled out in two ways: First, the Gospel lection is taken from the Sermon on the Mount, which is the best known of Jesus' five great sermons in Matthew; and second, the text is drawn from the Beatitudes, which constitute the best-known section of the Sermon on the Mount (5:1-12). On the last Sunday, the Gospel recapitulates the entire season of Epiphany and points ahead to the season of Lent by narrating the story of Jesus' transfiguration (Matt. 17:1-13). This story highlights the "person" of Jesus: For a second time, God declares Jesus to be "my beloved Son." It also points to Jesus' "work" and anticipates the season of Lent: God commands the three disciples to "hear" Jesus, that is, to attend to his prediction of his upcoming passion, death, and resurrection (17:5, 9-13).

Isaiah 49:1-7 constitutes the Second Servant Song. Two textual problems, however, undermine its coherence. Both problems arise from an identical confusion, namely, whether the Servant is to be understood as an "individual" or as the nation of "Israel." Before the Song can be preached, therefore, this confusion must be cleared up and the Song's coherence established.

To get at the two textual problems, we arbitrarily divide the Song into 49:1-4 and 49:5-7. In vv. 1-4, the Servant is explicitly said to be "Israel" (v. 3). In the other three verses, however, the Servant is depicted as an "individual" ("before I was born," "while I was in my mother's womb," v. 1; "I have labored in vain," "I have spent my strength," v. 4).

In 49:5-7, this same confusion between the Servant as Israel and the Servant as an individual reappears. It stems from an improper delimitation of the Song. The Song should have been ended at v. 6 but has been extended to include v. 7. Verse 7, however, is the source of the confusion. Thus, in v. 5 the Servant is manifestly an individual ("who formed me in the womb to be his servant"). But in v. 7a, the Servant is the nation of Israel: God is described as the "Redeemer of Israel," which means that God's "Holy One" also refers to Israel. Further, the references in v. 7b, d are to Israel: One "deeply despised, abhorred by the nations, the slave of rulers . . . chosen [by] the LORD."

This dual confusion between "Israel" and "individual" admits of no perfect solution. One does best, however, to construe the Servant not as Israel but as an individual. Verses 5-6 decide the matter: In both, the Servant is depicted as conducting a ministry to Israel ("Jacob," "Israel"), in which case the Servant is decidedly an individual. Admittedly, this makes for difficulty in interpreting v. 7a, b.

Having established the textual coherence of the Song, the preacher can concentrate on understanding the flow of the text. In 49:1a, b, the Servant calls upon the Gentiles to give ear to him. Next, however, he recapitulates his ministry to Israel. Before he was born, God elected him for ministry (v. 1c, d). God equipped him by endowing him with a tongue as sharp as a sword and as deadly as an arrow, and by keeping him safe (v. 2). In commissioning him to ministry in Israel, God bestowed on him the title of God's own "Servant," the one through whom God is to be glorified (v. 3).

At 49:4, the Servant suddenly changes his perspective. Instead of "looking forward" to ministry, he "looks backward" over a ministry already completed. He judges his ministry in Israel to have totally failed. God, however, honors his ministry (v. 5c). What is more, God commissions him to a much greater ministry: "I will give you as a light to the nations [Gentiles], that my salvation may reach to the end of the earth" (v. 6).

The various elements that make this second Servant Song a text to be read during Epiphany stand out plainly. The pattern of type and antitype occurs: The role of the Servant of God is fulfilled by Jesus Christ, the Son of God. The overarching schema of both the ministry of the Servant and of Jesus in the Gospels is the same: "to the Jews first" and "then to the Gentiles" (49:4, 5-6). The fundamental theme of "light" is sounded yet again: Just as the Servant of God is a "light to the nations [Gentiles]," so Jesus Christ is God's end-time light to the Gentiles (v. 6). Last, two more parallels between the Servant of God and the Son of God are apparent if v. 7 is interpreted as speaking of the Servant as an individual: First, the Son of God, like the Servant of God, is God's "chosen Holy One" (v. 7a, d); and second, the Son of God, like the Servant of God, will be worshiped by the kings and princes of the Gentile nations (v. 7c). Once the preacher has surmounted the problem of its coherence, this second Servant Song makes for a compelling Epiphany sermon.

> ONCE THE PREACHER HAS SURMOUNTED THE PROBLEM OF ITS COHERENCE, THIS SECOND SERVANT SONG MAKES FOR A COMPELLING EPIPHANY SERMON.

RESPONSIVE READING
PSALM 40:1-11 (RCL);
PSALM 40:1-10 (BCP);
PSALM 40:2, 4, 7-8, 9-10 (RC)

In all three variations, Psalm 40 is one of thanksgiving. In both structure and theme, it is almost self-explanatory. Verses 1-2 depict the terrible affliction the psalmist has endured; the mention of "waiting patiently" suggests that the disease or situation had lasted for some period of time. Verses 3-4 emphasize not only that one must "trust" in time of affliction but also that such trust is to be placed in none but God. Verse 6 draws a parallel between the psalmist's salvation by God ("my God") and the community's salvation by God ("your deeds toward us"). Verses 7-8 describe the way the psalmist first responds to God's salvation, by doing God's will. Verses 9-10 tell of the psalmist's second response, which is to announce to the whole community the glad news about God's saving help, love, and faithfulness. If v. 11 belongs to the text, it constitutes a prayer to God in

> THIS SONG OF THANKSGIVING HAS IMMEDIATE APPLICATION TO THE LIVES OF CONGREGANTS. IN A CONFLICTUAL AGE IN WHICH MOST EVERYONE BEARS THE SCARS OF LIFE, IT IS ESPECIALLY APT.

which the psalmist supplicates God so as to be spared from enduring such affliction ever again.

This song of thanksgiving has immediate application to the lives of congregants. In a conflictual age in which most everyone bears the scars of life, it is especially apt. As the text for an Epiphany sermon, however, the preacher will want to avoid the trap of talking in a private vein about "God and me." The salvation of which this psalm speaks so eloquently is made available to us Christians only in Jesus Christ.

SECOND READING

1 CORINTHIANS 1:1-9 (RCL, BCP); 1 CORINTHIANS 1:1-3 (RC)

However much Paul may be thought to have adapted the rules of letter-writing to suit his own purposes, he clearly made use of the conventions that governed such writing in the Greco-Roman world of his day. The structure of the opening verses of 1 Corinthians attests to this. "Paul" is the author, "Sosthenes" is his co-missionary, and the recipients are "the church . . . in Corinth" (1:1-2). Verse 3 is the "greeting," and vv. 4-9 constitute the "thanksgiving." Because Paul weaves into the thanksgiving mention of the various topics he will take up throughout the rest of the letter, we shall concentrate on the shorter version of the text (vv. 1-3).

Characteristic of Paul in his letters is that every word counts. Words are not throwaways, which is why commentaries on relatively short epistles get to be such thick books. Whereas 1:1-2 comprises a lengthy literary unit, it does not, until supplemented by v. 3, form a complete sentence. The term that binds this lengthy unit together is "called": Paul has been called to be an apostle of Jesus Christ, and the Chris-

> THE FORCE OF "CALLED" IS THAT IT IS NOT BY VIRTUE OF THEIR OWN DOING THAT PAUL BEARS THE TITLE AND OFFICE OF APOSTLE OR THAT THE CORINTHIANS HAVE BECOME SAINTS.

tians at Corinth have been called to be holy ones, or saints. The force of "called" is that it is not by virtue of their own doing that Paul bears the title and office of apostle or that the Corinthians have become saints. Instead, Paul is an apostle of Christ Jesus by the will of God (v. 1), and Christ Jesus is the one in whom the Corinthians have been sanctified (v. 2). Furthermore, the congregation in Corinth, though local, is nonetheless the entire church of God at this place, and the Corinthians, like saints everywhere, offer their prayers and worship to Jesus Christ, who is Lord of all saints (v. 2).

The greeting in 1:3, which completes the sentence begun in vv. 1-2, will be familiar to many preachers because they properly use it to greet their hearers at the beginning of their sermons. In Pauline theology, "grace" is the favor that God shows toward us sinners and all of fallen creation in Jesus Christ. "Peace" results from God's having graciously acted in the death of Jesus Christ to reconcile all of creation to Godself, that is to say, to do away with the hostility that a fallen creation shows toward God. Just as grace is grounded in God, who becomes our Father instead of our Judge, so peace is grounded in the reconciling death of Jesus Christ, who becomes our Lord.

This short text encompasses the whole of Pauline theology. If the preacher dwells on the "grace" of God shown to us in Jesus Christ, on the "peace" that God brings about through the reconciling death of Christ, and what it means for us Christians to be "called" not by ourselves but by God through Christ, one has all the ingredients that makes for a profound and well-rounded sermon.

THIS SHORT TEXT ENCOMPASSES THE WHOLE OF PAULINE THEOLOGY.

THE GOSPEL
JOHN 1:29-42 (RCL);
JOHN 1:29-41 (BCP);
JOHN 1:29-34 (RC)

On the First Sunday after the Epiphany, Matthew tells of the baptism of Jesus by John (3:13-17). On this Second Sunday, John tells of the witness to Jesus by John (1:29-42). In Matthew, "John the Baptist" is the antitype of whom Elijah is the type. As Elijah's antitype, John fulfills the end-time mission associated with Elijah: John goes before Jesus to prepare Israel through a baptism of repentance for the coming of Jesus (3:1-6; 17:9-13). In John, "John the Baptizer" is a voice who engages in the activity of baptizing so as to bear witness in Israel to Jesus as God's light of the world (1:6-8, 23, 31, 33). In Matthew, John the Baptist is thus the end-time Elijah who baptizes to prepare Israel for the coming of Jesus Messiah. In John, John is a voice who engages in baptizing to bear witness that Jesus is God's light.

The difference between the longer and shorter versions of the Gospel text is that whereas the longer version tells of both the "person" and "work" of Jesus (1:29-42), the shorter version tells only of the "person" of Jesus (1:29-34). To reveal the identity of Jesus within his story, the evangelist John pictures the Baptizer as designating Jesus as "the Lamb of God" (v. 29) and "the Son of God" (v. 34). Within the stories of Mark, Matthew, and Luke, the identity of Jesus and the mystery of his person are only gradually unveiled to human beings as various characters ask "who Jesus is." John, however, takes a different approach. Already in the prologue, he informs not only his readers of the deepest mystery of Jesus' person but also presents the Baptizer as knowing this. The Word who will become incarnate in Jesus of Nazareth (v. 14) is "the light" of humankind, and the Baptizer, who is sent by God, bears witness to the light so that, because of his witness, all may come to believe in the light (vv. 6-8).

Against the backdrop of John's prologue, therefore, it finally matters not that the Baptizer should designate Jesus as "the Lamb of God" or "the Son of God." Exalted as these titles are, they have already been defined. Whether as the Lamb of God or the Son of God, Jesus is essentially the Light. It is also the prologue, therefore, that informs us readers how to understand such words of the Baptizer as these: that Jesus "ranks ahead of me" and "was before me"; that "I came baptizing with water . . . that he might be revealed to Israel"; and that "I myself did not know him" (1:30-33). Jesus ranks ahead of, and existed before, the Baptizer because he is the pre-existent Word, the Light of humankind. The Baptizer did not know, and could not have known, who Jesus is, for any such knowledge must be revealed by God. To disclose to Israel that Jesus is God's Light to the world, the Baptizer baptizes with water.

In 1:35-42, the Gospel text turns to the "work" of Jesus. This is not to say, however, that Jesus' work has not already been touched on: Jesus "takes away the sin of the world" and, in contrast to the Baptizer, "baptizes with the Holy Spirit" (vv. 29, 33). Again, these words the Baptizer speaks in vv. 29 and 33 have already been interpreted for us in the prologue. As the Light of the world, Jesus takes away the sin of the world and baptizes with the Holy Spirit neither by shedding his blood (although he does this, too!) nor by actually baptizing people ("it was not Jesus himself who baptized," 4:2) but by "shining in the darkness" and "enlightening everyone" with knowledge of God (1:5, 9; 3:31-36). As the Light of the world, Jesus "saves" in John's Gospel by revealing God to benighted human beings: "Whoever has seen me has seen the Father" (14:9).

> WHEN THIS GOSPEL LECTION IS PREACHED AGAINST THE HORIZON OF JOHN'S THEOLOGY, IT IS SCARCELY IMAGINABLE THAT ANY TEXT COULD SURPASS IT IN FORCE AND DIGNITY.

Otherwise, the Gospel lection specifies the work of Jesus as that of calling disciples (1:35-42). In this connection, the Baptizer even participates in Jesus' work. He bears witness to Jesus, "Look, here is the Lamb of God!" whereupon two of his own disciples leave him to follow after Jesus. When this Gospel lection is preached against the horizon of John's theology, it is scarcely imaginable that any text could surpass it in force and dignity.

THIRD SUNDAY AFTER THE EPIPHANY / THIRD SUNDAY IN ORDINARY TIME

JANUARY 23, 2005

REVISED COMMON	EPISCOPAL (BCP)	ROMAN CATHOLIC
Isa. 9:1–4	Amos 3:1–8	Isa. 8:23—9:3
Ps. 27:1, 4–9	Ps. 139:1–17 or 139:1–11	Ps. 27:1, 4, 13–14
1 Cor. 1:10–18	1 Cor. 1:10–17	1 Cor. 1:10–13, 17
Matt. 4:12–23	Matt. 4:12–23	Matt. 4:12–23 or 4:12–17

In the lections for the Third Sunday after the Epiphany, the primary focus shifts from the person of Jesus to his work. Jesus begins with a public ministry in Israel, which Matthew characterizes as one of teaching, preaching, and healing (4:23; 9:35; 11:1). Not until Holy Week and Easter, however, will Jesus' public ministry culminate with his death on the cross and his glorious resurrection from the dead by God.

During Epiphany, Jesus is presented as God's light to the Gentiles. The texts for this Sunday point out that as Jesus takes up his public ministry in Israel, Gentiles sit in deep darkness. This motif of darkness and light pervades these texts. In the Old Testament and the Gospel lections, this motif is the featured element. In 4:14–16, Matthew highlights Isa. 9:1–2 as fulfilled prophecy by embedding it in a "formula quotation"; the emphasis on darkness and light is pronounced: "Galilee of the Gentiles—the people who sat in darkness have seen a great light, and for those who sat in the region and shadow of death light has dawned."

In the other readings, metaphors become the means by which this motif of darkness and light is projected. In Amos 3, darkness becomes Israel's unfaithfulness to God, and light shines not at all. In Psalm 27, darkness becomes fear of being assailed by evildoers and foes, and light becomes confidence in God's deliverance. In Psalm 139, darkness becomes separation from God, and light the experience of intimacy with God. And in 1 Corinthians, darkness becomes strife within the community of believers, and light the unity that results from the power inherent in the proclamation of Christ's cross.

ISAIAH 9:1-4 (RCL);
AMOS 3:1-8 (BCP);
ISAIAH 8:23—9:3 (RC)

Amos 3:1-8 is a text of unremitting darkness. It is "the word" that God speaks through the prophet "against the people of Israel" (v. 1). What prompts God's utter condemnation is that Israel is the one nation among all others whom God has chosen to be his people, yet Israel has been unfaithful to God (v. 2). Israel is without excuse, for God has revealed his will through the prophets (v. 8). God, therefore, is like a man who will indeed keep his appointment with another, or a lion roaring in the forest, or a snare springing up from the ground, or a trumpet blaring oncoming disaster (vv. 3-6). Faithless Israel is the one with whom God will keep the appointment, the prey that the lion has spotted or the snare caught, the city about to be stormed. In the face of divine disaster, fear is the order of the day (v. 8).

> DO WE NOT DELUDE OURSELVES INTO BELIEVING THAT OUR FREEDOM LIES NOT IN BEING UNDER GOD BUT IN BEING OUT FROM UNDER GOD?

This text delivers a harsh but salutary word of judgment. The implicit questions it raises are searching: Are we American Christians not losing our sense of the righteousness of God? Do we not tempt divine judgment in being so little fearful of God despite our iniquities? Do we not delude ourselves into believing that our freedom lies not in being under God but in being out from under God? And are we not all too ready to plead innocence in the face of all the evil we condone? This text brings close to home the terrible consequence of mocking God.

An opposite tone prevails in Isa. 9:1-4. It is a sunny text, for gloom no longer exists and the time of which it speaks is glorious, to wit: The nation of Israel increases, joy abounds, people exult, and slaves are freed. Nevertheless, this text does not proclaim cheap grace, and the reason is that it prophesies of Jesus Christ as the end-time light of God that has now shone on us Gentiles walking and living in deep darkness. The art of preaching this text lies in describing the "deep darkness" that surrounds and threatens us on the one hand and, on the other, the bright light of God's grace and forgiveness that shines upon us in Jesus Christ. (As a footnote, the difference between what seem to be two texts from Isaiah, 8:23—9:3 and 9:1-4, is not real but apparent: The first one follows the versification found in the Hebrew text [RC] and the other the versification found in Protestant Bibles [RCL].)

> THE ART OF PREACHING THIS TEXT LIES IN DESCRIBING THE "DEEP DARKNESS" THAT SURROUNDS AND THREATENS US ON THE ONE HAND AND, ON THE OTHER, THE BRIGHT LIGHT OF GOD'S GRACE AND FORGIVENESS THAT SHINES UPON US IN JESUS CHRIST.

RESPONSIVE READING

PSALM 27:1, 4-9 (RCL);
PSALM 139:1-17 or 139:1-11 (BCP);
PSALM 27:1, 4, 13-14 (RC)

Psalm 27 is a lament. A lament is distinguished by two fundamental elements, which in this psalm are juxtaposed to each other in two blocks of verses. One element is the plight of the suffering righteous person and the other is the righteous person's trust and confidence in God as deliverer.

In vv. 1-6, the suffering righteous person expresses complete confidence in God. God is light and refuge, so that the person is unafraid (v. 1). Indeed, from evildoers and adversaries, God protects the righteous person (v. 2). Even though the person were to be opposed by an entire army in a time of war, his or her confidence in God would not flag (v. 3). Having now found safety in the temple, the righteous person is secure and will, when delivered, offer sacrifice to God in thanksgiving (vv. 4-6).

In vv. 7-14, the suffering righteous person lays out in prayer before God his or her plight. Apparently, false accusations are being brought against the person (v. 12). These accusations have already separated the person from father and mother (v. 10) and threaten to do the person great personal harm ("false witnesses . . . breathing out violence," v. 12). The heartfelt plea of the righteous person is that he or she find intimacy with God, who is the "God of my salvation" (vv. 7-9). The psalm concludes on another note of confidence (vv. 13-14).

Psalm 139:1-17 is a hymn of praise. Hans-Joachim Kraus (*Psalms 60–150: A Continental Commentary* [Minneapolis: Augsburg, 1989], p. 514) identifies the setting as the situation in which a slandered or persecuted individual enters the temple area and submits to a test by God on the grounds that God alone knows a person's heart. Regardless of whether the psalmist still endures the test or has successfully completed it, he or she offers up a "doxology of judgment" in which God is praised for the divine omniscience (vv. 1-6), omnipresence (vv. 7-12), and omnipotence (vv. 13-17).

In vv. 11-12, the theme of Epiphany comes to the fore as the psalmist tells not only of darkness and light but of darkness as giving way to light: As far as God is concerned, "darkness is as light" and the "night is as bright as the day." If this psalm were used as the text for a sermon in Epiphany, the congregants might well find it refreshing if the preacher were to take up the divine attributes of omniscience, omnipresence, and omnipotence, which otherwise are so seldom mentioned. God has turned the darkness of us Gentile Christians into light by enlightening us through Jesus Christ, in whom the wisdom (omniscience), presence (omnipresence), and power (omnipotence) of God are made known to us.

1 CORINTHIANS 1:10-18 (RCL);
1 CORINTHIANS 1:10-17 (BCP);
1 CORINTHIANS 1:10-13, 17 (RC)

The darkness into which the Christians at Corinth have sunk is that of factiousness and divisiveness. The light with which Paul would dispel this darkness and heal the divisions is the unity of mind and purpose that can come only through the proclamation of the cross of Christ (1:10). This much in the text is clear. Beyond this, however, commentators tend to run in circles: To make sense of the text, they must tease out of the rest of the letter a picture of the situation at Corinth; but to get a picture of this situation, they must understand this text. Regarding details, see Roy A. Harrisville, *1 Corinthians* (Augsburg Commentary on the New Testament [Minneapolis: Augsburg, 1987]), pp. 33–36.

Harrisville understands the opponents of Paul at Corinth to be enthusiasts, that is to say, persons who believe that in the power of spirit, they could be whisked away from the conditions of time, space, and earth into a higher realm or sphere of existence (experience). In Paul's eyes, the difficulty with this is that if such a realm were thought to constitute true existence, then the cross of Christ would have no place within it. Paul was right, for his opponents were contemptuous of the cross (v. 18).

As reported to Paul by persons associated with an otherwise unknown person named Chloe, Paul's opponents had caused divisions ("schisms") within the church at Corinth (vv. 10-11). They had misled the Corinthians into assigning magical power to baptism. Factions had sprung up that rivaled one another for prominence by virtue of their "patron," whether Paul, Apollos, or Peter (v. 12). One faction even looked to Christ for spiritual exaltation, which denigrated the Christ of the cross (v. 12). Paul attacks such factiousness: Divisions, he asserts, do not exist in Christ, and he himself was neither crucified for the Corinthians nor was his ministry to them one of baptism (vv. 13-16). In saying this, Paul is not, of course, attacking baptism as

> THE DARKNESS THAT THREATENS TO EXTINGUISH THE LIGHT IN MOST OF CHRISTIAN AMERICA TODAY IS THE CONFLICTUAL NATURE OF OUR TIMES.

such (Rom. 6:1-4). Instead, he distances himself from it because it has been tied in to the "eloquent wisdom" his opponents (false evangelists) have spouted since coming to Corinth (v. 17). Paul contends that whereas his ministry brought him to Corinth to proclaim the gospel, the ministry of his eloquent opponents has reduced the gospel to nothing.

The darkness that threatens to extinguish the light in most of Christian America today is the conflictual nature of our times. Conflict of a personal, doctrinal, social, or cultural sort tears asunder families, congregations, denominations, and society itself. Never have the voices of stridency and hostility been so loud. In this text, Paul argues that the thing for Christians to do to overcome such conflict in their circles is to get back to the very basics of their faith, namely, the proclamation of the crucified Christ. From the light of the cross alone comes the power to banish the darkness.

The Gospel
MATTHEW 4:12-23 (RCL, BCP);
MATTHEW 4:12-23 or 4:12-17 (RC)

This Gospel reading (4:12-23) introduces the public ministry of Jesus in Israel by capturing as much of Jesus' activity as possible, namely, his move to Capernaum (vv. 12-16), the call of the first disciples (vv. 18-22), and the ministerial activity in which Jesus engages (teaching, preaching, and healing, vv. 17, 23). But it also strikes the theme of Epiphany in the expression "Galilee of the Gentiles" (v. 15). Two hurdles stand in the way of this excision: The public ministry of Jesus does not begin in Matthew until v. 17; and because "Galilee of the Gentiles" is not a reference to the Gentile nations but to the region of Galilee as such, the expression has virtually nothing to do with Epiphany. In the perspective of Matthew, vv. 12-23 constitute two distinct texts, one looking backward and one looking forward. Verses 12-16 look backward to 2:23 and narrate Jesus' resettlement from Nazareth to Capernaum, both of which cities are in Galilee; and vv. 17-23 look forward to Jesus' upcoming ministry in Israel (see 9:35; 11:1). As the basis for a sermon, the preacher does best to choose either the one part or the other.

If the preacher chooses to proclaim 4:12-16, it is the culmination of the entire first part of Matthew (1:1—4:17). The crucial element in the text is the formula quotation (4:14-16). Formula quotations in Matthew are a special breed, introduced by some form of the term "fulfilled." Including this text, the first part of Matthew contains a cluster of five of them (1:22-23; 2:15, 17-18; 3:3). In 1:1, Matthew declares Jesus to be the "Messiah, the Son of David, the Son of Abraham." As the

IN JESUS, THE MESSIAH, ALL OF ISRAEL'S "PROPHECY" FINDS ITS "FULFILLMENT."

Messiah, Jesus is the one in whom the history of Israel, which began with father Abraham and in which King David was the high point, reaches its culmination (1:17). Matthew underlines this very point through his use of formula quotations: In Jesus, the Messiah, all of Israel's "prophecy" finds its "fulfillment." The preacher who bases the sermon on 4:12-16 can develop a powerful message along these lines and not lose sight of Epiphany, whose lead text is also in the first part of Matthew, 2:1-12.

If the preacher selects 4:17-23 as the text for the sermon, then Jesus' broader activity of teaching, preaching, and healing (vv. 17, 23) becomes the framework for focusing on the calling of the first disciples (vv. 18-22). This text divides itself into two scenes (vv. 18-20, 21-22). The two scenes are parallel, even in structure, and each one lays stress on "following Jesus" (vv. 20, 22). The supreme authority with which Jesus summons disciples stems from the baptism (3:13-17) and is reinforced by the immediacy of the obedience with which those who are summoned respond. The cost of discipleship is reflected in the abandonment of profession (fishermen), goods (nets, boat), and family (father). This high cost is indicative, not of irresponsibility toward clients and relatives, but of the immense commitment involved in discipleship. In 8:18-22, Matthew returns to these topics. The applicability of these various features of the text to the hearers will be apparent.

IF THE PREACHER SELECTS 4:17-23 AS THE TEXT FOR THE SERMON, THEN JESUS' BROADER ACTIVITY OF TEACHING, PREACHING, AND HEALING (VV. 17, 23) BECOMES THE FRAMEWORK.

FOURTH SUNDAY AFTER THE EPIPHANY / FOURTH SUNDAY IN ORDINARY TIME

JANUARY 30, 2005

REVISED COMMON	EPISCOPAL (BCP)	ROMAN CATHOLIC
Mic. 6:1-8	Mic. 6:1-8	Zeph. 2:3; 3:12-13
Psalm 15	Ps. 37:1-18 or	Ps. 146:1-2, 5-7,
	37:1-6	8-9, 10
1 Cor. 1:18-31	1 Cor. 1:(18-25) 26-31	1 Cor. 1:26-31
Matt. 5:1-12	Matt. 5:1-12	Matt. 5:1-12a

Last Sunday, the focus of the Gospel reading shifted from the person of Jesus to his work. Jesus began his public ministry in Israel, which Matthew describes as one of teaching, preaching, and healing. The order in which Matthew cites these activities is not happenstance. As important as preaching may be to us today, teaching dominates in Matthew (4:23; 9:35; 11:1). Matthew bundles most of Jesus' teaching into five great discourses: the Sermon on the Mount (5:1—7:29), the Missionary Discourse (9:35—10:42), the Parable Discourse (13:1-52), the Church Discourse (18:1-35), and the End-Time Discourse (24:2—25:46). The crown of these jewels is the Sermon on the Mount, and the Gospel for this Sunday is the Beatitudes (5:1-12), which ranks among the best-known sections in all of scripture.

In one way or another, all of the scripture readings for this Sunday take their cue from the Beatitudes. Some emphasize the quality of righteousness: Mic. 6:1-6 prescribes the ethical life God requires of the chosen people; Zeph. 2:3 and 3:12-13 tell of the righteous remnant of Israel; and Psalm 15 virtually defines the concept of righteousness. The main feature of the Beatitudes, however, is the end-time "reversal of fortunes" such as that the poor in spirit inherit the kingdom of God, or that those who mourn will be comforted. This is the feature to which Pss. 37:1-18 and 146 point. It also appears in the contrast one finds in 1 Cor. 1:18-31 between the foolishness of human wisdom and the end-time wisdom of God that has been revealed in the proclamation of Christ crucified. Still, the intention that underlies all of the readings for the day is that of Epiphany, which is to let the teaching of Jesus, whether in prophecy or fulfillment, shine upon us Gentile Christians to guide us in our paths.

MICAH 6:1-8 (RCL, BCP);
ZEPHANIAH 2:3; 3:12-13 (RC)

Both texts deal in one way or another with the theme of righteousness. Zephaniah is thought to have been a prophet in the kingdom of Judah who was active in about the decade of 640–630 B.C.E. during the reign of King Josiah and consequently prior to the destruction of Jerusalem in 576. He is a prophet of the coming Day of the Lord, of God's wrath. In 2:3, Zephaniah envisages that God's wrath, which he predicts will come against the nations (vv. 4-15), should prompt Israel to

RIGHTEOUSNESS IS DEFINED IN TERMS OF JUSTICE, KINDNESS, AND HUMILITY BEFORE GOD.

"seek the Lord" by "seeking [to do] righteousness" (v. 3). In vv. 12-13, Zephaniah utters the oracle in which he looks to the future and identifies those who will have sought the Lord and done righteousness as the "remnant of Israel." This oracle has often been used to identity those in Matthew's first Beatitude who are said to be "poor in spirit" (5:3).

In Mic. 6:1-8, righteousness is defined in terms of justice, kindness, and humility before God (v. 8). Good commentary on this text can be found in James Luther Mays, *Micah* (The Old Testament Library; Philadelphia: Westminster, 1976), pp. 127-43. As Mays and the NRSV show, Mic. 6:1-8 falls into three parts: introduction (vv. 1-2), the "I Statement" of God (vv. 3-5), and the "I Statement" of Israel and God's reply (vv. 6-8).

In the introduction, the term "hear" is used three times as the device by which God calls Israel to trial before the mountains and the hills, which are the "foundations [or pillars] of the earth" (vv. 1-2); these have borne witness to the covenant God made with Israel. God is the aggrieved in this trial and Israel the one who aggrieves God (v. 2). In the "I Statement" of God, God reminds Israel of the grace he has shown it in history and especially in its redemption from slavery in Egypt; God also expresses divine exasperation because Israel has forgotten the "saving [righteous] acts of the Lord" (vv. 3-5). In its "I Statement," Israel responds to God (vv. 6-8). To atone for its forgetfulness, Israel anticipates that it can do something, such as offer sacrifice to God (vv. 6-7). God, however, wants Israel itself, namely, the righteousness (good) of doing justice, loving kindness, and walking humbly with God (v. 8).

RESPONSIVE READING

PSALM 15 (RCL);
PSALM 37:1-18 or 37:1-6 (BCP);
PSALM 146:1-2, 5-7, 8-9, 10 (RC)

The Beatitudes, together with the Sermon on the Mount, have been regarded in past interpretation as setting forth the ethics that makes for "entrance into the kingdom of God." Although the theology associated with this position has been heavily debated, Psalm 15 reflects something of this notion in that it sets forth what is required of those who would enter the temple to worship God. Such requirements are virtually a definition of righteousness, of alternating "do's" (vv. 2, 4) and "do nots" (vv. 3, 5) that tend to be self-explanatory. Notice the prohibition in v. 5 against usury. Because this prohibition has long since been dropped in Christian circles, the issue surrounding it is being raised again especially in connection with the debate over human sexuality and whether or not "laws of God" can be set aside.

Psalm 37 likewise sets forth a string of "do's" and "do nots" that tend to be self-explanatory. These commands and prohibitions also constitute a definition of what righteousness is. Unlike in Psalm 15, in this psalm the prohibitions are accompanied by explanations that follow the formula of "Do not do this . . . because" (vv. 1-2). The commands are accompanied by promises that follow the formula of "Do this . . . so that" (v. 3). The commands and prohibitions of this psalm, therefore, approximate more closely the structure of the Beatitudes ("Blessed are . . . because they will").

Psalm 146 differs from Psalms 15 and 37 in that the righteousness that is demanded of us humans in those psalms is, in Psalm 146, predicated to God. Psalm 146 is the "reverse" of those psalms: We children of the God of Israel (Jesus Christ) are blessed because our God is the Creator God who keeps faith forever, executes justice, gives food, sets prisoners free, and so forth (vv. 5-9). These three psalms will find their end-time fulfillment in the kingdom of heaven (God) that has become a present sphere of reality in the coming of the crucified and resurrected Jesus and will become a consummated reality at his second coming.

1 CORINTHIANS 1:18-31 (RCL);
1 CORINTHIANS 1:(18-25) 26-31 (BCP);
1 CORINTHIANS 1:26-31 (RC)

The second reading on the Second, Third, and Fourth Sundays after the Epiphany has been taken from the first chapter of 1 Corinthians. This text concludes that series. It contrasts the foolishness of human beings who will perish with the wisdom of God that is power unto salvation for those who hear and believe the proclamation of Christ crucified (vv. 18-25). It also applies this contrast to the members of the church in Corinth (vv. 26-31).

Such a contrast between the foolishness of humans and the wisdom of God in Christ parallels the contrast between the prohibitions and the commands to righteousness found in the psalms for the day. This contrast also reflects the Beatitudes by stressing the "reversal of fortunes": Whereas the wise, the Jewish scribe, and the Greek philosopher of this world together with the strong, the powerful, and the noble who boast in this world will perish, those chosen by God in Jesus Christ, who in this world are the foolish, the weak, and the low and despised, have already been made partakers of life by Christ. Christ, in fact, is the wisdom from God in whom are righteousness, sanctifi-

> THE CONTRAST BETWEEN THE FOOLISHNESS OF HUMANS AND THE WISDOM OF GOD IN CHRIST PARALLELS THE CONTRAST BETWEEN THE PROHIBITIONS AND THE COMMANDS TO RIGHTEOUSNESS FOUND IN THE PSALMS FOR THE DAY.

cation, and redemption. Note that in this text, Paul locates such a reversal of fortunes in this very age and as quickly as one hears and believes the gospel about Christ crucified.

THE GOSPEL

MATTHEW 5:1-12 (RCL, BCP);
MATTHEW 5:1-12a (RC)

The Beatitudes in Matthew are of such great theological and pastoral significance that they bear thorough study. In 5:1-2, Matthew describes the setting in which Jesus delivers the Sermon on the Mount. Mention is made of both the Jewish "crowds" and Jesus' "disciples" (v. 1). If the crowds or both crowds and disciples are construed as the addressees of Jesus' sermon, the interpreter could be misled into understanding the sermon as setting forth an ethics for society as a whole. Matthew, however, writes his Gospel for Christians, which means that the disciples are the principal hearers of the sermon and that both the end-time prom-ises and the ethics set forth are Christian.

Throughout Matthew's Gospel, Jesus is Emmanuel, which is translated as "God [is] with us" (1:23). Hence, what Jesus says or does throughout Matthew's Gospel is gracious in nature unless the text indicates it must be seen as judgmental. The Sermon on the Mount, therefore, is eminently gracious in character. Hence, com-mands and instructions Jesus gives to the disciples not only tell them what they are to do but also empower them to do these things.

The Beatitudes contain within them an end-time tension between the present and the future. In Matthew, the end-time begins with the conception and birth of Jesus (1:18, 20-21). Hence, in Jesus' person, words, and deeds, the kingdom of heaven (God) becomes a present reality in whose sphere his disciples already live. Nevertheless, the kingdom will not become a consummated reality until Jesus returns for judgment at the end of the age (25:31-46). Matthew, therefore, inter-prets the "end-time" as stretching from Jesus' appearance in history until the close of history.

This is the temporal dimension of the end-time. Because, however, Jesus is Emmanuel, "God with us," his disciples, in living within the sphere of God's end-time rule, live in the immediate presence of God. This lends two further qualities to life in the end-time, those of urgency and reversal. Life in the end-time is urgent because disciples are impelled to do the will of God as Jesus teaches it. Life in the end-time is marked by reversal because God's rule is the sphere wherein the "reversal of fortunes" has already begun and will proceed until the consummation. Thus, disciples who are poor in spirit and who are persecuted are blessed because the kingdom of heaven is already theirs (5:3, 10).

Matthew 5:1-12 is to be divided into four sections. The first section is the intro-duction (vv. 1-2); sections two and three constitute eight Beatitudes that follow the formula of "Blessed are . . . because (for)" (vv. 3-6, 7-10); and the fourth sec-tion constitutes a ninth Beatitude that follows the same formula (vv. 11-12). The reason the ninth Beatitude is not grouped with the previous eight is twofold: It repeats the theme of the eighth ("persecution"); and owing to the presence in it of other elements that disturb the style of the eight, it functions to describe the present situation in which Matthew's community finds itself.

A fine, readable commentary on the Beatitudes that will provide the preacher with insight into details is that of Robert A. Guelich, *The Sermon on the Mount* (Waco, Tex.: Word Books, 1982), pp. 62–118. The term "blessed" is both ethical and eschatological in character: ethical, because it is followed by the description of an "attitude" Christians are to exhibit in their lives, and eschatological, because it conveys a "promise" that, though enacted in the present, will come to full real-ization in the future. Whereas the term "the kingdom of heaven (God)" can connote a "spatial realm," especially in the case of God's consummated kingdom, it predominantly connotes the dynamic "ruling activity" of God as such.

The "poor in spirit" (5:3) are Christian disciples who may be economically poor but are particularly spiritually poor in that they "stand without pretense before God as their only hope" (Guelich, p. 75); under Christ, they already live in the sphere of God's end-time rule and, at the consummation, will come into full possession of it. "Those who mourn" (v. 4) are Christians who experience an intense sense of loss and helplessness (Guelich, p. 81). "The meek" (v. 5) are almost synonymous with "the poor," namely, Christians who "stand empty-handed before God in total dependence upon him" (Guelich, p. 82). "Those who hunger and thirst for righteousness" (v. 6) are Christians who sense the "dire need of a right relationship with God and others" (Guelich, p. 87). "The merciful" (v. 7) are Christians who "exercise mercy towards those who are in the wrong" (Guelich, p. 89). "The pure in heart" (v. 8) are Christians who will stand

> TO LOOK BACK OVER THE BEATITUDES IS TO REALIZE THEY EXPLAIN THE NEW LIFE OF THE CHRISTIAN THAT IN OUR DAY BEGINS AT THE BAPTISMAL FONT AND IS CONTINUALLY NOURISHED BY THE WORD AND THE LORD'S SUPPER.

in the presence of God on the Last Day and be accepted by him (Guelich, p. 91). "The peacemakers" (v. 9) are Christians who work to establish peace in the world because they have, in Christ, experienced the "demonstration of God's love in Christ" (Guelich, p. 92). And "those who are persecuted for righteousness' sake" (v. 10) are Christians who, because they do the will of God as Jesus has taught it, come into conflict with the Jewish or Greek standards of that day (Guelich, p. 93).

To look back over the Beatitudes is to realize they explain the new life of the Christian that in our day begins at the baptismal font and is continually nourished by the Word and the Lord's Supper. If the preacher turns the Beatitudes into demands for such-and-such behavior, the sermon will degenerate into moralism. To escape this, the preacher will bind the requirements of the Beatitudes to the empowerment to do them that Jesus makes available to us disciples in that he is Emmanuel, "God with us."

LAST SUNDAY AFTER THE EPIPHANY / THE TRANSFIGURATION OF OUR LORD / FIFTH SUNDAY IN ORDINARY TIME

FEBRUARY 6, 2005

REVISED COMMON	EPISCOPAL (BCP)	ROMAN CATHOLIC
Exod. 24:12-18	Exod. 24:12 (13-14) 15-18	Isa. 58:7-10
Psalm 2 or Psalm 99	Psalm 99	Ps. 112:4-5, 6-7, 8-9
2 Pet. 1:16-21	Phil. 3:7-14	1 Cor. 2:1-5
Matt. 17:1-9	Matt. 17:1-9	Matt. 5:13-16

On this last Sunday after the Epiphany, the theme of light still prevails. In the story of the Transfiguration and related texts, the light is Jesus himself (Matt. 17:1-9; Exod. 24:12-18; Psalms 2 and 99; 2 Pet. 1:16-21). The light, however, can also be the gospel about the crucified Christ (1 Cor. 2:1-5). Or the light can be the righteous or the practice of righteousness (Matt. 5:13-16; Isa. 58:7-10; Ps. 112:4-5, 6-7, 8-9). Or the light can be the righteousness that springs from faith and the "reversal of fortunes" this entails (Phil. 3:7-14). As is apparent, two major strains run through the texts selected to be read on this Sunday: Whereas those chosen by Protestants revolve around Jesus and the story of the Transfiguration, those chosen by Roman Catholics revolve around righteousness.

On this last Sunday, therefore, the light of Epiphany illuminates the person of Jesus and adumbrates his work of suffering, death, and resurrection. The texts on righteousness continue to build on texts from the previous two Sundays after the Epiphany. Recall that on the third Sunday, Jesus' public ministry was characterized as one of preaching, teaching, and healing. On the fourth Sunday, the teaching of Jesus was featured through his utterance of the Beatitudes. And on this last Sunday, both the uniqueness of Jesus' person and the life of righteousness that springs from faith in him stand out. On this Sunday, therefore, the whole of the Epiphany season aptly reaches its culmination.

ON THIS LAST SUNDAY, BOTH THE UNIQUENESS OF JESUS' PERSON AND THE LIFE OF RIGHTEOUSNESS THAT SPRINGS FROM FAITH IN HIM STAND OUT.

EXODUS 24:12-18 (RCL);
EXODUS 24:12 (13-14) 15-18 (BCP);
ISAIAH 58:7-10 (RC)

Exodus 24:12-18 focuses on the Old Testament counterpart to the Gospel story of Jesus' Transfiguration. In a sermon on this text, the preacher will want to work with type and antitype: Moses and Mount Sinai are the types, and Jesus and the Mount of Transfiguration are the antitypes. The link between Moses and Jesus is that God speaks face to face with each of them.

God commands Moses to ascend the mountain, where God will give him the two tablets of stone on which the Ten Commandments have been written for the sake of Israel's instruction (24:12). Whereas Joshua accompanies Moses, Moses commands the elders of Israel to wait below where Aaron and Hur will exercise oversight (vv. 13-14).

In 24:15-18, the exodus narrative offers what in Epiphany is prophecy of Jesus' Transfiguration. A cloud covers Mount Sinai, God's glory settles upon the mount, and on the seventh day God speaks to Moses from out of the cloud (vv. 15-16). The appearance of God atop the mount is seen by Israel below as a devouring fire (v. 17). For forty days and forty nights, Moses remains atop the mount (v. 18).

The emphasis in this text is on the relationship between God and Moses. God is holy, a devouring fire, whom no human can approach. Although Moses is God's chosen leader of Israel, it is possible for him to draw near to God only because God gives him the permission to do so (24:2). Notice how different Jesus' relationship to God is: Because Jesus is God's beloved Son, he needs no permission to stand in the presence of God. As Jesus' disciples, we, too, stand in the presence of God, and we do so every Sunday at worship. God gives us permission through our confession of sins and the absolution granted us for Jesus' sake.

The RC first lesson in Isaiah 58 encompasses two parts (vv. 7-9b and 9c-10). In each part, the light of Epiphany is righteousness. The righteousness of Israel is like light that breaks forth at the dawn or that rises as the sun (vv. 8, 10). To do righteousness is defined as feeding the hungry, giving shelter to the poor, providing the naked with clothing, and aiding one's relatives (v. 7). God's promise is that he will vindicate those who do righteousness and hear their prayers in time of trouble (vv. 8-9b). In the second part of the text, other acts of righteousness are enumerated (vv. 9c-10). Together, these several acts sketch the life of righteousness.

RESPONSIVE READING
PSALM 2 or PSALM 99 (RCL);
PSALM 99 (BCP);
PSALM 112:4-5, 6-7, 8-9 (RC)

In Psalm 112, the righteous are those who fear the Lord and delight in his commandments (v. 1). They are themselves a light to the upright, for they are gracious, merciful, and righteous (v. 4). Righteous behavior does not fail of its blessings (vv. 5-9). The term "happy" (v. 1) in the Old Testament is a correlate of the term "blessed" in the Beatitudes (Matt. 5:1-12). The expression "it is well with those" (v. 5) is the equivalent of "happy are those." The difference between "happy" and "blessed" is that whereas "happy" is noneschatological in nature, "blessed" is eschatological, to wit: The blessings poured out upon those who are "happy" are envisaged as accruing to them during their lifetime. The blessings poured out upon those who are "blessed" will not be fully realized until the consummation of the age. The preacher who bases the sermon on Ps. 112:4-9 will be readily able to apply both the righteous behavior and its attendant blessings to the hearers.

Just as the story of the Transfiguration deals with the relationship between God and Jesus, so Psalms 2 and 99 deal with God's relationship with his Anointed and with Israel. In Psalm 99, God is praised for his holiness, whereby he loves and enacts justice (vv. 1-5). This holy God, however, is also gracious toward Israel, hearing the cries of its priests and answering them in forgiveness of Israel (vv. 6-9). During Epiphany, we Christians praise the holy God for the grace he has, in Jesus Christ, shown toward us, his end-time (eschatological) people.

Psalm 2 is a royal psalm in which God's relationship with Judah's anointed (king) is described during an annual enthronement festival in Jerusalem. In an Epiphany sermon, the preacher will once again make use of type (anointed king) and antitype (Jesus, who is Messiah-King of the Jews). In vv. 1-3, the nations of the world are pictured as conspiring against God, the king, and against God's anointed king who is enthroned on Zion. The purpose of the nations' conspiracy is that they win freedom from the rule of God and God's anointed. In vv. 4-6, God derides the nations, threatens them with terrifying words of wrath, and warns them that he is the one who has established his anointed as king on Mount Zion. In vv. 7-9, God's anointed king speaks: He tells of the day of his enthronement as the day on which he has been "begotten" of God, which means that he lays claim to being the son of God; God has invested him, too, with God's terrible power. In vv. 10-11, God's son warns the nations of the earth that they are to serve God lest they perish because of their rebellion.

In a sermon on this text, Jesus is the antitype. At his conception and birth, he is begotten as the Messiah and the king of the Jews (Matt. 1:18-25; 2:2, 4). At his baptism (3:13-17), he is anointed by God with the Spirit for messianic ministry. At both the baptism and the Transfiguration, God declares Jesus to be the Son of God (3:17; 17:5). As Jesus descends from the Mount of Transfiguration, he embarks on a ministry that will place him in conflict with the rulers of the Jews and the prefect of the Romans. After they have killed him, God raises him from the dead, and he commissions his disciples to embark on a mission to make of all nations his disciples (28:18-20). Not destruction, therefore, awaits the nations, but salvation.

Second Reading

2 PETER 1:16-21 (RCL);
PHILIPPIANS 3:7-14 (BCP);
1 CORINTHIANS 2:1-5 (RC)

In all three of these texts, the light of Epiphany is either the message of the gospel, or righteousness, or discipleship. The text from 2 Peter presents Peter as telling the story of the Transfiguration. He reminds us that he, James, and John were eyewitnesses to the majesty of Jesus atop the mount (vv. 16, 18). There they heard God bestow honor and glory upon

> THIS MESSAGE IS LIKE A LAMP THAT SHINES IN A DARK PLACE UNTIL DAY DAWNS AND CHRIST, THE MORNING STAR, RISES IN THE HEARTS OF THOSE WHO HEAR IT.

Jesus through God's declaration, "This is my beloved Son with whom I am well pleased" (v. 17). Because the three had been eyewitnesses to the Transfiguration, they have received the prophetic message (gospel) whose truth is certain (v. 19). This message is like a lamp that shines in a dark place until day dawns and Christ, the morning star, rises in the hearts of those who hear it (v. 19).

Philippians 3:7-14 treats of Paul's righteousness and of his mission. For Paul, becoming a disciple of Jesus Christ has resulted in a "reversal of fortunes." Paul's life has been turned upside down. What he previously regarded as gain, he now counts as loss, as rubbish (vv. 7-8). What was gain but is now rubbish was his own righteousness that came to him through the law. What was rubbish but is now gain is the righteousness that has come to him through faith in Christ (v. 9). Such righteousness has made him want to be "like Christ," to want to know Christ: to know the power of his resurrection, to know his sufferings even to the point of becoming like him in his death, and to attain to the resurrection from the dead (vv. 10-11). With such knowledge as the goal of his ministry, Paul presses on toward this goal so that he may obtain the "prize of the heavenly call of God in Christ Jesus"

(v. 14). The application of this text to the lives of the hearers in his congregation is straightforward.

In the third text, from 1 Corinthians 2, the light of Epiphany is the gospel of the crucified Christ. If in the two Protestant lectionaries the series of texts from 1 Corinthians ended last Sunday after three readings, in the Roman Catholic lectionary this same series contains four readings, including this text. Remember that in this series, Paul has hit hard at the foolishness of human wisdom and the wisdom of God found in the "nothing gospel" of Christ crucified. It is Paul's "nothing gospel" that is a stumbling block to the Jews and foolishness to Gentiles. In 2:1-5, Paul continues this argument by asserting that he did not, like his opponents, appear in Corinth proclaiming the alleged "mystery of God . . . in lofty words

> IT IS PAUL'S "NOTHING GOSPEL" THAT IS A STUMBLING
> BLOCK TO THE JEWS AND FOOLISHNESS TO GENTILES.

of human wisdom." On the contrary, he came to Corinth in weakness, fear, and much trembling, and he preached "nothing" except Jesus Christ and him crucified. Unlike their lofty words, however, his gospel engendered faith, which is a demonstration of the Spirit and power of God. The sharp contrast in this text between "lofty words of human wisdom" and Paul's "nothing gospel" has the makings of an insightful sermon contrasting the values of the culture with the values of the gospel.

THE GOSPEL

MATTHEW 17:1-9 (RCL, BCP);
MATTHEW 5:13-16 (RC)

Within the context of the lections for this last Sunday after the Epiphany, the "light" in Matt. 5:13-16 is "righteousness." Just as salt that has lost its taste is good for nothing, so righteousness that has lost its integrity is good for nothing. Just as the light of a city built on a hill cannot be hid, and just as a lighted lamp is placed on a lampstand so that it can give light, so disciples of Jesus, who are the light of the world, must not hide their light but let it shine for all persons to see. When others see your light, or righteousness (good works), they will give glory to God, to the Father whose child you are. In dealing with this text, the preacher will not want to forget that the Jesus who speaks these words is the one in whom "God is with us" (1:23). Christian righteousness glorifies the Christ in whom God is to be found.

The story of the Transfiguration (17:1-9) is the lead text in which all texts selected for this Sunday find their culmination. At the heart of this reading is the voice of God that speaks from out of the cloud and says of Jesus, "This is my beloved Son with whom I am well pleased; listen to him" (v. 5). Along with the baptism (3:13-17), the Transfiguration marks the second time in Matthew's story that God bursts into the world of Matthew and makes this declaration.

Once again, "This is" is a formula of identity that makes a public declaration. The formula identifies Jesus as the beloved Son of God and declares this to both the three disciples atop the mount and us, the readers. That Jesus is the Son of God is the deepest mystery of his person. "The Son of God" connotes the intimacy that marks Jesus' relationship with God, the perfect obedience that Jesus renders to God, and the unparalleled authority that God entrusts to Jesus. Except for Jesus himself, no human being in Matthew perceives Jesus to be the Son of God until the confession of Peter and the disciples (16:16).

Despite their confession, however, the fact that God's voice from the cloud exhorts the three disciples, "Listen to him!" shows that the disciples do not understand that, for Jesus to be the Son of God, he must suffer, die, and be raised (16:21-23). Hence, not until Jesus dies on the cross is he properly confessed to be the Son of God (27:54). By thus uniting confession and death, Matthew reveals that the cross in

> THAT JESUS IS THE SON OF GOD IS THE DEEPEST MYS-
> TERY OF HIS PERSON.

Jesus' public ministry is the crucial event of salvation. It is on the cross that Jesus pours out his blood for the "forgiveness of sins" (26:28). If the preacher chooses to expound on the story of the Transfiguration, therefore, every element needed to proclaim the gospel is present: God's relationship with Jesus, the identity and dignity of Jesus, Jesus' mission of salvation, and wherein this salvation consists.

THE SEASON
OF LENT

DALE P. ANDREWS

Introduction

The power of the Lenten season can be felt from deep within its history. It is
a sacred time marked by spiritual disciplines rooted in ancient baptismal, catechumenal, and fasting practices. Trying to gather historical information on Lent
is a rather difficult way to inaugurate the season. Yet examining the obscure formation of the divergent practices that eventually conflated into a cohesive Lenten
season, as we know it, may be our best approach to introduce the multiple meanings involved.

A precise determination of the origins of Lent is elusive. While an in-depth historical consideration is not possible here, there are several important observations
that help us to understand this liturgical season. The earliest possible antecedents
to Lent may be ascribed to a pre-Nicene period. From Irenaeus, via the historian
Eusebius, we learn that a short, vigilant fast was observed generally over a one-
to two-day period prior to Easter Sunday. In some places this fast lasted for forty
hours. Only a short time later, Tertullian also draws attention to a strict fast. In
both instances, these references comprise early evidence of a paschal vigil. However, these fasts were not yet associated with Lent itself.

Our earliest evidence of an observance of forty days occurs in the canons of
the Council of Nicea in the year 325 C.E. While the exact determination of forty
days emerges later, this council did attach fasting to the paschal vigil, ending with
the resurrection celebration. Later, a forty-day fast is commended more explicitly
by the Council of Laodicea, soon after mid-century (ca. 360 C.E.).[1] Thereafter, the
particular observances between this forty-day fast and the paschal celebration,

comprising the season of Lent, are even more challenging to decipher. Still, a brief review of the divergent practices that eventually came together to form Lent helps us tremendously to capture the multiple meanings that demand our attention in the preaching task.

By the fourth century, the strict observance of three days marked the paschal celebration. (The term *pascha*, or the pasch, encompasses the passion and the resurrection of Jesus Christ.) The three-day period, called the Triduum, incorporated Good Friday, Holy Saturday, and Easter Sunday. Earlier fasting practices from the second century were eventually required on the first two days of the Triduum, Good Friday and Holy Saturday. The fast typically did not extend into the Easter celebration itself. Candidates for baptism were required to honor the fast in preparation for entry to the community in the Eucharist celebration. Members of the body also fasted faithfully in the paschal vigil.[2]

There is evidence to suggest that the association of the fast to preparation for baptism likely stems from various three-week catechumenal periods among many communities in Rome, Jerusalem, and North Africa, to name a few. In some places, this three-week period of preparation may have included Holy Week. In many others, baptismal preparation preceded it. Some historians note that this preparation period may have occurred at other times in the year in areas such as Alexandria and the East. In these traditions, baptism emphasized themes of rebirth relating to Jesus' own baptism. When baptism is placed within the paschal vigil, the focus moves to the death and resurrection of Christ.[3] The placement of baptism in this season calls attention to both the passion of Christ and the celebration of redemption. While the theological themes in the history of salvation, from creation to our need for redemption, still emphasize rebirth, they now turn our attention to the transformation of the cross and the resurrection. Here we see the impact of the early placement of baptism on Holy Saturday to be followed by the Eucharist celebration on Easter Sunday. Preparation for baptism ends during the paschal vigil, with an intense focus on God's transforming grace in Christ.

The liturgical tradition of a forty-day fast can be immediately correlated to the fast of Jesus in the wilderness. Other biblical correlations have been made with several events in Israelite history, the most common one being the Hebrews' forty years of wandering in the wilderness. In some communities, such as those in the East, a forty-day fast immediately followed the celebration of Epiphany. This fast commemorated Jesus' fast in the wilderness, which immediately follows the account of his baptism in the Synoptic Gospels.

With the growing association of baptismal preparation and fasting to the paschal vigil, the forty-day fasting period (though the number and actual days of fasting varied) was increasingly adjoined to the Triduum by the mid- to late fourth century. The forty-day observance began on the Sunday six weeks before Easter, called the *Quadragesima*, and extended to the Thursday before the Triduum. The eventual calculation of forty actual days of fasting complicated the matter. In the West, a six-week period excluded fasting on Sundays but eventually extended into the paschal vigil. In the East, Saturdays and Sundays were excluded, thus requiring a seven-week period that included Holy Week and in particular Holy Saturday. In either case, the numbered days of observance hovered at thirty-six. Although multiple calculations of the *Quadragesima* existed, in time the forty-day observance would be fortified by adding four days before the first Sunday, to begin with what we now call Ash Wednesday.[4]

The development of a forty-day fast reflects a strong movement to incorporate the community of the faithful. A predominate effect has been the strong attention given to ascetic exercises, particularly in penitence.[5] Prior to the Middle Ages, Christians celebrated new baptisms by remembering, fasting, and praying. With the arrival of the Middle Ages, more generations were born into the faith and baptized as infants. Increasingly, Christians entered the faith more so by birthright than by conversion. As fewer adult converts prepared for baptism during the time before Easter, preserving the practices of fasting and prayer became crucial. These practices helped deepen discipleship and renew the baptismal memory of Christians born into the faith and baptized in infancy. Over time, practices of preparation for Easter became more ascetic, emphasizing penitence more than baptism, calling believers to discipleship, and restoring the community's life with a deepened faith.

That the baptismal preparation would be linked with multiple meanings incorporating new life and restored life in the community should guide our attention in the season of Lent. The practices and themes of baptism, catechism, and penitence would transform Lent.[6] The interplay of the temptation and passion of Christ intensifies the season. Baptism still signifies a prevailing meaning for Lent in our rebirth, that is our dying and rising with Christ. However, the early placement of baptism in the paschal vigil also signifies deep meanings in the moral and relational commitments to life that the cross and resurrection demand. These ascetic developments, accenting the temptation of Jesus in the spiritual and physical discipline of fasting, unfold in self-scrutiny for penitents. They also intensify spiritual engagement in the community's life of faith. The demands of spiritual discipline engage us to confront sin and evil in ourselves and in the world and underscore the need for charity in the life of faith. Moreover, Lent reminds us through the life, passion, and resurrection of Christ that grace and mercy ought to distinguish our devotion from the perversions of self-interest or myopic asceticism.[7] The mystery of Lent

THE EARLY PLACEMENT OF BAPTISM IN THE PASCHAL VIGIL ALSO SIGNIFIES DEEP MEANINGS IN THE MORAL AND RELATIONAL COMMITMENTS TO LIFE THAT THE CROSS AND RESURRECTION DEMAND.

holds its deepest meanings when the historical themes of this liturgical season are held together: preparation, baptism, fasting, discipline, repentance, penitence, sacrifice, suffering, charity, mercy, devotion, new life, and restoration. All of these theological movements in the season's history work together in the demands Lent places upon individuals and the community.[8]

Notes to Introduction

1. W. J. O'Shea and T. Krosnicki, eds., "Lent," in *New Catholic Encyclopedia*, vol. 8 (New York: McGraw-Hill, 1967), 468–70. See also Herbert Thurston, "Lent," in *The Catholic Encyclopedia*, vol. 9 (New York: Appleton, 1910), 152–54; and, Thomas J. Talley, *The Origins of the Liturgical Year*, 2d ed. (Collegeville, Minn.: Liturgical, 1991), 216.

2. Patrick Regan, "The Three Days and the Forty Days," *Worship* 54, no. 1 (January 1980): 2–18.

3. Maxwell E. Johnson, "From Three Weeks to Forty Days: Baptismal Preparation and the Origins of Lent," *Studia Liturgica* 20, no. 2 (1990): 185–200.

4. Some limited evidence exists for this accommodation beginning in the fifth century, which later would serve more fluidly to draw stronger correlations between the fast of the *Quadragesima* and the liturgical season of Lent.

5. Talley, *Origins*, 214–25.

6. Catherine Gunsalus Gonzalez, "From Death to Life: Themes for Lenten Preaching," *Journal for Preachers* 14, no. 2 (1991): 11–15.

7. Regan, "Three Days," 2–18.

8. Eduard Richard Riegert, "The Lent-Easter Cycle," *The Lutheran Quarterly* 26 (fall 1974): 12–23.

ASH WEDNESDAY

FEBRUARY 9, 2005

REVISED COMMON	EPISCOPAL (BCP)	ROMAN CATHOLIC
Joel 2:1-2, 12-17	Joel 2:1-2, 12-17	Joel 2:12-18
or Isa. 58:1-12	or Isa. 58:1-12	
Ps. 51:1-17	Psalm 103 or 103:8-14	Ps. 51:3-4, 5-6,
		12-14, 17
2 Cor. 5:20b—6:10	2 Cor. 5:20b—6:10	2 Cor. 5:20—6:2
Matt. 6:1-6, 16-21	Matt. 6:1-6, 16-21	Matt. 6:1-6, 16-18

In many cultures, religious symbols and liturgical rituals sometimes become so common that they risk losing particular theological meaning in people's lives. At other times, those same symbols and rituals gather meaning into distinctive identities. For Christians, the cross is so central, whether in cultural identity or faith, that it has become simply ornate for some yet essential for others. Even when the symbols and rituals of our faith break into our lives renewed, we are caught amid multiple meanings. Does the cross indicate God's faithfulness in suffering or our thanksgiving for redemption? Understanding the imposition of ashes, in its ritual or symbol, shares in a similar struggle for meaning between the solemnity of penitence and the celebration of redemption. Even among the faithful, Lent becomes commonplace as our obedient acknowledgment, even while it attempts to break in upon us in preparation for the Easter celebration.

Yet the imposition of ashes—"Remember you are dust, and to dust you shall return" (Gen. 3:19)—makes its claim upon us. The ash is there, like a weight plastered to our foreheads. We feel it all day! That is the power of Ash Wednesday; it breaks into our lives. It marks a fast in the traditions of the church, it marks a season of preparation, and it disrupts the profane that increasingly characterizes even our faithfulness.

THESE PASSAGES CAUSE US TO REFLECT CRITICALLY ON THIS DAY'S "CALL" TO FAST, ON THE CHARACTER OF FAITHFULNESS, AND ON THE DIALECTIC IN CHRISTIAN LIFE AND MINISTRY BETWEEN PERSONAL PIETY AND CARE FOR OTHERS.

The growing liturgical practice of imposing ashes on the first day of the forty-day Lenten fast, Ash Wednesday, was officially adopted throughout the Western church with the Synod of Benevento in 1091, under Pope Urban II.[1] Most com-

monly, the ashes are gathered from burning the palms from the previous year's
Palm Sunday service. The ashes remind us of our mortality. It is in the humility of
our mortality that we prepare penitently for the resurrection celebration. The cat-
echumenate also remains central in preparing candidates for baptism. Our readings for today call for us to rediscover the paschal mystery in the passion and
resurrection of Christ.[2] These passages cause us to reflect critically on this day's
"call" to fast, on the character of faithfulness, and on the dialectic in Christian life
and ministry between personal piety and care for others.

FIRST READING
JOEL 2:1-2, 12-17 (RCL, BCP);
JOEL 2:12-18 (RC)

Interpreting the Text

The day of the Lord is proclaimed by the blustering sound of the *shophar*,
a ram's horn. In prophetic traditions, sounding the horn could mean sounding off
victory over other nations in the vindication of God. At other times, sounding the
horn also warned that God was turning judgment upon Israel in the hands of foreign nations.[3] In either case, the trumpet blare sounded an alarm of crisis. For Joel,
the sound of this trumpet warned the people of Judah of looming danger. The
peculiarity of Joel's announcement is that this danger comes directly from God.

Joel does not focus intently on the particular causes for God's apparent judgment. However, the subsequent call for repentance makes it somewhat clear that
human license remains the common culprit. The language of "return to me"
(v. 12) suggests questions of covenant life and worship.[4] Chapter 2 elicits attention
to the threat of devastation in a plague of locusts from the preceding chapter. Joel
moves into a description of the looming doom. We cannot be sure whether the
impending destruction is a theological understanding of natural events or the
metaphoric imagery of a foreign army. What is clear, however, is that the threat of
destruction looms large in the postexilic period in which this text likely echoes in
the sound of the shophar. The plague is destructive. This destruction spreads under
the voice of God. Who can endure judgment on the day of the Lord?

But there is a call for repentance. In the very threat of destruction, Joel declares
a fast and calls for a solemn assembly. Also among the traditional uses of the
shophar is the call to repentance. For example, the shophar commonly signals a
new month and in particular the new year. In the Feast of Trumpets, the new year
is ushered in by the memory of God's mercy. The trumpets blare in the call to
repentance or atonement in reliance upon God's memory of mercy and forgive-

ness. For Joel, God's memory is intact and issues the oracle to "return" to God in repentance. The prophet calls for the people of Judah to remember God's character made known to them before in mercy. To "rend your hearts and not your clothing" (v. 13), in the very effort to return to God, presupposes questions of covenant and how the people of Judah are to understand their struggles with catastrophe.

Attention to mercy in the memory of God comprises the message of hope in Joel's summons to repentance. Will God "relent" in the judgment upon Judah? That is to say, will God repent? The possibility of God repenting of God's own wrath or judgment is not new, even if it is confusing. In Exodus 32, Moses implores God to repent of God's anger, to repent of "evil." God repents in the memory of God's own commitment to God's people. Joel relies on the hope that God may repent in the memory of the covenant, if the people of Judah will return to God in a repentance that also calls upon their own memory of the covenant.[5]

Interestingly enough, the shophar signals introspection on multiple levels. All individuals are instructed to enter a fast of introspection and prayer. Yet this summons is to assemble the congregation, from the aged to the infant. The priests, or "the ministers of the LORD," are implored to offer intercessory prayer, even weeping, beseeching God to spare God's people of both their destruction and shame among the nations. Joel cares deeply that other nations would mock them and thereby their God (v. 17), saying, "Where is their God?" The call to repentance cannot be fulfilled by personal rending of clothing, but rather must be done in solemn assembly that will honor God publicly. The people of Judah are called to return to their public practice of worship that has waned in the shame or struggle with destruction.[6] And indeed God will have pity once more (v. 18).

Responding to the Text

The role of symbolism in the shophar offers the preacher several entry points in wrestling with this text. To warn of crisis, to signal battle, to celebrate new beginnings, to call for repentance, to remember God's mercy and forgiveness—all of these traditions seem to echo in the cacophany of meanings that blare in Joel's prophetic ministry.

As preachers, we often think we have a strong grasp on what God desires to do among us. We may even proclaim that we are sent to reveal how God works with us. The struggles of this prophet, however, should cause us pause. In many cultures, preachers who stand in privileged pulpits, and even not so privileged ones, sometimes proclaim that our privileges are blessings given in God's care for God's own people. Somehow we tend to concretize God into obligations. God seeks to bless God's people, and we create an equation obligating God. Therefore, human crisis simply means human unfaithfulness, marked by God's judgment or abandonment. Suddenly, our theology and preaching become very limited. Joel seems to have been very familiar with the struggle to break out of the reduction. A struggle for Joel weighs in balance the immediate experiences of the people of Judah and the apparent judgment of God. Similarly, the question for prophetic preachers today in times of crisis may be, "Has the covenant been forgotten or reduced?" It is vital to notice that Joel's call for repentance is more a reliance on the expansion of the covenantal relationship than it is a reduction of it. Joel called for the people of Judah to trust in the character of God. Can God change God's own mind? The people are called to trust in God's compassion rekindled in both the people's and God's memory of their relationship.[7]

Our caution should rise to resist our own theological reduction in preaching repentance. Does repentance obligate God in a rigid equation? The risk may be that we reduce God's "relent" to simply a confession-forgiveness ratio. Clearly God's repentance is a powerful and confusing theme. How do we interpret unrelenting catastrophe? When we wrestle with repentance, we wrestle with injustice and justice, with hurt and sorrow, with actions and desire. Joel turns to the character of God's relationship with the people of

> WE MAY NOT BE ABLE EVER TO CAUSE GOD TO RELENT, BUT WE CAN RELY ON GOD'S DESIRE TO BE IN RELATIONSHIP WITH US.

Judah. Repentance becomes an acknowledgment and a commitment to seek our own relationship to God. We may not be able ever to cause God to relent, but we can rely on God's desire to be in relationship with us. The pursuit of this relationship in repentance opens the future; it opens the present.[8]

ISAIAH 58:1-12 (RCL, BCP alt.)

Interpreting the Text

Consideration of the structure of this passage will help to interpret the prophetic message between sacrifices of worship and actions in worship. The first major section (vv. 1–5) deals directly with the rebellion and judgment of the worship life in the house of Jacob. During this early postexilic period, Third Isaiah challenges the integrity of worship with language about rebellion that is characterized by serving one's own interest and oppressing others (v. 3). The focus of these verses is the shallow understanding and even hypocrisy of worship that turns on expectations of God but does not live beyond one's own desires. It is a harsh reality when acts of piety are rebellious to God (v. 4). The descriptions of fasting and worship (v. 5) reveal the divine perception of the people's actions: "to bow down the head like a bulrush, and to lie in sackcloth and ashes." These descriptions are exaggerated similes to expose the contempt created by acts of worship that punctuate piety in place of covenantal life.[9]

We gain this insight to the character of covenantal living through a transition in the passage that depicts the fast or worship that God chooses (vv. 6-7). These verses comprise the divine corrective or instruction. In short, religious piety and worship are lived out, or rather lived into, through care of justice for the poor, the hungry, the disadvantaged, and the oppressed. The message is unambiguous. Only then can relief, healing, and vindication be expected to rise from God like the dawn breaking forth (vv. 8-9a). A comparison between v. 2 and v. 9a illustrates that even some of our most sacrificial acts do not engage God. God responds to sacrifices of worship that live in the relationships among the people themselves.

GOD RESPONDS TO SACRIFICES OF WORSHIP THAT LIVE IN THE RELATIONSHIPS AMONG THE PEOPLE THEMSELVES.

Worship that seeks only one's sincerest desire to effect change in one's own life does not alone fulfill covenantal life with God. Even sacrifices risk self-interest and participate by neglect in the oppression of others.[10] We receive redemption in the promises of God and we live into it in relationships of care.

The last section of the given text emerges from the promise, "Here I am." If-then clauses (vv. 9b-12) outline the fullness of God's promise, received when living into the fullness of God's covenantal life. In essence, the prophet returns to the notion that God's activity is often entwined with human activity. The work of worship is in the sacrifices that remove yokes of oppression, retract contemptuous conflict, and offer one's very sustenance in meeting the needs of others. God's blessings emerge in being present among us. Notice the language of the prophet's proclamation. The promise emerges in God's guidance (v. 11) and what God will be able to bring forth from within the people and through them (v. 12).

Responding to the Text

Perhaps the strongest challenge here for preachers lies in how we wrestle with religious piety. As with the Joel text, the proclamation is blaring. The image and sound of trumpets announce crisis in the voice of the prophet. Do we wrestle with religious piety that seeks to make us holy? Will our holiness draw forth God's activity or blessing? In answering these questions, preachers would be wise to define their understanding of piety and its purpose. To what extent do our efforts in the religious morality of personal conduct become part of our worship? Is holiness acquired in piety? How does God view piety? Surely, our sacrifices of time and attention to God must mean something significant to God. This passage in Isaiah joins the Joel text in calling for repentance in our actual worship. With Joel, we are reminded that we cannot earn or manipulate God's promises. God's compassion is a blessing that cannot be reduced to obligation. With Isaiah, we are challenged in worship to move beyond personal piety. Piety is not much more than self-indulgence when it does not live into relationships. Our worship or piety even risks offending God when it surrenders work for justice or when we care for others only out of our expendable abundance and not our sustenance. Care for others is perhaps the goal and nature of religious piety. In care for others, we live into the worship that comprises covenantal life. Our worship is challenged to return to God in heart and in hope that God's commitment to us endures.

RESPONSIVE READING
PSALM 51:1–17 (RCL);
PSALM 51:3–4,5–6, 12–14, 17 (RC);
PSALM 103 or 103:8–14 (BCP)

Psalm 51 begins with appeals to God's character—to have mercy—known to us in steadfast love. The appeal to God's steadfast loves speaks out of the psalmist's familiarity with covenant language. It is the basis for confessing the grief of sin consuming the speaker. According to the heading of the psalm, consuming awareness of sinfulness is David's response to Nathan, who confronts David's acts of adultery and murder (2 Samuel 12). This context only accents the depth of despair that affects humanity. We are not spared from lament. The foundation or power of repentance here reflects the Joel passage, "rend your hearts" and "return to the Lord, your God" (Joel 2:13). In both cases repentance is conditioned in God's mercy and steadfast love. We do not repent in the power of our own convictions or values. The psalmist is deeply convicted that only a "broken and contrite heart" will offer an acceptable sacrifice to God (v. 17).

Important questions grow out of the awareness of sin: Will our needs of God's mercy and renewal challenge our sense of autonomy? How may preaching repentance challenge our awareness? To read this psalm simply as personal confession to God, against whom "alone" we sin (v. 4), would miss an important understanding of how we often sin. Clearly, the psalmist recognizes the selfish character of sin that ignores or violates our relationship with God. As with David, the offense of our sinfulness often occurs in ignoring or violating our human relationships. While this psalm speaks from an individual voice, it speaks for human relations in covenant. When we violate each other, we sin against God. Our confession will appeal to God's character of steadfast love, which will be the source of our renewal.[11]

Psalm 103 also underscores God's compassion. Here the psalmist begins with blessing the Lord, who forgives and redeems in mercy and steadfast love. Of course, the very notion that we could "bless" the Lord suggests a peculiar relationship. The substance behind blessing God is God's forgiveness. The psalm spotlights or exalts God's steadfast love experienced in forgiveness (vv. 1-5). In the middle of this exaltation, the psalmist inserts attention to justice as a demonstration of God's forgiveness (v. 6). This psalm expresses great relief in God's righteousness (compare with vv. 17-18) that is experienced in God's forgiveness over injustice.

Forgiveness restores us to the covenant in justice.[12] The correlation between justice and God's forgiveness reflects the role of justice in Isaiah 58. Justice becomes a fulcrum in God's responses to repentance and praise alike. In Isaiah, God's mercy breaks forth in our attention to suffering around us. In Psalm 103, we remember that God's mercy thrives by not dealing with us as we deal with each other (v. 10). Ultimately, God remembers forgiveness in remembering our genesis and our finitude, "that we are dust" (v. 14).[13] When we remember our genesis and our finitude, we cherish God's mercy and steadfast love.

Second Reading
2 CORINTHIANS 5:20b—6:2 (rc);
2 CORINTHIANS 5:20b—6:10 (rcl, bcp)

Interpreting the Text

These readings are part of a slightly larger unit focused on reconciliation (5:11—6:10). Even the larger unit is part of an even broader piece that comprises Paul's defense of his ministry and expansion into authentic service to Christ (2:14—6:10). Paul's address on reconciliation to the Corinthians is somehow correlated to his own ministry of reconciliation. The verses for today's second reading are introduced by Paul's attention to the nature of salvation. The love of Christ is known in that "one has died for all" (v. 14b). The effect of salvation is that we no longer live for ourselves, "so if anyone is in Christ, there is a new creation" (v. 17a). God's objective is that we become transformed. The ministry of reconciliation and the nature of reconciliation are understood in this transforming work of Christ.[14]

Paul moves from attention to the saving grace of Christ into the nature of reconciliation (vv. 18-21). God reconciles us and also calls us to a ministry of reconciliation. The turn in this passage is Paul's appeal to be reconciled (v. 20b). Paul speaks as an "ambassador" of Christ. His shift to admonish the Corinthians to be reconciled is a fulcrum in this address. Another way to translate this appeal here is to "reconcile yourselves to God." A debate among scholars ensues in how we are to understand this appeal. Some argue for a passive agency in the verb, Paul thereby suggesting that the Corinthians allow themselves to be reconciled by God. Other scholars contend that a call for human agency drives the appeal. Evidence supporting the latter claim develops from 6:1-2. The caution against receiving God's grace in vain (6:1) carries the weight of agency. Paul calls for intentional action of some enterprise in reconciliation, spiritually or otherwise. The role of human agency is difficult to decipher but critical to understanding this passage. In the form of appeal, the admonition tips the scale in calling for assent and an active pursuit of transformation. Paul's citation (6:2) of Isaiah 49:8 places the present appeal in the middle of God's saving work in the past as well as in its eschatological future. The Corinthians are urged to live into God's grace and ministry of reconciliation.[15]

While the appeal in 5:20b provides the crux of Paul's address to the Corinthians in this passage, 6:1 gives attention to the ministry of reconciliation expressed in his role as an ambassador working together with God in the reconciliation realized only through Christ (v. 21). Verse 1 of chapter 6 marks a transition tying together Paul's defense of his ministry. Paul appeals to the Corinthians to claim

> PAUL CALLS FOR INTENTIONAL ACTION OF SOME ENTERPRISE IN RECONCILIATION, SPIRITUALLY OR OTHERWISE.

an agency empowered by grace, and defends his ministry both in rebuttal to dissenters and in illustration of one's essential work in reconciliation. Paul's defense moves into a list of hardships. For Paul, any attempt here to authenticate his ministry in spiritual gifts that spotlight outward appearances (5:13) or boast of blessing would be to live for himself and not for Christ (v. 15). Clearly, Paul finds that his detractors have fallen prey to misguidance. To illustrate the transforming call to live into reconciliation, Paul couches his defense in a love of Christ evidenced in the endurance of hardships (6:3-10). The role of suffering in Paul's theology reflects a particular mind-set on the passion of Christ. Suffering is not a goal but rather a reality of ministry. In this passage suffering also becomes the evidence of Paul's commitment to Christ and to the Corinthians. His suffering reveals his apostolic authority in Christ's passion. Scholars have found that Paul's list of hardships reflects some traditional apocalyptic literature, which points to a spiritual interpretation of the immediate experience. Paul's style may also resemble literary traditions in Stoic philosophy that relied on reversals of values. The reversals in Paul's list are illustrated by antitheses and comparisons. Without entering the extensive debate in comparing Paul's literary formula to these two traditions, Paul's defense of ministry here lies somewhere in the dialectic between his experiences and the values of service defined in Christ.[16]

Responding to the Text

Many preachers might be attracted to the lexis of "ambassadors for Christ" and "fellow workers with God." Surely, we interpret our call to the ministry in similar ways when reading how Paul underscored meaning for his ministry and its vindication in the very passion of Christ. We are tempted likewise to translate the struggles of our ministries and even the hardships among our congregations. Yet great risks rise when we uncritically esteem our "sacrifices" in ministry. Suddenly whenever we are challenged, our critics become adversaries rather than fellow workers. You can hear the reasoning: "God will certainly now bless us for our willing submission to ridicule," or "Resistance is the sign that we work for righteousness." In some strange way, it is equally difficult to understand how Paul reasons vindication out of his suffering. However, a closer look at the context of Paul's defense helps to illumine that the defense is also a correction. From the previous passage, we learn that Paul's defense is a response to those who claim divine election in ecstatic spiritual experiences. Paul's response is not to reject such blessings or even spiritual gifts. Instead, he places their honor in direct relation with God; he finds the vindication of ministry in the hard work of loving God's creation (5:13).

In turn, Paul's appeal to the Corinthians is no less strident, "be reconciled to God" (v. 20b). This charge is hardly a proclamation for conversion. Paul is writing to a Christian church in Corinth. As explained above, living into the integrity of God's grace (6:1) is the context for Paul's appeal to be reconciled. Reconciliation received, therefore, requires another pursuit. The appeal sounds almost like transformation called to pursue transformation. Spiritual gifts are not ends in themselves, nor are ecstatic experiences. Reconciliation lives in the ministry of reconciliation. It is in the struggle to live into reconciliation where Paul locates the work of grace. And Paul's admonition becomes his proclamation, "Now is the acceptable time; see, now is the day of salvation" (6:2). The work of reconciliation is the sign of God's grace among God's fellow workers in Christ.[17]

The Gospel
MATTHEW 6:1-6, 16-21 (RCL, BCP);
MATTHEW 6:1-6, 16-18 (RC)

Interpreting the Text

The Gospel reading is a continuation of what tradition calls the Sermon on the Mount. In the previous chapter, we receive the nine Beatitudes (5:3-12). The Beatitudes deal with character, action, and relations. More important, they reassure us that God is concerned with righteousness, which is differentiated in justice and relationships. And the continuation of these teachings from the mount into chapter 6 follows suit. There are three areas of redress in today's passages from Matthew: almsgiving, prayer, and fasting. A principal warning in v. 1 introduces them. Actually, the first verse in its entirety proposes the entire theme and struc-

ture of argument for these passages. The warning exposes the practice of piety that
seeks recognition and reward. The subject is piety; the offense lies in misguided
intention; and the consequence is the questionable character of reward. In each
teaching, the same structure guides a treatment of piety in each act. Similar to the
Beatitudes and teachings from the previous chapter, the word for piety here should
be understood in a connection between doing justice and pursuing righteousness.
Sanctification is clearly caught up in the character of our actions. God's responses
to acts of piety are caught up in our motivations and faithfulness.[18]

Each address in vv. 2-4, 5-6, and 16-18, respectively, begins with a warning
against acting like "the hypocrites." In short, the warning is against doing the right
things for the wrong reasons. Our goals then become twisted in recognition of
our righteousness, whether in just
actions of almsgiving or in pious prayer
and fasting. Human recognition itself
will be the only consequence as far as

THERE ARE THREE AREAS OF REDRESS IN TODAY'S PASSAGES
FROM MATTHEW: ALMSGIVING, PRAYER, AND FASTING.

God is concerned. Ultimately, blessings become as empty as the actions. The final
section of the Gospel passages for today (vv. 19-21) summarizes the nature of this
warning and message. One's heart is exposed by what one treasures. The warning
here echoes each warning above: we must pay heed to our intentions, values, and
treasures.[19] What are our treasures and what do we do with them? Or perhaps, concerning piety, what do we seek? Our treasures become corrupt when their value
and use remain in our own ends or purposes. As some scholars have observed,
Matthew projects a strong correlation between this text and Jewish teachings that
claim the pursuit of justice and righteousness places our treasure in the love of
God.[20] The "heart" of the matter is the "treasure" (v. 21).

Responding to the Text

Preachers may find in this Gospel text a provocative warning of the
"trumpet" (v. 2) in comparison with the Joel and Isaiah passages for today. Both
Joel and Isaiah employ the familiarity of trumpets in religious life to signify danger or caution (Joel 2:1; Isa. 58:1). Matthew also refers to trumpeting but implores
that we lay down our trumpets. In a sense this declaration is a reversal of the Joel
2:15, in which the prophet returns to the trumpet to sanctify a fast and call for
public assembly. However, these passages reverberate in a common theme. The
trumpet may be used for warning; it may be used to call for repentance; and it may
even be used for devotion and worship. Yet we sometimes raise trumpets in vio-
lation of these same uses. When we herald proclamations of our faithfulness, it is
time to lay down the trumpet. The teachings from the mount remind us of our
extraordinary capacity to confuse even our faithfulness. Isaiah cautions that we
serve our own interests, even with our fasts, and raises the question from God, "Is

this the fast that I choose?" (Isa. 58:5). Matthew extends the warning, "Do not sound the trumpet" when the trumpet declares our acts of righteousness. To free oneself to live into righteousness in both justice and worship, lay down the trumpet. The common theme is the integrity of faithfulness.

The integrity of faithfulness is underscored by two terms that stand out in the Matthew passage: "hypocrites" and "reward." The references to hypocrites carry with them the historical context of play actors and a stage. It is clear, however, that negative implications already were prominent in Matthew's historical context.

> MATTHEW EXTENDS THE WARNING, "DO NOT SOUND THE TRUMPET" WHEN THE TRUMPET DECLARES OUR ACTS OF RIGHTEOUSNESS.

Therefore, the allegation here is that hypocrites were actors, and their stage was their religion.[21] The language of reward carries forward the question of integrity in our motivations. Along with the early Christians, preachers today wrestle with the notion of reward. To what extent are our motivations driven by a misguided theology of rewards? Are our efforts to please God ever free from our desire to receive God's blessing? Do our efforts to love another rise above self-deceit? In Matthew, hypocrisy seems to extend beyond motivation into self-deception in one's own faithfulness.[22] The notion of "reward" is a disturbing concept that we cannot escape. Transformation of the heart holds an important key to overcoming hypocrisy. Perhaps, Paul's charge to "be reconciled to God" (2 Cor. 5:20b), that we may "become the righteousness of God" (2 Cor. 5:21), responds to the self-deception of hypocrisy and reward. We lay down the trumpet at the foot of the cross, not in defeat but to live into the resurrection of Christ.

Notes

1. Earl James Johnson, "Ashes, Liturgical Use of," in *New Catholic Encyclopedia*, vol. 1 (Washington, D.C.: Catholic University of America, 1967), 782.

2. Don E. Saliers, "Ash Wednesday through Lent: Practical Considerations," *Reformed Liturgy and Music* 24 (winter 1990): 16–18.

3. James H. Harris, Jerome C. Ross, and Miles J. Jones, *Lent*; Proclamation 6, Series B (Minneapolis: Fortress Press, 1996), 8.

4. Ronald A. Simkins, "'Return to Yahweh': Honor and Shame in Joel," *Semeia* 68 (1994): 41–54.

5. Thomas B. Dozeman, "Inner-biblical Interpretation of Yahweh's Gracious and Compassionate Character," *Journal of Biblical Literature* 108 (summer 1989): 207–23.

6. Simkins, "'Return to Yahweh,'" 41–54.

7. James L. Crenshaw, "Who Knows What YHWH Will Do? The Character of God in the Book of Joel," in *Fortunate the Eyes That See*, ed. Astrid B. Beck et al. (Grand Rapids: William B. Eerdmans, 1995), 185–96.

8. Terence E. Fretheim, "The Repentance of God: A Key to Evaluating Old Testament God-Talk," *Horizons in Biblical Theology* 10/1 (1998): 47–70.

9. Kwesi A. Dickson, "He Is God because He Cares," *International Review of Mission* 77 (April 1988): 229–37.

10. Bernhard W. Anderson, *Lent*; Proclamation 6, Series C (Minneapolis: Fortress Press, 1997), 12.

11. Patrick D. Miller, Jr. "Preaching Repentance in a Narcissistic Age," *Journal for Preachers* 21, no. 2 (1998): 3–8.

12. D. F. O'Kennedy, "The Relationship between Justice and Forgiveness in Psalm 103," *Scriptura* 65 (1998): 109–21.

13. Walter Brueggemann, "Remember, You are Dust," *Journal for Preachers* 14, no. 2 (1991): 3–10.

14. Jerome Murphy-O'Connor, *The Theology of the Second Letter to the Corinthians* (Cambridge, England: Cambridge University Press, 1991), 55–65.

15. Jan Lambrecht, *Second Corinthians*, Sacra Pagina Series, ed. Daniel J. Harrington, vol. 8 (Collegeville, Minn.: Liturgical Press, 1999), 90–115.

16. Chris Ukachukwu Manus, "Apostolic Suffering (2 Cor. 6:4-10): The Sign of Christian Existence and Identity," *Asia Journal of Theology* 1, no. 1 (April 1987): 41–54.

17. Richard K. Moore, "2 Corinthians 5:20b in the English Bible in the Light of Paul's Doctrine of Reconciliation," *Bible Translator* 54, no. 1 (January 2003): 146–55.

18. Warren Carter, *Matthew and the Margins: A Sociopolitical and Religious Reading* (Maryknoll, N.Y.: Orbis Books, 2000), 158–73.

19. Ibid.

20. George Wesley Buchanan, *The Gospel of Matthew*, New Testament Series, vol. 1, book 1 (Lewiston, N.Y.: Mellen, 1996), 319.

21. Ibid., 288-89.

22. Dan O. Via, "The Gospel of Matthew: Hypocrisy as Self-Deception," *Society of Biblical Literature Seminar Papers* no. 27 (1988): 508–16.

FIRST SUNDAY IN LENT

FEBRUARY 13, 2005

REVISED COMMON	EPISCOPAL (BC)	ROMAN CATHOLIC
Gen. 2:15-17; 3:1-7	Gen. 2:4b-9, 15-17, 25—3:7	Gen. 2:7-9; 3:1-7
Psalm 32	Psalm 51 or 51:1-13	Ps. 51:3-4, 5-6, 12-13, 17
Rom. 5:12-19	Rom. 5:12-19 (20-21)	Rom. 5:12-19 or 5:12, 17-19
Matt. 4:1-11	Matt. 4:1-11	Matt. 4:1-11

These readings for the First Sunday in Lent correlate strongly with the themes of Ash Wednesday. Humanity's struggle with sin and our need for forgiveness become the central themes that condition our understanding of penitence. The Gospel lesson sets the temptation of Jesus in the wilderness. With the forty days of fasting, it is easy to see how this text became prominent for the first Sunday, which once was the actual start of Lent before the extension back into Ash Wednesday. The Genesis texts contemplate the temptation of humanity. Here humanity falters, and the knowledge of evil and

> HUMANITY'S STRUGGLE WITH SIN AND OUR NEED FOR FORGIVENESS BECOME THE CENTRAL THEMES THAT CONDITION OUR UNDERSTANDING OF PENITENCE.

death result. Clearly, the victory of Jesus in our Gospel reading sets the stage of human sin and Christ's victory over temptation and eventually over death. The epistle reading draws forth Christ's reversal of judgment and death. Christ overcomes temptation and the knowledge of evil in humanity; Christ is our justification. The psalm readings pick up the lament and prayer for forgiveness from Ash Wednesday. However, they also add the thanksgiving for forgiveness. Our awareness of sin finds healing in God's steadfast love.

GENESIS 2:15-17; 3:1-7 (RCL);
GENESIS 2:4b-9, 15-17, 25—3:7 (BCP);
GENESIS 2:7-9; 3:1-7 (RC)

Interpreting the Text

The first readings for this Sunday share a common focus in the temptation of humanity and human sin or finitude (3:1-7). An entry point, however, has
been more difficult to determine. Each of the three lectionary traditions begins
with a different point of entry to the temptation of humanity. A transition in Gen.
2:4 initiates an introduction to a second creation narrative (v. 4b). Some textual
or linguistic changes distinguish this creation narrative from the one found in the
preceding chapter. Among the most obvious changes are a different sequence in
creating the world and the new term for God (YHWH *elohim*). The juxtaposition of two distinct creation narratives in chapters 1–2 should raise questions of
structural design and meaning. Making note of formulaic changes, some scholars
underscore 2:4b-7 as an introduction, with the main players being God and
humanity. Emphasis on what has been called a thesis of "lack" sets up the plot of
this narrative. The beginning of creation is outlined by what does not yet subsist
(v. 5). The lack is glaring in that "there was no one to till the ground." Here, the
plot thickens as we encounter the theme of this narrative—the toil of humanity.[1]

The narrative begins to unfold with the creation of humanity in v. 7. God
plants a lush garden, and amid all the beauty and nourishment, God places both
the tree of life and the tree of knowledge of good and evil. This creation narrative
now develops more importantly as a context for the plot of temptation to unfold
(vv. 7-9). God created humanity from the barrenness of dust, breathed the breath
of life into humanity, and planted a garden for our needs and pleasure. Still the
question of toil remains unanswered. The negative formula "not yet" from v. 5
draws our attention to problems of lack that will be redressed in the narrative.[2]
Similarly, the negative command structure of vv. 15-17 thickens the plot in attention to the potential contrast of life inside the garden with life across the earth.
The theme of toil should not be simply understood as work. In v. 15, God places
humanity in the garden to till it. Remember from v. 5 that the need for someone
to till the ground was a factor in understanding God's acts of creation. Humanity
is deeply connected with the creation of the world (or earth in the language of
this narrative). Even part of the eventual judgment of humanity would come by
way of a curse on the ground (3:17-18).[3] Though God's command is a prohibition, there is no indication of conflict between God and humanity. In fact, humanity works with God in care of the garden.

Interestingly, chapter 2 ends with a very different kind of lack—a lack of shame. But shame does not really capture the full essence of how nakedness is used here. Shame implies embarrassment or dishonor of one's person. The lack here certainly includes these meanings of shame but may be more fully understood also with language describing a lack of vulnerability. Notions of sexuality are not central here. Nakedness involves a lack of protection or the capacity to protect. When the man and woman become aware of their nakedness, they cover themselves, and they seek cover from the Lord God (3:7-8). Vulnerability and security are at stake. God's response reminds humanity of their dependence as well.[4] One scholar suggests "for the first time the human couple were able to see themselves through the eyes of God, and they perceived their weakness, fragility and dependence."[5]

Some internal parallel structures of events or language reflect thesis-antithesis developments throughout this narrative.[6] The role of nakedness in the narrative well illustrates this dynamic, which gets at understanding the temptation of humanity (3:1-7) as part of this creation narrative. The serpent and woman are held in tension. Both emerge from creation and contend with one another in discerning the options available to them in life. Obedience and knowing are in tension. Both the woman and the man are disobedient and become aware of evil. The "fall" to temptation, though, results in more than an awareness of vulnerability. The woman and man become aware of a sudden estrangement in their very being. The tension results in estrangement from God. They actually seek to protect themselves.[7] A stark irony of tragic "knowledge" emerges in seeking protection between one another and from God. The state of estrangement extends into God's intentions for creation, relations between humanity and God, and also within human relationships themselves.

Responding to the Text

The garden scene or, in its common characterization, the "fall" narrative poses some difficult questions for the preacher. Let us start with the obvious: How does the "fall" language actually capture the meaning of this story? In an odd twist, it is actually the desire of wisdom and attainment of knowledge that characterize the "fall." For the human couple, "the eyes of both were opened." Perhaps the discussion of estrangement in the section above will help preachers find alternative ways to make sense of what has been traditionally called the fall of humanity. In the garden narrative, the estrangement of humanity results from a pursuit and awareness of one's own interest that usurps the primacy of relationship with God. The desire to know good and evil is to be like a god, not to be with God. We are not used to preaching that a desire to be "wise" may estrange us from God. The nature of this

THE DESIRE TO KNOW GOOD AND EVIL IS TO BE LIKE A GOD, NOT TO BE WITH GOD.

wisdom, however, is the acquisition of power to be like a god and distinctly independent from God. One scholar identifies this independence within themes of separation in this narrative.[8] The relationship between God and humanity changes drastically. The human couple becomes estranged as well. They each cover themselves. And note how Adam defends his offense before God. It would be almost comical if it were not so tragic: "The woman whom you gave to be with me, she gave me the fruit from the tree, and I ate" (3:12). Our estrangement from God and one another mark our fall.

There are at least two looming queries the preacher may wish to treat, but with caution. First, how should we understand the role of the "tree of life" in the garden? The caution comes in working with 3:5. When combined with the "tree of knowledge," how does humanity become like God? From the ensuing reaction (3:22), even God is alarmed. It is the combination of immortality and knowledge that appears to cause alarm. Expulsion from the garden in this subsequent scene changes the nature of our toil in the earth and characterizes our mortality. Humanity's need for God does not cease but changes dramatically. And perhaps the need for God is a driving theme in understanding this passage for Lent.

Next, how should we understand the role of the serpent? Clearly, the immediate role is antagonistic. The serpent is the tempter. Notice that the serpent is only referred to as one of the wild animals (3:1). This narrative does not refer to the tempter as Satan. Interpretations of this creature as Satan began to emerge in later scriptural allusions to this passage (cf. Wisd. of Sol. 1:16) and became more commonplace in Christian traditions and New Testament texts (cf. Rev. 12:9).[9] Perhaps, as the notations in the NRSV suggest, the enigma of the serpent thrives in its ancient symbolism of beguilement or even immortality. The caution comes in the latter suggestion. The serpent is part of God's creation and by implication one of the creatures named by humanity. Temptation comes from within creation. Preachers may do well to wrestle with the import of this internal quandary.

Responsive Reading
PSALM 32 (RCL);
PSALM 51 or 51:1-13 (BCP);
PSALM 51:3-4, 5-6, 12-13, 17 (RC)

Psalms 32 and 51 are penitential psalms dealing with the realization of our sinfulness. For a review of Psalm 51, see the comments on the responsive reading for Ash Wednesday. Let it suffice here to repeat that David's lament begins with confession and is followed by pleas for forgiveness. In the prospect of restoration, the psalmist commits to teach and give witness to the joy of God's merciful deliverance.

Psalm 32 also speaks of restoration. However, here the psalmist sings from the perspective of restoration received. The psalm begins with thanksgiving in the form of blessing. While it is particularly important to hear the psalmist singing the thanksgiving of forgiveness, preachers should observe the transition into a struggle of penitence in v. 2: "Happy are those . . . in whose spirit there is no deceit." Self-deceit might be a more explicit connotation in this passage. The psalmist distinguishes the destructive capacity of sinfulness in the power of self-deceit. The deception is what some have called impenitence.[10] The ravages of sin and self-deception are felt in many areas of our lives. Preachers will need to discern theologically how they will interpret the ravages of sin in view of this psalm. Some will be tempted to suggest that the destructive experiences of sin are part of God's judgment. However, the psalmist here considers the pain and guilt of sin to be the caustic effects of sin itself (vv. 3-5). The same question may arise in v. 10 when considering "the torments of the wicked." Reformed theology may help with the question of judgment or effect; the awareness or acknowledgment of sin comes from God's in-breaking grace. Verses 8-9 speak of God's instruction and counsel. Like thanksgiving, confession of sin is a response to God's grace, empowered by God's grace.[11] Similarly, Roman Catholic doctrine stresses that the grace of God is necessary for us to exercise faith.[12] God's love for us moves to restore us in the image of God and in relationship to God. The psalmist ends with an important assurance to others of God's steadfast love. In the experience of forgiveness, the psalmist's liturgical charge to us echoes in the same joyous thanksgiving that began the song: "Be glad in the LORD and rejoice" (v. 11).

SECOND READING

ROMANS 5:12-19 (RCL);
ROMANS 5:12-19, 20-21 (BCP);
ROMANS 5:12-19 or 5:12, 17-19 (RC)

Interpreting the Text

This passage confronts us with multiple contrasts. At least in structure and language, the most striking contrast is the juxtaposition of one person who introduces us to sin and death (v. 12) and another person who introduces the free gift of grace (v. 15). The very humanity of Christ is weighed in response to the human condition determined through Adam's inaugural encounter with sin. More than a contrast or juxtaposition, it is helpful to distinguish the syntax of sin and grace in this

DEATH RAISES THE QUESTION OF JUDGMENT; JUSTIFICATION IN CHRIST IS GOD'S FREE ANSWER.

pericope as a question-answer dialectic. Humanity experiences judgment of death in response to sin. Sin does not merely refer to acts but to a more pervasive human capacity or culpability. God's own response to the judgment of humanity steps forward freely in justification through Christ. Sin presents a question of the human condition; grace depicts God's response. Death raises the question of judgment; justification in Christ is God's free answer (vv. 16-17). One cannot escape the struggle to understand the human condition. Adam clearly exemplifies our efforts to understand human toil and death. Christ overcomes all that to which Adam succumbs. Grace thereby overcomes sin; the free gift of justification overcomes the condemnation of death. Christ's humanity is part of God's answer to humanity. Eternal life in Christ is the dominion of grace that overcomes the dominion of sin in the judgment of death (v. 21).[13]

Responding to the Text

This text is one that requires dialogue with historical interpretations. In particular, Augustine's doctrine of original sin relied heavily on this passage in Romans. Preachers today will need to grapple here with the notions of sin and judgment. Augustine argued that humankind inherited sinfulness through the act of Adam and therefore inherited God's judgment as well. Augustine interpreted the last phrase of 5:12 to read ". . . 'in whom' all sinned." Scholars largely agree that Augustine made an exegetical error stemming most likely from the Latin text on which he relied. The Greek text is more appropriately translated here as "in that" or "because that." This distinction raises questions for the doctrine of original sin or original guilt.[14] An orthodox understanding holds that the apostle Paul viewed sinfulness to be an imputed condition stemming from the act of sin by Adam (Eve is subsumed within the misogyny of male dominance in human identity). Dispute ensues on whether human sinfulness and judgment are best understood as inherited conditions from one person's act. Does Paul hold human sinfulness apart from individual accountability? The language in v. 12 charges that the judgment of death "spread to all because all have sinned." Therefore, despite Augustine's emphasis on imputed sinfulness, even very early exegetical work in the modern era finds that Paul seems to have both human nature and individual accountability in mind.[15] In defense of Augustine, however, it is more difficult to draw the above distinction in v. 19, where Paul maintains that by the act of one person, "the many were made sinners." The preacher will not be able simply to dismiss the language of original, or imputed, guilt.[16]

One's biblical theology is at stake here. Clearly, the apostle reads the creation and temptation narrative in an orthodox tradition that sees a more unembroidered account of scripture. In this passage, scriptural interpretation for Paul is more concerned with understanding how Christ revisions or fits within biblical traditions.

This passage undoubtedly attempts to reason out theologically the nature of human sinfulness, death, and salvation in Christ. Preachers will have to clarify their biblical theology of the creation and temptation narratives. Notwithstanding, the most salient question may ask how might this passage be understood if the Genesis narratives in consideration focus more intently on the nature of human toil, death, and sinfulness than on a theology of punishment. The address or attention of God's judgment will then weigh heavily in discerning God's response to human sinfulness in the grace of Christ. Our attention during Lent to our own sinfulness no less involves our response to the free gift of grace.

The Gospel
MATTHEW 4:1-11 (RCL, BCP, RC)

Interpreting the Text

The temptation of Jesus in the wilderness follows directly upon his baptism (3:13-17). Any consideration of the temptation narrative must consider the role of the Spirit between Jesus' baptism and temptations. First, the Spirit descends upon Jesus, accompanied by a voice of approval. Without transition, chapter 4 then begins with the Spirit leading Jesus into the wilderness to be tempted. The obvious implication is that divine intention lay behind the ensuing temptations. However, the meaning seems to be more than a simple providence designed to show forth Jesus' power in human and spiritual conflict. Most scholars agree that Matthew's account underscores the "sonship" of God. And with this identity comes the struggle to understand Jesus' calling and role within humanity.[17] Let us consider, then, the more prominent features and meanings in the temptations of Jesus that point to his human and divine roles together.

The structure of this narrative and correlations with Israelite traditions help immensely to interpret this pericope. The temptations test Jesus in three areas: his needs, divine favor, and the object of his faith. In response to each temptation, Jesus cites a passage from Deuteronomy: 8:3; 6:16; and 6:13, respectively. This dependence on the Hebrew scriptures represents a narrative midrash—a reliance on particular words, content, or structure from prior scriptures.[18] In the first temptation, the devil challenges Jesus in his human needs or, more specifically, his hunger. The Deuteronomy text supplies the backdrop of context and language. The wilderness experience of the Israelites was the testing ground for their trust that God was the source and supplier of their needs (Deut. 8:3). For both the Israelites and Jesus, it is a test of obedience. Exodus 16:3-4 also depicts the Israelite experience in the wilderness with hunger as God's test of obedience. The Israelites would have to rely on God for a daily fulfillment of very real needs.

With a second temptation, Jesus is swept away to the "holy city" and the temple. Jerusalem is the holy city, and the messianic implications of placing Jesus on the "pinnacle" of the temple may reflect early rabbinic teachings. In consideration of his identity, we ponder over Jesus' authority: Does God's favor extend to Jesus' whims and desires? Or does God's favor imply a role and a relationship with Jesus, which in turn would require his submission? Will Jesus test God's promises or God's faithfulness? The Israelites were warned in Deut. 6:16 not to test God as they had at Massah and Meribah. From Exodus 17, we learn of the Israelites' demand of Moses, and therefore God. If God would be the Israelites' provider in the wilderness, then they would require that God show forth in quenching their

JESUS' OBEDIENCE RESISTS THE TEMPTATION TO TURN HIS RELIANCE ON GOD INTO A TEST OF GOD'S FAITHFULNESS.

thirst. Though one could rightly call this a need-based test, the temptation challenges their reliance on God. Jesus' obedience resists the temptation to turn his reliance on God into a test of God's faithfulness.

Resorting to even more audacious temptation, the devil attempts directly to educe worship from Jesus. To show Jesus "all the kingdoms of their world and their splendor" from a high mountain was to tempt him with power and riches. Jesus' lot would be one of control and privilege. It is possible that the Gospel writer here wished to redefine Jewish presuppositions that the Messiah would be a ruler or vindicator of the nation with political autonomy. Jesus defines his rule in straightforward service to God (Deut. 6:13). This temptation and response draws upon God's covenantal relationship with the Israelites in Exod. 20:2-6, where we receive the first commandment to worship YHWH only. Exodus 32 displays the Israelites' disobedience with the golden calf. In contrast, Jesus stands in obedience, and in so doing is able to claim authority.

The use of narrative midrash should be quite observable. Interpretation of the temptation narrative needs to weigh carefully how this Gospel identifies and defines the nature of Jesus as the Son of God. Our understanding of Jesus as the Christ is developed through just how Jesus' humanity comes to grip in the wilderness with God's will and his own divine nature.[19]

Responding to the Text

Great temptation lies in wait for the preacher to reduce this passage to modeling behavior in a Manichean wilderness of good versus evil. Here confrontation involves more than "resist the devil and he will flee" (James 4:7). Another temptation is to focus too narrowly on a spiritual power in the simple recitation of scripture. Much has been made of the devil's own citation of scripture in tempting Jesus to test God. A third temptation for preachers rests in mistaking the power of obedience. The risk is that we begin to view our obedience as obligating God to respond in terms of our own interests or intentions. The wilderness experience is far more complex, as these temptations should indicate. While wilderness theology in Israelite history and this text certainly accents testing, the wilderness is more about revealing the character of our hearts and the nature of faith.[20] We are tempted to raise rather myopic questions: Does God intend testing today? Are we led into the wilderness to be tested? These kind of questions focus more on reasoning out the "Why?" of our wilderness encounters and risk neglect of "How?" do we live through those places. In short, this passage would be too narrowly defined if our focus only perceives questions about theodicy and conquering evil; it is more about understanding obedience or faith within a dynamic trust in God.

> THIS PASSAGE WOULD BE TOO NARROWLY DEFINED IF OUR FOCUS ONLY PERCEIVES QUESTIONS ABOUT THEODICY AND CONQUERING EVIL; IT IS MORE ABOUT UNDERSTANDING OBEDIENCE OR FAITH WITHIN A DYNAMIC TRUST IN GOD.

The obedience of Jesus helps to reveal the identity of Christ by reorienting our assumptions about his power and ministry. Romans 5:12-21 reminds us that Christ's obedience counteracts, or rather overcomes, the disobedience of humanity as given in the garden narrative of Genesis. Jesus is obedient to a way of living intended for humanity. His identity as the Son of God is certified in his baptism; the character of messianic office is revealed in his living—and as we learn from the Gospel—even unto death.[21] It will be a difficult challenge for the preacher to interpret obedience for us, particularly during this season of Lent. Surely our obedience in fasts and prayers during these forty days of spiritual wilderness echoes efforts of faithfulness found in Jesus' obedience. We struggle to understand when and how God responds to our obedience. In Lent we seek to renew and strengthen our faithfulness. God's faithfulness is in Christ. Our vindication and restoration is in Christ's obedience and resurrection.

Notes

1. Stephen Kempf, "Introducing the Garden of Eden: The Structure and Function of Genesis 2:4b-7," *Journal of Translation and Text Linguistics* 7, no. 4 (1996): 33–53.

2. Terje Stordalen, "Man, Soil, Garden: Basic Plot in Genesis 2-3 Reconsidered," *Journal for the Study of the Old Testament* 53 (March 1992): 3–25.

3. Ibid.

4. Jonathan Magonet, "The Themes of Genesis 2–3," in *A Walk in the Garden: Biblical, Iconographical, and Literary Images of Eden*, ed. Paul Morris and Deborah Sawyer (Sheffield, England: Sheffield Academic Press, 1992), 39–46.

5. Roberto Ouro, "The Garden of Eden Account: The Chiastic Structure of Genesis 2-3," *Andrews University Seminary Studies* 40, no. 2 (autumn 2002): 236.

6. Ibid., 219–43.

7. Magonet, "Themes of Genesis," 39–46.

8. Ibid.

9. Marvin E. Tate, "Satan in the Old Testament," in "Perspectives on Satan," ed. Charles J. Scalise, *Review and Expositor* 89 (fall 1992): 466–67.

10. Robert W. Jensen, "Psalm 32," *Interpretation* 33 (April 1979): 172–76.

11. John Calvin, *Institutes of the Christian Religion*, 3.3.2.

12. Vatican Council II, *The Conciliar and Post Conciliar Documents*, 58.I.5.

13. Leslie Houlden, "Fall and Salvation: A Case of Difficulty," *Expository Times* 109, no. 8 (May 1998): 234–37.

14. Philip L. Quin, "Disputing the Augustinian Legacy: John Locke and Jonathan Edwards on Romans 5:12-19," in *The Augustinian Tradition*, ed. Gareth B. Matthews (Los Angeles: University of California Press, 1999), 233–50.

15. Stuart Moses, trans., "DeWette's Commentary on Romans 5:12-19," *Bibliotheca Sacra and Theological Review* 5, no. 18 (May 1848): 263–83.

16. Quin, "Augustinian Legacy," 233–50.

17. William Loyd Allen, "Matthew 4:1-11: The Devil at the Crossroads," *Review and Expositor* 89 (fall 1992): 529–33.

18. George Wesley Buchanan, *The Gospel of Matthew*, New Testament Series (Lewiston, New York: Mellen, 1996), 157.

19. Ibid., 155–69. See also William Richard Stegner, "Wilderness and Testing in the Scrolls and in Matthew 4:1-11," *Biblical Research* 12 (1967): 18–27.

20. Stegner, 18–27.

21. Lamar Williamson, "Matthew 4:1-11," *Interpretation* 38 (January 1984): 51–55.

SECOND SUNDAY IN LENT

FEBRUARY 20, 2005

REVISED COMMON	EPISCOPAL (BCP)	ROMAN CATHOLIC
Gen. 12:1-4a	Gen. 12:1-8	Gen. 12:1-4a
Psalm 121	Ps. 33:12-22	Ps. 33:4-5, 18-19, 20, 22
Rom. 4:1-5, 13-17	Rom. 4:1-5, (6-12) 13-17	2 Tim. 1:8b-10
John 3:1-17	John 3:1-17	Matt. 17:1-9
or Matt. 17:1-9		

We might comprehend faith more clearly if we accept that it increasingly unfolds in the course of life. The Second Sunday in Lent proclaims transformation in Christ. This transformation, however, is both an event and a process. We are sojourners who have been transformed by grace and placed on a journey of faith in Christ that seeks to transform life itself. We live into the paschal mystery.[1] Lent intensifies our attention to the transformation and journey of living out of, and yet into, faith. The readings for this week deal with the gift of redemption and character of faith. In one Gospel reading, we encounter the glory of the Transfiguration. Like the disciples, we only begin to grasp the paschal mystery. The other Gospel lection redefines the life of faith in Christ. We are born into a new life of the Spirit. Inasmuch as we are transformed, we are called to trust in God's promises. Both the Genesis passage and psalms speak of trust in God's faithfulness to fulfill God's promises. We increasingly experience God's steadfast love as we live into the call to faith. The second readings affirm that the life of faith depends on grace in Christ and is God's call upon our lives.

FIRST READING

GENESIS 12:1-4a (RCL, RC);
GENESIS 12:1-8 (BCP)

Interpreting the Text

Abram's call and promise of blessing might suggest to some that God had given up on much of creation and decided to form a people wholly committed to God in a faith distinct from that of other peoples. Surely the flood narrative (Genesis 6–8) illustrates God's utter frustration with humanity. But as sure as God's frustration rises, so does God's resolve to nurture a covenant relationship with humanity and the growing nations (Genesis 9–10). However, humankind's capacity for self-interest or self-indulgence increases in the pursuit of power (Tower of Babel, Genesis 11), apparently driven by anxiety over security or self-determination. Dependence upon God seems to be at stake. Biblical redaction places Abram's call following the creation narratives, the establishment of a covenantal relationship with humankind, and the development of nations. With the end of chapter 11, Genesis 12 marks a transition from biblical, primeval human history into the development of patriarchal traditions. Abram is called forth from among the nations, and God begins again the work of restoration.[2]

This transition is no small response to the Babel narrative. Humankind's relationship with God experiences a tragic rupture, which also results in broken unity among human relationships. God responds in a new work. Restoration here becomes a process. The fragmentation of fellowship with God and the splintering of human relations reveal God's motivations in Abram's call. Abram is called into a pilgrimage. His pilgrimage is marked by the insecurity of any unknown journey. God calls Abram with a voice of promise. It is not a threat of anger or judgment. This call is to evoke trust in God's word. The

> AS SURE AS GOD'S FRUSTRATION RISES, SO DOES GOD'S RESOLVE TO NURTURE A COVENANT RELATIONSHIP WITH HUMANITY AND THE GROWING NATIONS.

promise is that God will bless Abram and transform Abram into a blessing for others. Promise and fulfillment do seem to shape trust. Abram's obedience is a measure of his trust in God's promises. Risk of travail is not removed from the pilgrimage. As we learn from the ensuing passage of Abram and Sarai's excursion into Egypt (vv. 10-20), their pilgrimage encounters extreme difficulty between faith and fear. Where trust is challenged, God does require faithfulness. Abram's pilgrimage is to live into divine calling; he is called to a way of life that depends on God's faithfulness and blessing.[3]

Responding to the Text

The emphases on blessings in this passage are significant. Blessings are not simply promised to a task-oriented obedience from Abram. They are promised in a process to restore relationship with God. Abram's call is a response to broken relations with God and alienation throughout humankind. Abram's pilgrimage itself comprises God's resolve to restore humanity. Personal blessing is all caught up in blessings for others. The promise of greatness (v. 2) is subordinate to the ultimate intentions of God's blessing. God will make Abram's name great "so that" he will become a blessing. Abram's call sets in motion the patriarchal narratives, which are most appropriately viewed in response to broken fellowship with God and human relations.[4] God is looking ahead.

When God makes a covenant with Abram (chapter 17), God changes his name to Abraham. The pilgrimage of restoration leads to transformation. Preachers may help people grasp blessing in pilgrimage when considering our own liturgical traditions of naming within the baptismal rite, or renaming in confirmation into the faith. We do not make a name for ourselves—that would be to repeat the construction of Babel. Greatness must be redefined into a trust in God's faithfulness to restore humanity. Naming or renaming in our liturgical traditions is to receive a faith identity. Fulfillment comes in God's faithfulness in humanity's pilgrimage of trust. Ultimately, the blessing we receive actually finds further fulfillment in the blessing of others. Abram's name will be great in the meaning his pilgrimage will carry for humanity. Even the language of curse (v. 3) is subordinate to blessing. The point is not that we live under a threat of judgment, but rather that we live into God's commitment to restore humanity. The motivation is blessing, not judgment.[5]

RESPONSIVE READING
PSALM 121 (RCL);
PSALM 33:12-22 (BCP);
PSALM 33:4-5, 18-19, 20, 22 (RC)

Psalm 121 is one of the Songs of Ascents, used in pilgrimage to Jerusalem. During the year, Jews were expected to travel to Jerusalem for several feasts, such as the Feast of Unleavened Bread or the Feast of Tabernacles. These songs were likely formed in a postexilic period. This particular song is not one of duress under political threat but one of joyous celebration on a journey. Still, the Songs of Ascents do not comprise a single focus. They variously comprise laments, praise or thanksgiving, as well as wisdom songs. Psalm 121 has been classified as a song of trust. Throughout this song, the faithfulness of God is proclaimed.

Most experts agree that there are two primary voices in this psalm, one being the pilgrim and the other being a priest. Despite some speculation that the psalm might represent an internal mental dialogue of a pilgrim, distinct voices are made clear in the language of the text. In v. 1, the pilgrim lifts up a rhetorical question that sets up an affirmation of faith in v. 2. Both the question and answer speak in the first-person singular. The pilgrim's help does not come from any gods that may reside in the mountains or hills of the ancient world, as many cultures of the age held. The pilgrim's help comes from the Creator, YHWH. It is an affirmation of faith in the care of God. The speaker changes in v. 3 to a priest addressing the pilgrim in the second person, "you." Notice the repeated emphasis that God "keeps" the pilgrim. God's faithfulness is evidenced directly in how God "keeps" Israel.

Many exegetes draw a correlation here with the exodus narrative. God is ever present. Verses 5-6 further characterize God as the pilgrim's "keeper." God is a "shade" in both the heat of the sun and the ominous folklore of the moon's light. The priest attests to God's steadfastness. One scholar translates "keeper" as "minder." The emphasis is that God watches over us.[6] Ultimately, the priest pronounces God's continual or future blessings (vv. 7-8). God's blessings extend over one's very being as well as over the daily activities in "going out" and "coming in."[7]

Verse 7 may present the greatest difficulty for us during Lent: "the Lord will keep you from all evil." If we take this verse to mean that we are spared all evil, the evil we actually encounter can throw us into existential crisis. We seldom escape the evil of our own hearts, not to mention the evil of suffering at large. Instead, the assurance of this priestly voice lies in God's care for us. Preachers will want to address the meaning of God's care for us in the face of evil. In what manner does God keep us from all evil?

Psalm 33 also begins with attention to God's faithfulness. God's love is known throughout the earth in righteousness and justice (vv. 4-5). The psalmist illustrates God's faithfulness in looking over humanity; God watches over us all from heaven. Moreover, God directly looks after those who place their hope in God's unyielding love (v. 18). Like Psalm 121, this psalm rests in trust of the Lord. We may struggle, but our trust is in God who seeks to help us. Our help lies in God's steadfast love (v. 22). The language of deliverance of the faithful from death, whose hope finds life in God's love (vv. 18-19), has also been interpreted with a christological lens—God's steadfast love is fulfilled in Christ's passion and resurrection.[8] In essence, this psalm calls us into praise because God redeems creation with faithful love.

Second Reading
ROMANS 4:1-5, 13-17 (RCL);
ROMANS 4:1-5, (6-12) 13-17 (BCP)

Interpreting the Text

Chapter 4 begins with a controversial verse. The NRSV translates it as "What then are we to say was gained by Abraham, our ancestor according to the flesh?" This translation is a liberal one in that it adds the words "was gained by." The translators are trying to wrestle with questions of Paul's reliance on a rhetorical question. Paul frequently drives his arguments forward by raising potential oppositions or objections. In this case, his question points to how we ought to understand the patriarchal narrative. Abraham is the "father figure" for the Jewish faith. Paul's question attempts to get at just how he became that figurehead and to whom his example fully applies.

This is not the place to outline in detail the fascinating nuances in translating v. 1. We can, however, determine the driving issue that this rhetorical question is designed to illumine. In the previous two chapters, Paul has just gone through an elaborate treatment of the law, although the real issue has to do with boasting over one's place with God. The role of circumcision addresses the plight of Gentiles in the faith. In the closing passages of chapter 3, Paul turns to "the faith *of* Jesus Christ" (vv. 21-26). The NRSV translates the above phrase as "faith *in* Jesus Christ." With the former translation, at least one exegete highlights Paul's reliance on Christ's faithfulness.[9] Grace is a gift offered through the faith of Christ. We are therefore justified by the faith of Christ, who demonstrated his righteousness through his own obedience and his sacrificial death and redemptive faithfulness.[10] In this light the query into boasting over one's place with God is thoroughly transformed. God is the God of the Jews and the God of the Gentiles. Christ does not simply nullify the law. The law is ultimately fulfilled or transformed in the faith of Christ (vv. 27-31).

With chapter 4, Paul attempts to show that this role of faith is not a new one to the Jews. And this is where the rhetorical turn to Abraham becomes instructive. The point of the rhetorical question in v. 1 is shaped by Paul's attention to the role of faith. Is Abraham the "ancestor" or progenitor of the faith due to circumcision, the line of natural heritage, or some combination of the two? Paul wishes to show that justification by faith has been part of the Jewish inheritance even with the ancestor of the faith. From Genesis, Paul underscores the role of faith in God's promises to Abraham. Verse 3 cites Gen. 15:6: "Abraham believed God and it was reckoned to him as righteousness." Abraham's obedience in works did not render him righteous; it was that he "believed God." Paul illustrates in vv. 4-5 that trust in God is faith. In v. 9, therefore, faith distinguished Abraham's righteousness

ABRAHAM IS AN EXAMPLE OF HOW FAITH EMPOWERS LIFE WITHIN GOD'S OWN FAITHFULNESS.

before the law, before circumcision, before his seed-promise was fulfilled. The function of faith makes Abraham the ancestor of faith for both Jews and Gentiles alike. The promises of God called Abraham forth in grace and blessed him and the nations (v. 17; cf. Gen. 12:2, 17:5). Abraham's faith lived into the gift of grace. Abraham is an example of how faith empowers life within God's own faithfulness. By the end of chapter 4, Paul ties the function of faith back into the faith of Christ. Through Christ we are justified by faith.[11]

Responding to the Text

Verse 3 poses an interesting stance, "Abraham believed God." Why not say that Abraham believed in God or even hoped in the promises of God? Preachers may wish to track the implications further. Abraham's trust in God is vital to

Paul's understanding that faith functions as righteousness before God. Obedience in works does not "reckon" us righteous. Rather, obedience derives from some other affect or effect. Are we obedient in fasting and prayers during Lent because we fear God? At times, we must admit that fear can encourage obedience. Maybe "obedience" is not a sufficient term. One may suppose that trust can produce obedience; but more likely, trust generates commitment, reliance, investment, and even belief. Abraham believed God. Abraham's belief grew out of God's call and promises. As one writer describes this dynamic, Abraham was persuaded by God's promises.[12] Verses 13-17 summarize that God mediates God's promises by procuring faith.[13] We come to know or trust God's promises through God's effort to reach us. God is revealed in God's own word and activity. We know God because God calls us forth and promises to bless us. When we say that we believe in God, we more accurately proclaim that we believe God. Faith breaks forth from the activity and promises of God. In turn, God fulfills God's promises through engaging our faith. Our very faith relies completely on the gift of grace that God reveals in the faith of Christ. Our faith is that we believe God. We live into that faith as God engages us in trust of God's word and promises.

2 TIMOTHY 1:8b-10 (RC)

This "pastoral epistle" begins with terms of endearment for Timothy. While the authorship of the letter remains in question, Paul claims apostleship through the will of God and in "the promise of life that is in Christ Jesus (v. 1).

However, in this letter the emphasis on Christ lies in his earthly life. Verse 10 stresses the grace given to humanity was made known in Christ's earthly life and death. This very human Jesus illumined the promise of life restored. Therein, we not

> THE LIFE OF CHRISTIAN MINISTRY TRUSTS IN THE POWER AND LOVE OF GOD IN CHRIST TO TRANSFORM OUR WORKS AND EVEN OUR SUFFERING IN SERVICE TO GOD'S GRACE FOR HUMANITY.

only encounter revelation in Christ, but also discover the power of God for our own living (v. 8b). With Timothy, we are reminded that our apprehension of the gospel does not liberate us from the toils of living. In fact, the letter points out that we may suffer for the sake of the gospel message. We are called into God's purpose in the promise of grace fulfilled (v. 9).

This passage addresses the exigencies of faithful ministry. The dismay of suffering is transformed by the divine calling. In remembering the gift of grace given through Christ's earthly ministry, we are empowered by the love of God as evidenced in that grace (v. 7; 2:1). Oddly enough, this passage is intended to encourage. The encouragement comes to light in the life of the gospel promise (vv. 1, 10). The life of Christian ministry trusts in the power and love of God in Christ to transform our works and even our suffering in service to God's grace for humanity.[14]

The Gospel
MATTHEW 17:1–9 (RC, RCL alt.)

Interpreting the Text

In the Episcopal and Revised Common lectionaries, this passage is the same Gospel text used for Transfiguration Sunday, preceding Lent (for a comparison by liturgical seasons, see the comments on the Gospel for the Last Sunday after Epiphany/Transfiguration of our Lord/Fifth Sunday in Ordinary Time, February 6, 2005). Matthew's narrative is the primary Gospel reading for the Roman Catholic lectionary. And it is with this repeated usage that our attention begins. The Transfiguration of Jesus narrative fits nicely within the Epiphany season, because the glory of Christ is revealed to the disciples and, through them, to us. A repetition of the baptismal revelation, when the voice from heaven proclaims, "This is my Son, the Beloved, with whom I am well pleased," (3:17), is no small matter. This echoed proclamation now follows at least one disciple's affirmation of Jesus' messianic identity. Who is Jesus? Well, Peter declares that he is the Messiah (16:16). In the mountain scene of Transfiguration, Peter is among the select few allowed to accompany Jesus. The revealed glory of Jesus marks a transition in this Gospel. The proclamation from the cloud is divine disclosure. The mystery of Christ is set forth in disclosing further the nature of Jesus' human pilgrimage.[15]

God's disclosure takes place on a high mountain (v. 1). Frequently in biblical literature, mountains provide a significant milieu to represent God's self-revelation. The vision of the Transfiguration scene depicts a "bright cloud" that "overshadowed" the disciples. A dramatic experience unfolds when God's voice emanates from a bright and yet overshadowing cloud. While the disciples respond with awe to the images of Moses and Elijah speaking with Jesus (v. 3), they respond with fear to the revelation from the cloud. As one scholar helpfully observes, the cloud image is revealing and yet mystifying; it is an image of "knowing and unknowing" in the same instance.[16] Theophanie descriptions in the exodus narratives (chapters 24 and 34) function similarly within Moses' Mount Sinai encounters.[17] The glory and the veil of God's self-disclosure operate dynamically together in our encounters with God. One cannot escape this dynamic in the transfiguration narrative. The glory of Christ is revealed and, in a mysterious suppression of the phenomenon (v. 9), Jesus points beyond this event to the full revelation of the resurrection. Our task here is to interpret the passion and death of Jesus under the shadow of his glory.

Reasonable interpretations not only point forward to the messianic identity of Christ but also may consider the impact on Jesus directly in his pilgrimage to Jerusalem. The glory of Christ is reaffirmed in the Transfiguration. It is no great leap of faith to imagine the impact the experience would have in preparing Jesus in contemplating his imminent passion. Actually, as one preacher put it, the Transfiguration narrative transforms the earthly ministry of Christ.[18] The point here is that the teachings and earthly ministry of Jesus must be understood in terms of his divine glory. Just prior to the Transfiguration scene in Matthew, Jesus explains to the disciples that he must endure great suffering and die but will rise again (16:21). Here, this Gospel turns to face Jerusalem. The Transfiguration points to the glory of Christ in his passion and resurrection.

The Transfiguration in Lent compels us to view Jesus, his passion, and his death in the revelation of his resurrection. Jesus' disciples had to wrestle with this very understanding. Notice that after Peter's attestation of Christ (16:16) and the Transfiguration pronouncement (17:5), wherein Christ's glory is revealed to the disciples, they are "ordered" to tell no one about the messianic revelation as yet (16:20; 17:9). Here, the significance of the clouded vision within the mountain scene may prove helpful: "knowing and not yet knowing." The disciples would need to experience the resurrection to understand more deeply Jesus' earthly ministry and the messianic glory of his "sonship"—both as the Son of Humanity (17:9) and as the Son of God (16:16; 17:5). We also understand

> THE IMPACT OF THE TRANSFIGURATION IN LENT IS POWERFUL BECAUSE THE REVEALED GLORY OF CHRIST NOT ONLY REDEFINES THE PASSION IN VIEW OF THE RESURRECTION, BUT ALSO SUSTAINS US IN THE EXPERIENCE OF SUFFERING.

the passion of Christ more deeply through the glory of the resurrection. The impact of the Transfiguration in Lent is powerful because the revealed glory of Christ not only redefines the passion in view of the resurrection, but also sustains us in the experience of suffering.[19] Perhaps then, we may grasp more clearly our earthly discipleship (16:24-26) in the promise of salvation fulfilled in the resurrection.

JOHN 3:1-17 (RCL, BCP)

"We just don't get it!" And neither does Nicodemus! We marvel at the miracles of Jesus. We often pray for miracles in our lives. Some of us have resigned ourselves to the conclusion that miracles belonged to the ministry of Christ and the apostolic age—that is, if ever they truly existed. Still, scripture affirms that God desires to bless us—you name it . . . God's creation . . . the people of God . . . the children of God. We spin God's promises to bless into God's purpose in our lives. This Gospel passage, like many in John, projects the uncertainty of our assumptions. Nicodemus suspects that more lies behind the miracles of Jesus than he grasps. His language of "signs" is instructive (v. 2). Signs point to something else. Miracles, then, are meant to be instructive or to point beyond what is evident in their immediate effects. At the very least, this perspective seems to steer Nicodemus through the blindness of night to press Jesus for some answers. But why does Jesus have to be so incessantly vague? You must be born "anew," or born "from above"; you must be "born of water and Spirit" (vv. 3, 5). That Nicodemus represents

EVEN WHEN WE CAN IDENTIFY CLEARLY GOD'S BLESSINGS AMONG US, WE OFTEN FAIL TO SEE THEIR FULL INTENT.

the religious leadership should not be minimized. Even when we can identify clearly God's blessings among us, we often fail to see their full intent. As Jesus charges, we can testify to what we know and see and still fail to comprehend the blessing (vv. 11-12). To grasp the blessings in our lives, we must perceive God's intent to restore us. The signs point to God's intent to restore and nurture relationship with us and among us, through Christ.[20] For God so loved the world!

Notes

1. Adolf Adam, *The Liturgical Year: Its History and Its Meaning after the Reform of the Liturgy*, trans. Matthew J. O'Connell (New York: Pueblo, 1981): 100–101.

2. Calvin E. Shenk, "God's Intention for Humankind: The Promise of Community; Bible Study on Genesis 12," *Mission Studies* 5, no. 2 (1998): 13–20.

3. Ibid. See also Patrick D. Miller, "Syntax and Theology in Genesis 12:3a," *Vetus Testamentum* 34, no. 4 (October 1984): 472–76.

4. Allan K. Jenkins, "A Great Name: Genesis 12:2 and the Editing of the Pentateuch," *Journal for the Study of the Old Testament* 10 (1978): 42, 46, 53.

5. Miller, "Syntax and Theology," 472–76. See also John Ellington, "Translating God's Promises to Abraham," *The Bible Translator* 45 (1994): 201–7.

6. Phillip R. Davies, "Yahweh as Minder," *Old Testament Essays* 11 (1998): 430.

7. David G. Barker, "'The Lord Watches over You': A Pilgrimage Reading of Psalm 121," *Bibliotheca Sacra* 152 (1995): 163–81.

8. Geoffrey Wainwright, "Psalm 33 Interpreted of the Triune God," *Ex Auditu* 16 (2000): 101–20.

9. Luke Timothy Johnson, *Reading Romans: A Literary and Theological Commentary* (New York: Crossroad, 1997), 59.

10. Ibid., 60.

11. Richard B. Hays, "'Have We Found Abraham to Be Our Forefather according to the Flesh?' A Reconsideration of Rom. 4:1," *Novum Testamentum* 27 (January 1985): 76–98. See also Thomas H. Tobin, "What Shall We Say that Abraham

Found? The Controversy behind Romans 4," *Harvard Theological Review* 88 (October 1995): 437–52.

12. Richard Holst, "The Meaning of 'Abraham Believed God' in Romans 4:3," *Westminster Theological Journal* 59, no. 2 (fall 1997): 319–27.

13. Tobin, "What Shall We Say," 448–49.

14. Jerome Murphy-O'Connor, "2 Timothy Contrasted with 1 Timothy and Titus," *Revue Biblique* 98 (July 1991): 403–18.

15. Albert Curry Winn, "Worship as a Healing Experience: An Exposition of Matthew 17:1-9," *Interpretation* 29 (January 1975): 68–72.

16. Henry F. Knight, "The Transfigured Face of Post-Shoah Faith: Critical Encounters with Root Experiences—Ex. 24:12-18 and Mt. 17:1-9," *Encounter* 58 (spring 1997): 138–39.

17. Ibid., 129-30. For a brief overview of the comparisons between these exodus narratives and the Transfiguration narrative, see also Warren Carter, *Matthew and the Margins: A Sociopolitical and Religious Reading* (Maryknoll, N.Y.: Orbis Books, 2000), 347–49.

18. Peter J. Gomes, *Lent*; Proclamation 6, Series A (Minneapolis: Fortress Press, 1995), 38.

19. Knight, "Transfigured Face," 147.

20. Sharon H. Ringe, "Homiletical Resources on the Gospel of John: The Gospel as Healing Word," *Quarterly Review* 6, no. 4 (winter 1986): 84–85.

THIRD SUNDAY IN LENT

FEBRUARY 27, 2005

REVISED COMMON	EPISCOPAL (BCP)	ROMAN CATHOLIC
Exod. 17:1-7	Exod. 17:1-7	Exod. 17:3-7
Psalm 95	Psalm 95 or 95:6-11	Ps. 95:1-2, 6-7, 8-9
Rom. 5:1-11	Rom. 5:1-11	Rom. 5:1-2, 5-8
John 4:5-42	John 4:5-26, (27-38) 39-42	John 4:5-42 or 4:5-15, 19b-26, 39a, 40-42

God is the source of life. If we struggle to grasp just how thoroughly that is the case, it should not be for neglect in this week's readings. We thirst for life, but we often seek our own means of fulfillment. We quarrel with God over how and when to meet our apparent needs and essentially fail to perceive God in our lives. The readings for this week cover the whole range. Similarities between the exodus narrative and the Gospel lection run rampant in streams of living water. Water is so indispensable to natural life that the wilderness narrative and biblical metaphors in these readings expose how desperately our lives of faith are need-driven. The extent to which we recognize God as our provider and source of life is in question. We deeply understand that our felt needs impel us in so many capacities. The substance of God's presence as the deepest source of life is the focus in today's hymn from the Psalms. The second reading proclaims that God is our source and provider unto eternal life, through Christ. On this Sunday in Lent, God meets us in our needs.

FIRST READING

EXODUS 17:1-7 (RCL, BCP);
EXODUS 17:3-7 (RC)

Interpreting the Text

The Israelites have experienced some amazing things. The great Passover in Egypt has spared them because of their trust in God's promises (Exodus 12). God continually leads them, ever present in a pillar of cloud during the day and one of fire through the night (Exodus 13). At the sea, they have been delivered from the stalking threat of destruction by the hands of the Egyptians (Exodus 14). These sojourners have tasted sweetened water (Exodus 15), and God has been making the heavens rain bread each day for the sustenance of the Israelites in the wilderness (Exodus 16). They are well on their journey to Sinai, but they seem to be going nowhere on their pilgrimage. The Israelites have grumbled with impatience in each of these occasions, and yet God has responded to such indignation with mercy and blessing. Whenever their circumstance has produced risk or has threatened hardship, the Israelites have "complained" against Moses and God. Chapter 17 presents such an occasion. The wrangle is not a new one. In fact, the complaint by now has become somewhat of a refrain: "Why did you bring us out of Egypt . . . to kill us and our children?" The refrain echoes in the Israelite's panic under the Egyptian pursuit (14:11), in their disgust over the bitter water at Marah (15:24), and in cries of outraged hunger in the wilderness (16:3). Now, in the wilderness of Sin, the Israelites find no water when they camp at Rephidim (17:1). And they quarrel once more. Will God respond again with mercy? It has only been a couple of months since their departure from Egypt. Their memory could not be so frail to doubt God's resolve—or perhaps it is! Verse 7 raises this very question: "Is the Lord among us or not?"

This passage has a parallel narrative in Num. 20:1-13. Among the repeated themes, several comparisons stand out that help us interpret Exodus 17. While the Numbers narrative occurs after nearly forty years in the wilderness (the actual the Hebrew title for this book translates as "In the Wilderness"), the Israelites continue to respond to adversity with resentment. In both stories, need drives the Israelites to question God's faithfulness. The rehearsed refrain appears again. We can imagine that after nearly forty years of wandering, we might hear ourselves in the question, "Why would God let us wither unto death?" God again responds to the Israelites with mercy; and with the staff of Moses, God draws forth water from the rock. Some scholars have been tempted by the parallels between Exodus 17 and Numbers 20 to conclude that they refer to the same event. However, the differences between these passages seem to indicate distinctive events and particular meanings. The parallels serve to illumine recurrent themes or lessons in the life of the Israelites. One such theme is illustrated in the patterns of risk and distrust.[1]

God continues to respond with mercy, but God does not ignore the distrust. Herein, we gain insight to the differences between the two narratives. The Israelites' repeated distrust leads to defiance. After arriving at Sinai, the Israelites fashion a golden calf. Their endeavor becomes desperation seeking security. The blessing-risk-quarrel-blessing plot of the early wilderness sojourn in Exodus, as represented in today's reading (Exod. 17:1-7), depicts the struggle of trust the

> NEED DRIVES THE ISRAELITES TO QUESTION GOD'S FAITHFULNESS.

Israelites experience in their renewed life of faith. The culmination of this struggle is an utter breakdown of trust in God's presence and promises. The Israelites intend to elect a new "captain" to lead them back to Egypt (Num. 14:4). God forgives but responds to their unrelenting distrust by prohibiting this generation to enter the land promised (Num. 14:20). Trust has to define the life of faith. Moses, in turn, exhibits distrust in Numbers 20 when he decides to wield God's authority (represented by the staff) beyond God's measure. He goes beyond God's instruction and strikes the rock instead of pronouncing the given command. And worse yet, he augments the offense by striking twice. Moses receives mercy but will not enter the promised land either (Num. 20:12). We perceive the offenses committed in Numbers more clearly because of the exodus parallel. The Numbers' authors would have been familiar with the exodus narrative, so the differences seem intentional. The differences between the passages expose the plots of distrust. In Exodus 17, the Israelites thirst to thrive, yet a quarrelsome distrust depletes all faith in their Sustainer. Relationship with God requires a life of faith that trusts God's presence and promises.[2]

Responding to the Text

Can we remove the element of risk from the life of faith? One might think that given the glory of God's deliverance, any risk the Israelites may have felt would have been alleviated altogether. Still, the threat that insecurity perpetuates is very real. How do we live into faith? The Israelites dealt with the stark realities of insecurity—risk, lack, and dependence—odd realities of deliverance indeed.[3] The early wilderness sojourn seems almost like a head game. If God would go to the extreme of miraculous deliverance, would God ignore sustenance? This question is so important that preachers need to exercise great care to avoid trivializing people's needs. Between Exod. 15:25 and 16:4, we learn that God tested the Israelites. The idea that we could live up to a test from God seems almost ludicrous. And perhaps the Israelites shared the sentiment. Like Moses in the Numbers passage, preachers risk wielding the authority of God beyond God's directive if we portray the purposes of God as mere demonstrations of power or demands of submission. God exercises power for the purpose of deliverance and redemption. Even when the wrath of God's judgment is at stake, God responds with restoration and redemption. Exodus 17 illustrates that God responds to our contemptuous insecurity with mercy. However, the exodus narratives together illustrate that God is busy building a relationship of trust. The life of faith is a relationship of trust in God. The exodus narratives make it ultimately clear that as afar as this relationship is concerned, God will not compro-

> EVEN WHEN THE WRATH OF GOD'S JUDGMENT IS AT STAKE, GOD RESPONDS WITH RESTORATION AND REDEMPTION.

mise. We infect that trust when, like the Israelites (17:2), we test God. Testing God is more self-interest–minded than relationship building. The exodus narratives reveal that deliverance and redemption are not independent goals; they are God's means of restoration and relationship.

RESPONSIVE READING

PSALM 95 (RCL);
PSALM 95 or 95:6-11 (BCP);
PSALM 95:1-2, 6-7, 8-9 (RC)

The most glaring observation to consider is the sharp turn this psalm takes in the middle of v. 7. Verses 1-7a comprise a liturgical call to worship. This section contains a thanksgiving and doxology. Psalm 95 opens with an invitation to join together in joyous singing to God (v. 1). It is an invitation to come together before God (v. 2). The context for this psalm, therefore, appears quite intentionally to be worship that begins outside of the temple and then moves inside in a procession. Notice the change of activity in worship. The psalmist or priest, in leading worship, beckons for the community to bow down and kneel (v. 6). These acts indicate the transition inside. The hymn of thanksgiving that opens the psalm includes an affirmation of God's greatness (vv. 3-5). With the progression of worship inside the temple, the liturgical language includes confession of our relationship to God (vv. 6-7a).[4]

The progression of the psalm, along with the liturgical procession, raises intriguing reflections regarding historical context. The psalm is likely postexilic, and the stages of call to worship suggest the renewal of the temple. Some scholars arrive at these conclusions when comparing the first section of Psalm 95 with its closest parallel, the preexilic Psalm 100. Psalm 95 repeats the language of Psalm 100 very closely (compare the thanksgiving of 95:1-2 with 100:1-2, 4; then compare the confession of relationship of 95:6-7a with 100:3). The omission of a parallel in Psalm 95 with Ps. 100:5 causes at least one commentator to interpret a postexilic hesitance to declare God's faithfulness to "all generations" without attention to immediate history.[5] The call to worship is contextual, both historically and relationally. We shape liturgy and rites to reflect church traditions representing God's historical Word and acts among us. Notwithstanding, we also shape worship to help people give expression to their theological discernment within their sociopolitical lives.

With v. 7b, this psalm shifts quite dramatically in voice and focus. One does not have to be a seasoned exegete to notice the redirection. Suddenly, a call for obedience interposes a new focus. The voice of the psalm becomes a direct address, reminiscent of the prophetic office. Verses 8-9 directly reference the wilderness experience of the Israelites at Massah and Meribah (Exodus 17 and Numbers 20). The imperative is clear. Do not test or quarrel with God! Deuteronomy referents also appear to be significant in determining here the contention and testing influences of Meribah and Massah (Deut. 6:16; 9:22-24; 33:8).[6] These scriptural references within the psalm help us to define the focus of this call to obedience in vv. 7b-11. We receive a call to worship in vv. 1-7a. We give thanks for being in God's presence (v. 2). We kneel before God in affirmation of God's presence in our lives (v. 6). And now we are admonished not to repeat the insult of questioning God's presence or testing God's faithfulness, as in Massah and Meribah (v.8). Or truly, we shall not enter the "rest" of the Lord (v. 11; cf. Deut. 12:9, Num. 14:20-23).[7] In worship we give thanks and affirm the presence of God in our lives. This psalm speaks to us in times of difficulty. God is present and active in our lives even in the wilderness of exile—relentlessly seeking to restore us in the life of faith.

Second Reading

ROMANS 5:1-11 (RCL, BCP);
ROMANS 5:1-2, 5-8 (RC)

Interpreting the Text

This passage is a fulcrum in the development of the epistle. It almost feels wedged into the progression of Paul's reasoning on the justification of faith. The chapter begins by drawing a conclusion, "Therefore, we are justified by faith" (v. 1). Paul has just shown that Abraham's faith was regarded as righteousness (4:3, 22). Moreover, as underscored in last week's second reading, we are justified in Christ because the faith *of* Christ reveals the righteousness of God. Hence, we too are "reckoned" in righteousness when we trust in Christ (4:24-25). Jesus was raised for the sake of our justification. Chapter 5 pivots on justification and attempts to explain its effects.[8] For Paul, justification here is not forensic; that is, it is not based on the law. God is the acting architect of justification. Our faith is a trust in the faith of Christ. Like Abraham before us, we believe God. We are justified by the faith of Christ and the faithfulness of God. The effects of justification that Paul develops in this passage rely directly on God's initiative and Christ's agency.[9]

> WE ARE JUSTIFIED BY THE FAITH OF CHRIST AND THE FAITHFULNESS OF GOD.

Through Christ we have peace. We also gain access to the grace of God (v. 2). Then Paul makes an audacious claim: we "boast in our hope of sharing in the glory of God." How can we possibly share in God's glory? Paul certainly rebuffs any prideful notion of works performed (3:27). The boasting that Paul advocates here actually points beyond us to the glory of God. We may boast in the promise of God's glory. Our hope rests in the gift of grace. We can boast in our hope because it is a gift of restoration in God's glory. Our hope points beyond ourselves to the eschatological culmination of God's work of grace in Christ.[10] Eschatology speaks of our future, but it defines our present. We boast in the impact of hope realized in Christ. Still our boasting does not stop there. Paul moves from the audacious to the absurd. We boast "in our suffering" (v. 3). A closer consideration of the prepositional phrase is helpful. The preposition refers to circumstance and therefore might be better understood with the phrase "in the midst of suffering."[11] Paul points to the circumstance of suffering that can result in hope. Verses 3-5 employ a rhetorical strategy of building climax. This strategy links phrases with a progression of repeated terms.[12] The progression in this text is: sufferings—endurance, endurance—character, character—hope. Hope is the eventual effect of faith in the midst of sufferings. Ultimately, even boasting in suffering leads to boasting in the "hope of sharing the glory of God." Hope thrives because we receive God's outpouring of love through the Holy Spirit.

The love of God is known in Christ. The final section of this passage, vv. 6-11, explains that the ultimate effect of justification is reconciliation. For while we were "weak". . . "sinners," and . . . "enemies," God redeemed us (vv. 6, 8, and 10). God responds to God's own wrath by restoring relationship with humanity through a love that would die for us (vv. 8-9). Paul's meaning is pivotal. We encounter God's love in the faith of Christ, who died for us. Christ's death is God's act of love, not wrath. God's love overcomes even God's wrath. Paul's explanation of reconciliation (vv. 10-11) centers in the restoration of life. This concentration on reconciliation emphasizes the desired relationship between humanity and God. The gift of grace restores relationship.[13]

Responding to the Text

The last segment of v. 10, "saved by his life," is difficult to understand. The disputed choices in interpretation include the resurrection life of Christ or eternal life in God. The resurrection life seems consistent with the if-then clause of v. 10. Still, most scholars feel the language remains ambiguous. For our purposes, the ambiguity is instructive. The resurrection life of Christ and eternal life in God come together in the restoration of relationship—reconciliation.[14] Restoration of life entails relationship between God and humanity as well as throughout humanity. From the beginning of this letter, Paul seems to have been working quite carefully at developing both meanings. In fact, his attention to the heritage of faith between the Jews and Gentiles illustrates dramatically the foundation of our relatedness in Christ and our relationship to God. Faith is a means of restoration. The faith of Christ restores us to share in the glory of God. Restoration draws us together. Throughout this passage, Paul uses unifying language. The pervasive use of "we" in chapter 5 has been called a "rhetorical bridge."[15] Paul intends for the "we" to be unifying among all believers. We are reconciled to one another through reconciliation with God in Christ. Reconciliation with God demands human reconciliation. Our hope is indeed to *share* in the glory of God.

THE GOSPEL
JOHN 4:5-42 (RCL);
JOHN 4:5-26, (27-38) 39-42 (BCP);
JOHN 4:5-42 or 4:5-15, 19b-26, 39a, 40-42 (RC)

Interpreting the Text

It is significant that the Gospel of John includes direct attention to both Jews and Samaritans. In the early years of the Johannine tradition, there existed considerable concern among the Jews over Christian worshipers in their synagogues. Those who confessed belief in Christ were expelled (9:22). Exposure and expulsion of Christians were sometimes accomplished by invoking a rite in public worship that contained an anti-Christian blessing of sorts. Failure to participate openly in the blessing-curse would result in expulsion. The context behind this Gospel tradition would include Christian Jews. Concern would continue also for those Christians still quietly worshiping among the Jews. Similarly, attention to converted Samaritans would stem from controversial relations between Jews and Samaritans.

From the Gospel narrative, we learn of a number of Samaritans who became part of the Johannine Christian community (4:42). Of course, care for Jewish traditions and how to understand the gospel of Christ were central in the early years. By the time of the Gospel's formulation, focus would increasingly turn to developing Christian

> THE COMPLICATED SPECTRUM OF RELIGIOUS CULTURES AND RELATIONS THAT CONSTITUTE THE BACKDROP OF THIS GOSPEL ACCOUNT ALSO CONSTITUTE ITS EVANGELISTIC ATTENTION.

communities, especially in light of growing persecution. In short, the complicated spectrum of religious cultures and relations that constitute the backdrop of this Gospel account also constitute its evangelistic attention.[16]

The dialogues in today's passage speak from the divergent contexts of religious cultures between the Samaritans and the Jews. Verses 5-38 constitute two dialogues woven together in a narrative unit, designed apparently to create a comparable address of the gospel message to each religious tradition. The first dialogue is between Jesus and the Samaritan woman. From the start Jesus engages the woman,

but the passage begins by setting the stage at the well of Jacob in Samaritan territory (v. 5). Both the enmity and shared history between the Jews and the Samaritans dynamically fill in the narrative scene. With the metaphor of living water, Jesus
shares the good news of his unfolding messianic revelation. He relies on the
woman's religious heritage not only to draw a connection with her, but also to
bridge the divide between their religious traditions of revelation. For example, the
role of the mountain is quite different here from that in the Synoptic Gospels. Verses
20-21 demonstrate the Gospel's concern over divine revelation in the context of
worship: on the Samaritan mountain (Mt. Gerizim) or in Jerusalem. Jesus wants to
redefine worship and revelation between their two religious cultures. God's revelation in Christ will bring them together "in spirit and truth" (v. 23). Jesus reveals
his messianic role with an eschatological message, "the hour is coming, and is now
here" (v. 23). In like manner, the second dialogue, between Jesus and the disciples,
reveals Jesus' messianic role among his Jewish disciples. Although the dialogue is
hardly direct address, vv. 34-36 employ familiar biblical language and images of
sowing and reaping. The disciples would be well familiar with the biblical metaphor
and Jewish traditions. Here too, Jesus defines the messianic message with eschatological vision, "the reaper is already . . . gathering fruit for eternal life" (v. 36). The
intent to address the two religious cultures is made apparent in the immediate attention given to the Samaritans coming to believe that Jesus is the Savior (vv. 39-42).
The table below is provided to give a snapshot or overview of the parallel dialogues
internal to the narrative unit. Particularly when reviewed together, these dialogues
reflect the concerns of the Johannine Christian community.[17]

Samaritan Woman's Dialogue (vv. 7-26)	Disciples' Dialogue (vv. 32-38)
v. 8 Jesus requests a drink	v. 31 Disciples urge Jesus to eat
vv. 10, 13-14 Living water; never thirst	v. 32 Food you do not know
vv. 11-12, 15 Woman does not understand	v. 33 Disciples do not understand
vv. 16-22 Grasping who Jesus is?	v. 34 Grasping who Jesus is?
vv. 23-26 Eschatological impact	vv. 35-36 Eschatological impact

Responding to the Text

Thirst and hunger (water and food) are such dominant symbols in this
passage that preachers can ill afford to neglect them. That Jesus explores these symbols obviously speaks to more than creating associations within relevant agricultural and trade cultures. As natural elements of survival, water and food signify
theological meaning in our spiritual sustenance. The power of symbols taken from
ordinary life is that they offer deeply personal connections. Thirst and hunger are
experiences that we can easily translate into questions or other needs we feel in

life. Once we move into felt needs, we imbue these symbols with theological significance. Certainly, the evangelist understood the power of natural symbolism. Even partial understanding of symbols opens door to understanding. Both dialogues in the Gospel reading illustrate how even familiar metaphors have to work us over before we begin to grasp their meaning. As the dialogues illustrate, our witness is partial because our grasp is partial.[18] The season of Lent calls for some intentional time to grow in comprehension of God's revelation in Christ and the life of faith. Fasting and prayer focus attention on our sustenance in life. God is our sustainer and provider in Christ. God reaches out to us in grace. These symbols break through the walls we build between us. In these dialogues, preachers will find a means to break through barriers of culture, gender, or even religious traditions. God's revelation in Christ is the source of our sustenance or, more accurately, the source of our restoration to life.

Notes

1. Tikva Frymer-Kensky, "Moses and the Cults: The Question of Religious Leadership," *Judaism* 34 (fall 1985): 444–52.

2. Lim Teng Kok, "Parallel Scripts, Paradigm Shifts," *Biblische Zeitschrift* 42 (1998): 81–90.

3. Frymer-Kensky, "Moses and Cults," 444–52.

4. Gwynne Henton Davies, "Psalm 95," *Zeitschrift für die Alttestamentliche Wissenschaft* 85, no. 2 (1973): 183–95.

5. Dennis W. Tucker, Jr., "Psalm 95: Text, Context, and Intertext," *Biblica* 81, no. 4 (2000): 533–41.

6. Davies, "Psalm 95," 194.

7. Ibid. See also Tucker, "Psalm 95," 540.

8. Theodore Pulcini, "In Right Relationship with God: Present Experience and Future Fulfillment, An Exegesis of Romans 5:1-11," *St. Vladimir's Theological Quarterly* 36, nos. 1–2 (1996): 61–85.

9. Leander E. Keck, "Romans in the Pulpit: Form and Formulation in Romans 5:1-11," in *Listening to the Word*, ed. Gail R. O'Day and Thomas G. Long (Nashville: Abingdon, 1993), 77–90.

10. Ibid.

11. Pulcini, "Right Relationship," 70.

12. Luke Timothy Johnson, *Reading Romans: A Literary and Theological Commentary* (New York: Crossroad, 1997), 80.

13. Ibid., 83–86.

14. Pulcini, "Right Relationship," 61–85.

15. Patricia M. McDonald, "Romans 5:1-11 as a Rhetorical Bridge," *Journal for the Study of the New Testament* 40 (October 1990): 81–96.

16. Raymond E. Brown, *An Introduction to the Gospel of John*, ed. Francis J. Moloney (New York: Doubleday, 2003), 62–71. See also Sharon H. Ringe, "On the Gospel of John: The Gospel as Healing Word," *Quarterly Review* 6, no. 4 (winter 1986): 75–103.

17. Gail R. O'Day, *Revelation in the Fourth Gospel: Narrative Mode and Theological Claim* (Philadelphia: Fortress Press, 1986), 49–92.

18. Fred B. Craddock, "The Witness at the Well," *Christian Century* 107 (March 7, 1990): 243.

FOURTH SUNDAY IN LENT

MARCH 6, 2005

REVISED COMMON	EPISCOPAL (BCP)	ROMAN CATHOLIC
1 Sam. 16:1-13	1 Sam. 16:1-13	1 Sam. 16:1b, 6-7, 10-13a
Psalm 23	Psalm 23	Ps. 23:1-3a, 3b-4, 5, 6
Eph. 5:8-14	Eph. 5:(1-7) 8-14	Eph. 5:8-14
John 9:1-41	John 9:1-13, (14-27)	John 9:1-41
	28-38	or 9:1, 6-9, 13-17, 34-38

We often think of Lent as a time when we return to God. We make sacrifices of fasting and prayer in reverence to God. We spend time in penitential meditation, repenting from sinfulness, to recommit our lives to God. We focus our attention upon the passion and resurrection of Christ in thanksgiving to God. Lent is a time for remembering and renewal. The readings for today proclaim that God reaches out to us in Lent. God calls us forth and anoints us to service. The Lord guides us forward, remains with us, protects and cares for our souls. In Christ, the love of God transforms us. And the light of Christ saves us from the darkness. Lent is a season of restoration in Christ, God's gift of grace. Thanks be to God!

FIRST READING
1 SAMUEL 16:1-13 (RCL, BCP);
1 SAMUEL 16:1b, 6-7, 10-13a (RC)

Interpreting the Text

The Lord was sorry for having made Saul the king over Israel (15:35). Chapter 15 ends with deep regret. However, Samuel's grief is much more than regret. Samuel grieves over God's decision to remove Saul from office. We are not told the nature of Samuel's grief over Saul. Loss is obviously the central factor, but it is not clear if the object of his grief is directly Saul or the nation's loss of its king. What we do discover is somewhat a reproof of Samuel in his unrelenting grief (16:1). The speech here sounds more like the lament language one might find in the Psalms or prophetic literature, "How long will you grieve over Saul?" If not for the next couple of lines in God's address, we would not be sure whether God is dismayed by Samuel's grief or angered. The rest of v. 1, however, makes it clear that God has already moved on to the business of choosing the next king and wishes that Samuel would move on as well. Samuel grieves over God's recalcitrant rejection of Saul as king. Even Saul's repentance cannot change God's mind (15:24-31).

The reader can empathize with Samuel's grief. God apparently does change God's mind, since God regrets placing Saul over Israel. But God will not recant the decision to replace Saul. God has dealt with disobedience before and shows mercy even when judgment follows an offense. Much of Israelite history bears witness to how God's wrath does not operate without an essential measure of mercy. Certainly God understands the sting of rejection. Saul's anointing as the first king over Israel came at the expense of rejecting God as their king. They wanted to be like other nations (8:7-8, 19-22). God's rejection of Saul does not appear to be an "I told you so!" since God's immediate reaction is to anoint another king. The message here is fairly direct. Even in the deepest confusion over the events in life, God is already pointing to the future while we still seek to understand God's actual presence. We are left to struggle deeply along with Samuel.

> EVEN IN THE DEEPEST CONFUSION OVER THE EVENTS IN LIFE, GOD IS ALREADY POINTING TO THE FUTURE WHILE WE STILL SEEK TO UNDERSTAND GOD'S ACTUAL PRESENCE.

We will have even more confusing revelations in the stories of Saul and David. Within the very next passage, we may be able to perceive how God might remove the spirit of empowerment from Saul, but to torment him with an evil spirit is beyond our grasp (16:14). What happens with Saul's repentance (15:24-31)? Does God withhold forgiveness? The Samuel narratives place Saul's disobedience and corruption at the heart of the matter. In these passages, we learn about the offices of prophet and king before the Lord.[1] However, we also learn more about our own grief before God. Samuel grieves over Saul's corruption of the heart and removal from office. We are left with Samuel to contemplate how God responds to Saul's corruption and repentance.

Matters of the heart abound in this text. God makes it clear that Samuel's reaction to the eldest son (cf. 1 Chron. 2:13) of Jesse the Bethlehemite is not within God's divine purview. Eliab was of fine stature, but God cautions that appearance is not an important criterion in God's selection of the next king (vv. 6-8). Now, we must conclude that Samuel was not completely deluded or enamored. Appearance was an integral factor in selecting Saul as the first king (9:1-2). In fact, Saul's stature is the only quality presented before the people of Israel for his inauguration (10:23-24). With the selection of Saul, the most important criteria for God appear to be stature and a willingness to comply with the statutes outlined for a theocratic monarchy (8:11-18; 10:25). Saul's heart was apparently a problem from the start, so much so that early on God "gave him another heart" (10:9) and endowed him with God's own prophetic spirit (10:10). Apparently, the change of heart did not preclude the corruption to come. So now in chapter 16, it seems reasonable that Samuel would be drawn to the same traits in Eliab that once appeared acceptable to God in Saul. But the revelation to Samuel is that God is concerned with the heart of the king, not the outward appearance (v. 7). In the end, David, the youngest child and keeper of the sheep, is anointed; and in a dramatic capacity, he receives the spirit of God (v. 13). We are never told why David's appearance receives such attention in v. 12. We are again left confused over God's criteria. God's actions are ambiguous throughout these narratives, from the passive deception in electing a king (vv. 2-3) to deciphering the criteria in selecting a king (vv. 6-12). Perhaps God had a change of heart in the anointing and function of the next king. Notwithstanding, the text only says that God looks to the heart (v. 7).[2]

Responding to the Text

Samuel's grief should reflect our own. God's unrelenting rejection of Saul in the face of abject repentance should be enough to drive us all into anguish. When God is not moved by repentance, we should indeed grieve with despair. By what criteria does God forgive, if not by mercy? Samuel aches over Saul. The flow of events in Saul's demise was set in motion by Saul's disobedience. Preachers need to take note that little discussion ensues over delineating levels of disobedience or calculating obedience, as one commentator observes.[3] God is clear that the distrust displayed in disobedience does drive God's disdain. But God remembers God's promises. God remembers God's love for God's people. God does remember forgiveness for the repentant heart. When repenting of sin in seeking a king other than God, Samuel assures the people of Israel to "serve the LORD with all of your heart . . . for the LORD will not cast away God's people" (12:20-24), although the people still receive a warning that God's mercy does not ignore corruption (12:25). God did not alter the decision of the people to attain a king, but neither did God withhold mercy. So, why not also with Saul? We cannot determine a precise answer, because only God knows the heart—and that is exactly the point. God does look at the heart. Hence, one comment to Samuel in Saul's repentance suggests ambiguity: "Then Saul said, 'I have sinned; yet honor me now before the elders of my people and before Israel and return with me, so that I may worship the LORD your God'" (15:30). Many questions emerge for any preacher, but two stand out: Why does Saul seek honor? Why does Saul seek the protection of Samuel to approach God? We learn in David's future that God is capable of forgiving the king of grievous acts. God considers the heart that repents in a life seeking faith within a life of faith. Only God knows the heart. Samuel does not grieve alone. God grieves over broken relationships, and our grief should weigh deeply that God suffers with us. As with Samuel, God calls us to restoration. We place our trust in God to have mercy. Only God knows the heart.

RESPONSIVE READING

PSALM 23 (RCL, BCP);
PSALM 23:1-3a, 3b-4, 5, 6 (RC)

Though opinions of authorship and time of origination differ greatly, the structure of this psalm is commonly held between two images of God as shepherd and then as host. How the two images of God function together in this psalm has proved critically important for interpretation. From vv. 1-4, we are given powerfully moving descriptions of God's manner with us. God provides for our daily needs. God leads us, as would a guide who is familiar with the paths that safely bring us to needed replenishment. God is an intimate shepherd to our souls. The psalm expresses our deepest trust in God's care. From vv. 5-6, we also perceive God as a host who receives us with bounty. God is full of generosity and grace. We are more than guests; we are blessed to commune with our host. The two images combine to build a psalm of trust and dependence in God. That David has been suggested as the author should not be surprising given his own upbringing as a shepherd boy. He certainly would have been deeply familiar with the concern a shepherd holds for the flock. While authorship remains in question, the prevailing meanings do not; God is our caretaker and guide in the life of faith.[4]

Some scholars have tried to reconcile the two broadly defined structural units of the psalm into one image of God. Two suggestions help us weigh the psalm more deeply. One suggestion involves textual criticism. The images of shepherd and host have pivoted on v. 5a, "You prepare a table before me in the presence of my enemies." Stemming from the rod and staff symbols of shepherding in v. 4, an alternative translation for v. 5a emerges in the protection a shepherd might provide, "You array a spear in front of me in the presence of my enemies." This translation unifies the psalm with images of shepherding. The subsequent anointing with oil would be consistent with balm treatment a shepherd might tender. We cannot resolve the exegetical viability of this translation here, but the exegetes who proffer this interpretation rely on a textual variant that raises an intriguing perspective.[5] God is a shepherd who guides, protects, and heals. These traits or images reflect for some scholars a unifying metaphor throughout the psalm.

Three facets of the psalmist's encounters with God extend the argument for a unified image of shepherd. These substructures comprise different manners in which the psalmist deeply experiences God. God leads in front of us (v. 3); God is with us (v. 4); and God follows us (v. 6). The images here of shepherding create a procession or pilgrimage, which may suggest a postexilic emphasis on exile and restoration.[6] Here the shepherding paradigm develops a faith pilgrimage out of the psalmist's intimate relationship with God. Ultimately, Psalm 23 assures us of God's guidance and care. God restores our souls (v. 3).

SECOND READING

EPHESIANS 5:8-14 (RCL, RC); EPHESIANS 5:(1-7) 8-14 (BCP)

Interpreting the Text

This reading lacks some of the specificity that we typically find in Paul's letters. It is generally suspected that authorship belongs to a disciple of Paul, perhaps from Colossae. Early transcripts do not even indicate a particular community of address. Instead, the opening reads something like, "To the saints who are also faithful in Jesus Christ" (1:1). This general background to the epistle helps us to understand its intended function as a letter of advice or admonition to converts around the area.[7] Particular literary forms that dominate in today's passage are consistent with this intent. The forms that concern us directly are the hortatory structures in the context of chapters 4–5. As part of the epistle's address to the baptized, the pericope in 4:17—5:2, which for some scholars might extend to 5:5, develops into a structural outline of vices and virtues between the preconversion way of life and now the postconversion or virtuous way of life. Verses 6-14 continue with language of opposition between darkness and the light. Though these verses focus predominantly on listing behavior and values, the intent is to draw out a way of life for believers. Segments of these verses even reflect liturgical rites for baptism. Believers must "put away" the vices of corrupted life (4:22, 25, 31) and live into the virtues of life in Christ, to be "imitators" or "children" of God (5:1).[8]

As children of God, we are no longer darkness but now are light (v. 8). Notice the language of association. It is not enough to understand that we live under conditions of corruption or enlightenment. We either *are* darkness or light existentially. The impact of such a claim lies in the function of darkness and light. We know darkness and light by how they affect us. These verses address our affect on others. How one lives affects others.

The subsequent verses (vv. 11-14) are much more difficult to decipher. Problems of interpretation stem from use of the word "expose" (vv. 11, 13). At face value, one is tempted to interpret the intended usage to mean uncover. It is not clear, however, if the purpose then would be to reprove someone or simply to bring something to light for the benefit of introspection. By way of explanation,

vv. 11-12 begin building an argument with dependent clauses: we take no part in darkness, "for" it is shameful; "but" (v. 13) the function of exposure is to make things visible; "for" (v. 14) what becomes visible ultimately becomes light. Still, when we interpret "expose," we cannot escape some notion of affecting others. The author seems to have more in mind than the mere consequence of being a good witness. Some scholars argue that the exhortation of this passage is a call for believers to distinguish themselves as children of light and thereby disempower darkness. While this meaning seems at least inferred, we must still speculate from the direct association that we become light; in fact, "everything that becomes visible is light" (v. 14). Whatever the light exposes can be transformed into light. As children of the light of Christ, how we live does affect ourselves and still yet others.[9]

Responding to the Text

Obviously, we cannot escape the reality that we live in community. The interchanges within this text between vices and virtues, between darkness and light, presume communal engagement. Despite an admonition to disassociate from the disobedient, "do not be associated with them" (v. 7), the directive is to expose those persons and "unfruitful works" of darkness to light (v. 11). We are "to find out what is pleasing to the Lord" (v. 10). By the end of the passage it becomes "visible" that the light engages darkness within us and around us. The influences of early baptismal liturgy within this text expose the demands upon one's personal being and communal responsibility.[10] We are baptized into the community of faith. In the same liturgy, community members are invited typically to reaffirm their faith and make a spiritual commitment to nurture the newly baptized.

> THE INTERCHANGES WITHIN THIS TEXT BETWEEN VICES AND VIRTUES, BETWEEN DARKNESS AND LIGHT, PRESUME COMMUNAL ENGAGEMENT.

We often claim to feel enlightened in this life of faith. Is the light internal only? We pursue the virtues of enlightenment, but to what ends? Preachers certainly have an important task to illumine the need to live in obedience to the life of faith in Christ (4:17—5:2). However, preachers also have an overwhelming task to elucidate the purpose of being light (vv. 8-14). We commonly misunderstand the function and purpose of religious piety that seeks to live in the light of Christ. We mistake piety for holiness. And we make holiness a goal of our own being. Piety does not produce holiness. Holiness belongs to the glory of God. We pursue holiness when we pursue God. Piety is a product of our relationship with God, because we seek what is pleasing to God (v. 10). To be the light is to be in relationship with God, and therefore the pursuit extrapolates into relationship with others. Much of what we call piety concerns the treatment of others.

Religious piety thoroughly involves religious ethics. It is living in the desire and light of Christ—a life of faith living into relationship with God and others. Rejection of piety among believers risks rejecting care for restoration. And that would be darkness!

THE GOSPEL
JOHN 9:1–41 (RCL);
JOHN 9:1–13, (14–27) 28–38 (BCP);
JOHN 9:1–41 or 9:1, 6–9, 13–17, 34–38 (RC)

Interpreting the Text

We have observed in the second reading that the metaphors of light and darkness powerfully contrast life in Christ with life before that enlightenment. Moreover, in the Lord we are the light (Eph. 5:8). The Johannine story of the blind man also relies heavily on the dualism between light and darkness. Jesus is "the light of the world" (9:5), and the blind person of this story lives in darkness. But darkness has many forms, as we will learn. In the preceding chapter, Jesus had already claimed that he was the light of the world. Those persons who will follow Jesus will no longer walk in darkness but will live in the light of Christ (8:12). The Jews (more accurately, the religious leaders) react by questioning Jesus' identity and authority, which engrosses the remainder of the chapter. Darkness rears its head in this discussion in the form of sin. The power of sin is that it enslaves (8:34) a person, even unto death (8:21, 24). When discussing theological matters such as his identity, authority, or mission, the Johannine Jesus often speaks in ambiguous language with potentially conflicting meanings. Ambiguity becomes a tool for the Gospel writer. The point is to challenge assumptions or normative thinking among the characters of the narratives. We are invited into the narrative as observers who already share at least some partial understanding. The narratives and teachings unfold the ambiguity or irony to reveal the Christ. Hence, the dualism we commonly find in John's Gospel is a literary device frequently serving the ironic interplay.[11] With this understanding, we encounter revelation in the Gospel's narrative of the blind man.

The blind man narrative has been outlined into as many as seven scenes. Each exchange of dialogue comprises a unit: (a) the healing, vv. 1–7; (b) the neighbors' inquiry, vv. 8–12; (c) the Pharisees' interrogation, vv. 13–17; (d) the family background investigation, vv. 18–23; (e) another interrogation, vv. 24–34; (f) a reencounter with Jesus, vv. 35–39; and (g) Jesus' exposing of blind Pharisees.[12] While the breakdown of this passage is helpful, an overview of the dualism that brackets the narrative and the ironic ambiguity in the central dialogues will prove more immediately useful for the preaching interpreter.

First, notice that the dualism of light and darkness persists in the events of seeing and different forms of blindness. Between the first two opening scenes, Jesus (the light) heals the blind man, but in turn the neighbors are suddenly "blind" to the identity of the "seeing" man (vv. 1-12). Irony fills in the dualism. This dynamic is repeated in the two closing scenes. The blind man's sight continues to improve with Jesus. Jesus seeks out the faithful man and reveals his identity more clearly, and the man sees his healer more sharply. The Pharisees, instead, grow

> THE DUALISM OF LIGHT AND DARKNESS PERSISTS IN THE EVENTS OF SEEING AND DIFFERENT FORMS OF BLINDNESS.

blind. Even their affront is an exasperation of irony itself: "Surely we are not blind, are we?" Jesus confirms their confusion; they are blind to their own sin. The narrative therefore ends in an ironic reversal. Those who claim to possess sight grow in the blindness of sin (vv. 35-41). The light of Jesus is our sight.

Next, the central dialogues comprise the three middle scenes with the Pharisees described above. The Pharisees interrogate the sighted man but remain conflicted over Jesus' actions (v. 16). The narrator lets us overhear their debate: Jesus could not be from God because he worked a miracle on the Sabbath; yet, how could he be a sinner and perform such miracles of God? Ultimately, they will not believe he had been blind, but his parents set them straight (vv. 18-21). In frustration, the Pharisees call the man back for yet another interrogation. However, this time the man cannot restrain his sarcasm (v. 27): "Why do you want to hear it again? Do you also want to become his disciples?" And in a huff of self-inflated blindness, the Pharisees expel the man from the temple (v. 34). These dialogues are filled with comedic and tragic irony. Religious leaders are confused; the blind can see the sign of God. Teachers do not discern the revelation of God; the blind teach and discover redemption. Through the dialogues we are invited into the narrative of Jesus and the blind man to discover redemption in the revelation that God is with us.

Responding to the Text

To be born blind and then suddenly see! One might think that everyone would remember you. But then again, how often do we look past those around us who disturb our inner peace with nothing more than their own struggle? It is selective blindness. Sight can be awfully painful. With sight, we must face suffering. With sight, we must face evil. With sight, we must face ourselves. Blindness from birth, indeed! The tragic irony is that the healing of sight can be painfully blinding when our darkness is suddenly exposed to the light. Preachers may find the baptism imagery in the pool of Siloam (v. 7) rather appealing. The symbolism of baptism into new life speaks strongly to redemption from sin. Liturgical language for baptism in the early church referred to baptism as enlightenment.[13] In this regard, healing our blindness exposes us to new life in the light of Christ. Both the water and light symbols in this narrative signify theological meanings of restoration. However, preachers should exercise caution to avoid naming all blindness as sin. We must inquire into the nature of sin that renders blindness. Clearly the blindness of the religious leaders in this narrative is human sin. The text is careful to say the blindness of the man was quite different. Still, the claim that blindness is the opportunity for God's revelation is terribly perplexing. The ambiguity and darkness for us begin here. We pray for the light of Christ to heal our blindness.

Notes

1. Martin Kessler, "Narrative Technique in 1 SM 16:1-13," *Catholic Biblical Quarterly* 32 (October 1970): 543–54.

2. Lyle Eslinger, "A Change of Heart: 1 Samuel 16," in *Ascribe to the Lord*, ed. Lyle Eslinger and Glen Taylor (Sheffield, England: JSOT Press, 1988), 341–61.

3. David G. Hester, *First and Second Samuel*; Interpretation Bible Studies Series (Louisville: Geneva Press, 2000), 46–55.

4. Gene Rice, "An Exposition of Psalm 23," *Journal of Religious Thought* 52 (summer–fall 1995): 71–78.

5. Julian Morgenstern, "Psalm 23," *Journal of Biblical Literature* 65, no. 1 (March 1946): 13–24.

6. Mark S. Smith, "Setting and Rhetoric in Psalm 23," *Journal for the Study of the Old Testament* 41 (June 1988): 61–66.

7. Wayne A. Meeks, ed., *The Writings of St. Paul* (New York: Norton, 1972), 121–32.

8. David E. Aune, *The New Testament in Its Literary Environment* (Philadelphia: Westminster, 1987), 194–98.

9. Troels Engberg-Pederson, "Ephesians 5:12-13: *Elenchein* and Conversation in the New Testament," *Zeitschrift für die Neutestamentliche Wissenschaft und die Kunde der Alteren Kirche* 80, nos. 1–2 (1989): 89–110.

10. James A. Harnish, "Listening in Time," *Quarterly Review* 15 (winter 1995): 427–40.

11. Gail R. O'Day, *Revelation in the Fourth Gospel: Narrative Mode and Theological Claim* (Philadelphia: Fortress Press, 1986), 1–10.

12. R. Alan Culpepper, *The Gospel of John and Letters of John* (Nashville: Abingdon, 1998), 174.

13. Adolf Adam, *The Liturgical Year: Its History and Meaning after the Reform of the Liturgy*, trans. Matthew J. O'Connell (New York: Pueblo, 1981), 102.

FIFTH SUNDAY IN LENT

MARCH 13, 2005

REVISED COMMON	EPISCOPAL (BCP)	ROMAN CATHOLIC
Ezek. 37:1-14	Ezek. 37:1-3, (4-10) 11-14	Ezek. 37:12-14
Psalm 130	Psalm 130	Ps.130:1-2, 3-4, 5-6, 7-8
Rom. 8:6-11	Rom. 6:16-23	Rom. 8:8-11
John 11:1-45	John 11:(1-16) 17-44	John 11:1-45 or 11:3-7, 17, 20-27, 33b-45

Death looms large as we approach Holy Week. All around us, life is filled with destruction and death. If ever we need a reminder of the devastation of sin, we need only to weigh the destructive capacity of humanity or the despair of hopelessness. In Lent we thrash against death. Fasting, prayer, and penitence meet up with thanksgiving, praise, and hope in worship. The gospel message is our lifeline; in the death and resurrection of Christ, God is glorified and we receive the gift of eternal life. As Paul proclaims, through Christ, the Spirit of God dwells within us. No longer do we live according to the power of sin in the flesh, but according to the Spirit. We join the psalmist in the comfort that God restores our souls. We find grace in the knowledge that no account of sin or death holds ultimate authority even in the valley of dry bones. A prophetic voice cries out in Lent; the Lord breathes the breath of life into humanity. God's faithfulness is mercy. And in the love of Christ, we live.

FIRST READING

EZEKIEL 37:1-14 (RCL);
EZEKIEL 37:1-3, (4-10) 11-14 (BCP);
EZEKIEL 37:12-14 (RC)

Interpreting the Text

The first section of this passage is vv. 1-10. A powerfully disturbing image of dismembered bones strewn across a valley consumes the prophetic vision (vv.

1-2). God's rhetorical question is intimidating: "Can these bones live?" In the face of such an overwhelming scene, Ezekiel answers timidly, "O Lord God, you know" (vv. 3-4). Vast remnants of bones remain from a "slain" people (v. 9). God will recondition flesh upon the bones of the valley and enliven them with something more than air . . . the "breath" of life (vv. 5-6, 10). The spirit of God is the resource of life. With Ezekiel we recognize that the activity of the spirit bears the prophetic meaning of the vision. God will breathe new life into the dead. And God will be known (v. 6).

Verse 11 is the transition to the next unit. What we have here is a wonderful gift of interpretation within the vision itself. The house of Israel lies strewn across this valley floor of despair. Hope itself has been slain. Verse 11 becomes the fulcrum of the prophetic vision, naming the direct object of this revelation, "the dried out and broken" house of Israel. The death trap of despair has choked the life out of their hope. Ezekiel's perspective of these decayed bones of the slain reflects a perspective of the exiled community and projects theological interpretations from exiled life. In the ancient Near East, deceased persons were thought to be cursed if they had not received a proper burial. Their exposed bodies would otherwise become prey to scavenging beasts. Often this curse would be exacted on persons who broke solemn agreements or treaties.[1] Hence, the power of Ezekiel's vision would have an overwhelming impact on the exilic community. The curse of breaking covenant with God fills their understanding of exile. God's faithfulness exceeds even the hope of the exiled. The death valley of broken bones, broken trust, or broken faith will have to release the skeletons of broken lives. God will resurrect life and the hope of salvation.

> GOD WILL BREATHE NEW LIFE INTO THE DEAD. AND
> GOD WILL BE KNOWN.

Verses 12-14 translate the vision for us. Israel will be resurrected from the grave and receive the spirit of life. Ezekiel receives again an edict to proclaim the promises of God. These verses repeat the language of vv. 4-6 and bear a striking resemblance to Ezek. 36:26-28.[2] This earlier passage proclaims the restoration of Israel. God will give the house of Israel a new heart and a new spirit. Israel's heart has become like stone, and God will replace it with one of flesh. Restoration is completed, though, only when God's spirit enters in order to generate faithful obedience. The reflection of these verses in today's vision explains further the restoration of Israel. Let there be no confusion, Israel's return to promise is sculpted by the re-creative hands of God. Creation language pulsates and breathes within this prophetic vision. Recall creation: God formed humanity from the dust of the earth and "breathed the breath of life" into us, and we became living beings (Gen. 2:7). The spirit of God will breathe new life into God's re-creation of Israel.[3]

Responding to the Text

181

FIFTH SUNDAY
IN LENT
─────────────
MARCH 13

"Can these bones live?" What do you say about the capacity of God to resurrect the dead? We know that God does not simply act in our lives; God inter-acts within our lives. God is not looking for our opinion or trying to showcase. Our reticence to answer the question before God reflects our fear to commit beyond our imagination or, in this case, beyond our vision. The vision is a panorama of our broken faith. When God inter-acts within our lives, we re-encounter just who God is. The preaching event is another re-encounter in which God breathes revelation into our lives for our restoration or renewal. Preachers may turn to Ezekiel's vision to catch sight of God's intent. Restoration of life in Ezekiel was not simply a return to a corrected state of preexilic life. Ezekiel's prophecy was restoration to the knowledge of God (vv. 6, 13-14). This knowledge, however, was not a former knowledge. Israel would know God's faithfulness to God's promises, which creates new life and reveals new knowledge of God. Empowerment to live a new life of faith comes from the revelation of God.[4]

RESPONSIVE READING
PSALM 130 (RCL, BCP, RC)

"Out of the depths, we cry" (v. 1) in lament. The Psalms often communicate our strongest sentiments and theological convictions. They also convey our confusion or confidence, as the occasion might determine. Within the worship context, the Psalms are commonly understood in two broad terms, either praise or lament. Inasmuch as these are emotion-laden terms, they are theologically understood in their liturgical expression. The speaker or direct addressee of the Psalms may be either an individual or a communal voice. In either instance, the Psalms give expression to our ways of being and responses to God.[5] At times, they voice God's address to us. Psalm 130 is largely an individual lament, but with a communal component. Among the biblical, liturgical traditions, it is a Song of Ascents. For the church, it has become a penitential psalm, finding its place within the Lenten season.

Verses 1-2 cry out in anguish. The psalmist speaks from the depths of experience. Modern interpretations stress the internal angst or despair of the psalmist's language. As we identify with the psalmist, we acknowledge the deep emotion of guilt and a fear that we are cut off from God's hearing. The biblical imagery of "depths" deposits us in chaotic waters.[6] We join the psalmist in the despair of stormy seas that encompass our lives. For us the depths usually express the internal vacuum of despair that erupts into anguish. The psalmist, however, feels engulfed by some tumultuous waters, lost in the wake, and tossed far from the shores of the promised land. Will God hear the outcry? A fierce, utter separation seems best to describe the depths. The lament begins with a petition for God to hear or to be present. We gain sight of the storm in vv. 3-4. On this occasion the lament does not echo from the calamities of life, but from the frigid seas of sinfulness. The psalmist knows God is righteous, and it seems that guilt and a fear of separation drive the despair. Here, a paradox defines the despair. It is the psalmist's knowledge of God's character that feeds the fear of separation, but the psalmist also knows the only possible hope of recovery rests in that very character of God. With the psalmist, we are utterly dependent on God's character. From the depths we latch on to our only hope, that with God there is forgiveness.[7]

> IT IS THE PSALMIST'S KNOWLEDGE OF GOD'S CHARACTER THAT FEEDS THE FEAR OF SEPARATION, BUT THE PSALMIST ALSO KNOWS THE ONLY POSSIBLE HOPE OF RECOVERY RESTS IN THAT VERY CHARACTER OF GOD.

The address changes with vv. 5-6. Previously, the psalmist called out to God and addressed God. Now, hope finds its voice in a declaration of trust. When we place our hope in God, we declare trust in God's character. This hope is not simply a future vision. When hope is confined to the future, it lacks trust. Hope in a future with God changes the present. A declaration to wait on the Lord is a projection on the future, but the immediate "depths" experience is altered. Hope is active in some capacity, whether in struggle or expectation. On the word of God, the psalmist latches (v. 5).[8]

While yet in the waiting tower, the voice of the psalmist shifts again. The psalmist takes on a priestly voice and lifts a charge to Israel (vv. 7-8). As a Song of Ascents one can begin to hear this psalm on the communal pilgrimage. This psalm moves through individual lament and takes on a communal appeal.[9] The two join in hope for restoration. The people of God can trust in God's redemptive love. We can rely on God to forgive sin. "For with the LORD there is steadfast love" (v. 7). In the life of faith, hope trusts in the character of God.

SECOND READING

ROMANS 6:16-23 (BCP);
ROMANS 8:6-11 (RCL);
ROMANS 8:8-11 (RC)

Interpreting the Text

Today's second readings are part of a large section of Romans dealing with sanctification. The section itself includes at least chapters 6–8. In fact, 6:22

directly states that the advantage we enter when freed from sin is sanctification through relationship with God. The substance of these chapters is to explain this new relationship. Newness is a pervasive theme (6:4). Being made righteous in Christ, however, does not result in sudden human perfection. While new life in Christ begins with an event, one lives into a new nature in the power of God.[10] Grace exercises power in our lives, which in Christ frees us from the power of sin and frees us into eternal life (5:21). The thematic movement in the letter is from justification to sanctification.

Paul drives the argument forward with a rhetorical style of questioning (6:1): "Should we continue in sin in order that grace may abound?" Paul explains this newness of life in Christ through baptism and death. He uses death and burial symbolism to define baptism in Christ and therefore the ethical impact of Christ's righteousness upon our lives. In Christ, we die to sin. Herein Paul builds a direct correlation with the death and resurrection of Christ. We are freed from the power of sin. Christ frees us to live into life resurrected (6:2-11).[11] Paul's attention therefore turns to understanding freedom, the law, and life in the Spirit. His task in the remainder of this section is to explain sanctification, largely mirroring the chapter's opening question (cf. 6:1, 15).[12]

Paul develops his treatment of sanctification in a structural series of points (6:16-23). In brief, the structure is a diatribe that repeats the argument but in a progression of rhetorical objections and responses.[13] The passage here can be described as a preconversion and postconversion diatribe. Are we obedient to sin or obedient to righteousness (v. 16)? We were once enslaved by sin but now submit to righteousness (v. 17-18). Though once we enslaved ourselves to impurity, we submit to sanctification (v. 19b). Paul's argument continues in vv. 20-23 but weighs ethical behavior. We are ashamed of the fruits we have produced in sin, but now we are free from the chains of sin to pursue sanctification (vv. 20-22). Sin leads to death, but life in Christ leads to eternal life (v. 23). Paul's argument in this passage develops theological exhortation for ethical living defined by a life of faith in Christ.

> WE FIND PEACE IN LIFE WHEN WE LIVE ACCORDING TO THE SPIRIT; ONLY THEN CAN WE BEGIN TO PLEASE GOD.

By the time we move through chapter 6 to the end of chapter 8, it becomes clear that sanctification is Paul's means of developing Christian ethics. In chapter 8, Paul recapitulates that we do not live under the threat of condemnation (v. 1). Sanctification, then, is living in the love of Christ and life of the Spirit. This life in the Spirit concerns how we function daily. For Paul, we no longer live at the behest of the flesh in sin and death (v. 5a). Life in the flesh is "hostile" to God (v. 7a). We find peace in life when we live according to the Spirit; only then can we begin to please God (vv. 6b, 7b). When introducing the possibility "to set the mind" on the Spirit (vv. 5-6), Paul emphasizes choice. When we belong to Christ, we are empowered unto righteousness by the Spirit that dwells within us (vv. 9-11). It all sounds spiritually pragmatic until we remember Paul's own inner discord (7:15): "For I do not do what I want, but I do the very thing that I hate." Ultimately, we must understand that the power from within is the Spirit of God. The very inner compulsion to live according to the Spirit is a gift of grace from God, through Jesus Christ.[14]

Responding to the Text

Romans 6 employs disturbing symbolism from slavery (although we take some solace in the possible translation of "slaves" as "servants"). As observed above, Paul stresses that we are no longer bound to the power of sin but instead are bound to righteousness. The power of sin in our lives has been broken and usurped by Christ. Righteousness holds sway over us, so much so that we are driven into obedience by an inner call from God. We belong to God and have been transformed into a desired obedience.

Preachers must use caution with the images of slavery. I am not sure there has ever been an age when slavery could be considered an appropriate image for illustrating God's role in our lives—except to free us from it. Our world today can ill afford casual references to slavery from the pulpit. Simply put, any attempt to find theological meaning in slavery cannot escape the evil of its reality. Lest the reader here dismiss this as excessive ranting, note that Paul himself could not rest with the functional image of slavery (6:19). He certainly appears driven by such difficulty that he is eager to press beyond it into a deeper relational dynamic (8:15): "For you did not receive a spirit of slavery to fall back into fear, but you have received a spirit of adoption." God is not our slavemaster—figuratively, theologically, or otherwise. God desires relationship with humanity. We join with Paul's struggle for a truer expression of our new life in Christ; God is our creator and parent. We are restored to intimate relationship with God. If we are enslaved after the bonds of sin have been broken, we are enslaved only by the struggle to live with transformed hearts, with the love of God compelling us to seek righteousness. The Spirit of Christ dwells within us (8:9) as God's free gift of grace. And then, yes, as heirs we can confess with thanksgiving (8:17) that we are "possessed" by the love of Christ.[15]

JOHN 11:1-45 (RCL);
JOHN 11:(1-16) 17-44 (BCP);
JOHN 11:1-45
or 11:3-7, 17, 20-27, 33b-45 (RC)

Interpreting the Text

Like other Johannine narratives, the structure of the Lazarus narrative is an important factor in understanding the story's function in John's Gospel. Jesus sets the stage. Upon receiving the message that Lazarus is deathly ill, Jesus informs his disciples that "this illness does not lead to death; rather, it is for God's glory, so that the Son of God may be glorified through it" (v. 4). Jesus even waits a couple of days before leaving for Bethany, seemingly just

> THIS STORY IS A SIGN OF THE GLORY TO BE REVEALED SOON IN THE DEATH AND RESURRECTION OF CHRIST HIMSELF.

to accent the pending message. The narrator has just given the reader an initial clue to the function of the ensuing story. These events anticipate the glory of Christ to be revealed. This intent is confirmed near the end of the narrative when Jesus reminds Martha with some frustration that God will reveal his glory in raising Lazarus (v. 40). These verses almost serve as bookends for the narrative. The reader knows what the characters do not quite grasp. This story is a sign of the glory to be revealed soon in the death and resurrection of Christ himself. The glory of God in Christ is the central theme.[16]

Jesus still relies on deep symbols to illustrate the underlying theological interpretation of his identity and mission. In vv. 9-10, the symbolism of light and darkness reemerge. Despite the looming danger, Jesus will go to Judea once again. Now is the time to work in the light of his ministry to the world. Still, it is important that the narrative at some point state its message straightforwardly even if it will not be fully comprehended. In dialogue with Lazarus's grief-stricken sister, Martha, Jesus proclaims, "I am the resurrection and the life" (v. 25). It would seem in the context of the narrative that his message would be received. Yet, in typical Johannine fashion, his meaning is wrapped in mystery. Verses 25-26 continue in what has been described as promises by some readers and enigma by others: If we believe, in spite of death we shall live, and anyone who lives and believes will not die. The promise and enigma of "life in the very face of death" work together to demonstrate the thematic function of the narrative. The narrative illustrates that we are promised new life in the death and resurrection of Christ.[17]

If we are honest interpreters, we have to concede that we are slow to comprehend the full revelation of Christ. Though we are granted inside knowledge as readers of the Gospel, we see ourselves within the characters of the narrative, who struggle between belief and inadequate understanding. The disciples struggle to understand Jesus' earthly ministry (vv. 7-16). Martha claims to understand the resurrection and professes belief but cannot get past her perceptions of a divine Teacher and the stench of death (vv. 24, 27-28, 39). Her sister, Mary, responds to Jesus without question but is consumed by grief (vv. 29, 32-33). The crowd of consolers knows that Jesus performs miraculous signs, and some begin to believe in him, even though many cannot see beyond death (vv. 31, 37, 45-46). All the characters struggle with limited understanding of Jesus' identity and mission. And to seal the narrative in John's trademark irony, when the news of Jesus raising Lazarus from the dead gets out, the religious leaders conspire in planning for Jesus' own death (vv. 45-53). With both promise and mystery, the Johannine narrator crafted the story to forecast salvation in the full revelation of Christ through his impending death and resurrection.

Responding to the Text

As a matter of interpreting and responding, v. 35 presents one of the most intriguing expressions in the Gospel, "Jesus began to weep." Some translations more forcefully exclaim, "Jesus wept." In either translation the power of understatement is the tour de force. Many preachers have commented on the pastoral power of Jesus weeping for us. A close consideration of the context may offer some theological foundation for its pastoral significance. Jesus saw Mary weeping over the death of her brother, Lazarus, and he became both greatly disturbed and deeply moved (v. 33). The original language suggests a tone of anger in these emotions. Some exegetes have tried to capture this quality by translating the emotions as groaning or grief.[18] The narrative context is particularly instructive here. The Lazarus resurrection narrative points forward to the death and resurrection of Jesus (vv. 4, 25-26). This miraculous event is a sign of Christ's power over both life and death. But here, too, John relies on the partial understanding of the reader. We are left to question the nature of the sign and its function. Some scholars find that the disturbed emotions of Jesus in this sign-narrative parallel those occurring in the spirit-exorcism narratives of the Synoptic Gospels. If so, the Lazarus account shares the theme of new life in Christ. New life is identified in the power of Christ over the forces in life and the consequence of death.

The emotional disturbance in this narrative anticipates Jesus' own encounter with death. Yet we see that his disturbance is deeply rooted in our own encounter with death (vv. 33, 38). With the grief experienced by humanity (v. 33), Jesus encounters death with humanity (v. 35). The glory of God is demonstrated in the Lazarus narrative through the resurrection of new life. With humanity, Jesus faces death with building emotions. Christ is revealed in his humanity, death, and resurrection. Truly the glory of God is revealed in the power of God over death and life—in the love of Christ.[19]

In Jesus weeping, we have one of the most powerful images for Christology. It is tempting to consider only the pastoral meanings accessible in Jesus' emotional identification with humanity before giving direct attention to his death and resurrection. Certainly, God's compassion is personified in Jesus. We do discover significant theological meaning in the miraculous signs Jesus performed. These signs are an important component of the Gospel story. Moreover, we gain spiritual strength in knowing that God's presence is visceral. "God with us" (Matt. 1:23) is empowerment in life—and is life itself (John 1:4). The Spirit of God ministers to us because Christ knows our condition and has mercy. Jesus does not merely weep for himself; he weeps for human life so tragically defined by death (vv. 17-37). His impending death is so much a part of ours. In these depths of Christology, this narrative has been affectively compared to Jesus' grief at Gethsemane in the Synoptic Gospels.[20] Jesus grieves in the face of death. Christ is really revealed in his passion, to which the Lazarus narrative turns our attention. Perhaps he is also disturbed by our lack of faith (vv. 38-40). But here too Jesus' life and death are caught up in ours. In either case, "God with us" in Christ claims new life in the resurrection. The passion and resurrection of Christ reclaim humanity.

> JESUS DOES NOT MERELY WEEP FOR HIMSELF; HE WEEPS FOR HUMAN LIFE SO TRAGICALLY DEFINED BY DEATH.

Notes

1. F. C. Fensham, "The Curse of the Dry Bones in Ezekiel 37:1-14 Changed to a Blessing of Resurrection," *Journal of Northwest Semitic Languages* 13 (1987): 59–60.

2. Leslie C. Allen, "Structure, Tradition, and Redaction in Ezekiel's Death Valley Vision," in *Among the Prophets: Language, Image, and Structure in the Prophetic Writings*, ed. Philip R. Davies and David J. A. Clines (Sheffield, England: JSOT Press, 1993), 127–42.

3. Christopher R. Seitz, "Ezekiel 37:1-14," *Interpretation* 46 (1992): 53–56.

4. Jacqueline E. Lapsley, *Can These Bones Live? The Problem of the Moral Self in the Book of Ezekiel* (Berlin, Germany: de Gruyter, 2000), 169–71.

5. Claus Westermann, *The Living Psalms*, trans. J. R. Porter (Grand Rapids: Eerdmans, 1989), 1–20.

6. Leslie C. Allen, *Psalms 101–150*, Word Biblical Commentary, vol. 21 (Waco, Tex.: Word Books, 1983), 195.

7. Patrick D. Miller, Jr., *Interpreting the Psalms* (Philadelphia: Fortress Press, 1986), 138–43.

8. Ibid. See also Westermann, *Living Psalms*, 119–20.

9. Allen, *Psalms 101–150*, 193-96. See also Westermann, *Living Psalms*, 120–21.

10. John B. Polhill, "New Life in Christ: Romans 6–8," *Review and Expositor* 73 (fall 1976): 425–36.

11. C. Clifton Black II, "Pauline Perspectives on Death in Romans 5–8," *Journal of Biblical Literature* 103, no. 3 (1984): 413–33.

12. Luke Timothy Johnson, *Reading Romans: A Literary and Theological Commentary* (New York: Crossroad, 1997), 94–138.

13. Ibid., 12–13.

14. Barbara Ann Hedin, "Romans 8:6-11," *Interpretation* 50, no. 1 (January 1996): 55–58.

15. Frank W. Beare, "On the Interpretation of Romans 6:17," *New Testament Studies* 5 (April 1959): 206–10.

16. Mark W. G. Stibbe, "A Tomb with a View: John 11:1-44 in Narrative-Critical Perspective," *New Testament Studies* 40 (January 1994): 38–54.

17. Ibid. See also Paul S. Minear, "The Promise of Life in the Gospel of John," *Theology Today* 49 (January 1993): 485–99.

18. Stibbe, "Tomb with a View," 38–54.

19. Barnabas Lindars, "Rebuking the Spirit: A New Analysis of the Lazarus Story of John 11," *New Testament Studies* 38 (January 1992): 89–104.

20. Fred B. Craddock, "Jesus Wept: John 11:32-44," *Journal for Preachers* 23, no. 3 (Easter 2000): 36–38.

HOLY WEEK

ALICE L. LAFFEY

Introduction

Fifteen years ago I wrote a commentary on Lenten lections, Year B, for the Fortress Press Proclamation series. At the time I read the texts and made what I thought were appropriate comments, including historical information intended to aid both comprehension and appreciation of the readings. Now, writing on Holy Week for Year A, I have a much greater consciousness of the centrality of the events recorded in the readings. Believing that the passion, death, and resurrection of Jesus effected, once for all, human redemption is the context that gives meaning to Christian lives. The details of our own lives derive their importance from our value, a value confirmed by Jesus' life, death, and resurrection. Love, sin, forgiveness, and repentance

> BELIEVING THAT THE PASSION, DEATH, AND RESURRECTION OF JESUS EFFECTED, ONCE FOR ALL, HUMAN REDEMPTION IS THE CONTEXT THAT GIVES MEANING TO CHRISTIAN LIVES.

are integral to the sacred story that we hear over and over again each year—God's love, our sin, God's forgiveness, and our repentance. It is a new year and a slightly different telling of the story from last year's version, but it is a timeless story that took place in time yet also transcends time.

Prime Time

The phrase "prime time" may have been used for the first time by television ratings' companies who recognized that certain hours in the evening almost always had more viewers than other hours. The time during which a program was aired was at least as important as the quality of the program or the popularity of its performers. Our lives also have prime time. Graduations, weddings, births, the purchase of one's first house—these are times that are prepared for and anticipated, but they are also times that later are remembered and whose details are recounted.

While deaths may not be anticipated, surely they too are prime-time events. Depending on whose death and what the relationship had been, everything changes.

Holy Week is perhaps the most important prime time. The liturgical year begins with preparation for the birth of Jesus (Advent), and is followed by Christmas and Epiphany, the celebration of Jesus' baptism and his family. Occurring shortly thereafter is preparation for the suffering, death, and resurrection of Jesus (Lent), followed by those events of Jesus' life celebrated liturgically as Holy Week. The time after Easter, thirty-four weeks, is identified by some traditions as "ordinary time" and comprises more than half the year (other traditions refer to this half-year as the "Sundays after Pentecost").

Christmas is fittingly prime time; no one can die who has not been born. But whereas there is no record of Jesus' choosing his birth, in each of the Synoptic Gospels Jesus explicitly chooses to do the will of his Father (Matt. 26:39; Mark 14:36; Luke 22:42), knowing that he is about to be handed over to death. This is truly prime time. Jesus accepts the end to which the values, words, and actions of his life led. Selfless and sinless, his self-sacrificing love defeats sin. The king of the Jews triumphs over death by surrendering himself to death. Those who believe in him die in his death and are raised at his resurrection. The victory changes everything.

Symbols

Each of the four Gospels tells a story of Jesus' suffering, death, and resurrection. Details vary among the versions, but the main story line is constant. Historical criticism asks questions such as which version came first and which is most authentic, while liturgical reading hears the text as it experiences the liturgy, as the past made present in the now and pointing toward the future. Reflecting on biblical texts used in liturgy, then, causes us to ask what the community of believers was trying to express and what tools they used that they believed would best convey their message. Whether an event occurred in exactly the way it is recorded becomes less important than how the record functions to express the faith of the community. As we walk through the readings of Holy Week together, we will meet details that express power and priority, honor and praise, submission and sacrifice—details whose ultimate meanings are symbolic.

Associative Memory

The biblical texts were built upon one another. Persons, places, incidents, language, even minute details can trigger and evoke connections. Whereas scholars have tended to see Matthew's community especially, and, to a lesser extent, the communities that produced the other Gospels, as trying to show how Jesus fulfills Old

Testament prophecy, the community may not have been so intentional. They may simply have drawn on the linguistic world in which they lived to say what they believed and wanted to express. If one asks, "Who would name a flower 'Jacob's Ladder'?" the answer must surely be a person who was familiar with Genesis 28 and connected the flower's visual appearance with the ladder described there. Who would suggest after several days of rain that God be reminded of the promise of a rainbow? The answer could only be a person who knew the Genesis story of Noah, his ark, and the flood. As I prepared comments on the readings that follow, I became ever more deeply conscious of the fact that many of the details in the Old Testament readings prompted the images and perhaps even some of the narratives themselves in the New Testament. In the same way, the images and incidents in both the Old and New Testaments, like Jacob's ladder and Noah's ark, prompted connections made later in a Judeo-Christian culture. It is more than juxtaposition that connects the Old and New Testament readings used together for Holy Week. The New Testament authors used Old Testament references and allusions, common language and common knowledge, to relate something new, that is, to show similarity and difference so that their audience could properly understand what they wanted to say. In a similar manner, contemporary liturgists have chosen the particular readings from the Old and New Testaments for each day of Holy Week so that we might more fully grasp Jesus' suffering, death, and resurrection and how they are linked to Jesus' own past and to the Jews' past, and that that past is our own.

SUNDAY OF THE PASSION/PALM SUNDAY

MARCH 20, 2005

REVISED COMMON	EPISCOPAL	ROMAN CATHOLIC
Liturgy of the Palms	*Liturgy of the Palms*	*Procession of the Palms*
Matt. 21:1-11	Matt. 21:1-11	Matt. 21:1-11
Ps. 118:1-2, 19-29	Ps. 118:19-29	Psalm 24 or Psalm 47
Liturgy of the Passion	*Liturgy of the Word*	*Liturgy of the Word*
Isa. 50:4-9a	Isa. 45:21-25 or	Isa. 50:4-7
	Isa. 52:13—53:12	
Ps. 31:9-16	Ps. 22:1-21 or	Ps. 22:8-9, 17-18,
	22:1-11	19-20, 23-24
Phil. 2:5-11	Phil. 2:5-11	Phil. 2:6-11
Matt. 26:14—27:66	Matt. (26:36-75)	Matt. 26:14—27:66
or 27:11-54	27:1-54 (55-66)	or 27:11-54

This year the Gospel account that we hear for the procession of palms, the account of Jesus' passion on Palm/Passion Sunday, and the account of Jesus' resurrection read at the Easter Vigil is Matthew's. The authors of Matthew's Gospel preached to a Jewish community who knew the Hebrew scriptures and alluded to them constantly.

PROCESSION WITH PALMS
THE GOSPEL
MATTHEW 21:1-11 (RCL, BCP, RC)

While the narrative depicts Jesus riding triumphantly into Jerusalem as Israel's king and stands in stark contrast to the suffering Jesus in the Gospel account that follows, one is tempted to ask, "Did this event even take place?" and, if so, "Did it take place as described?" A more substantive question need be asked: "What did Matthew's community want to say about Jesus that prompted them to record the incident in this way?" Let us look at the details.

Jesus arrives at the Mount of Olives. The place from which he journeys to Jerusalem in triumph as king is the same place from which the soldiers, after Judas's kiss, will take him to Caiaphas. The liturgy that introduces a Jesus being honored by the people concludes with a Jesus being taken into custody—and the Mount of Olives is the place from which the two very different events originate.

Jesus sends his disciples to fetch a donkey and a colt, an overt reference to Zech. 9:9:

> Rejoice greatly, O daughter Zion!
> Shout aloud, O daughter Jerusalem!
> Lo, your king comes to you;
>   triumphant and victorious is he,
> humble and riding on a donkey,
>   on a colt, the foal of a donkey.

Commentators point out that Jesus' riding on two animals is a misunderstanding of poetic parallelism on the part of the New Testament writer. The Zechariah passage intends only one animal, and the point becomes not what Jesus rode but that he is king and that the New Testament writer believes that Jesus is the king who will bring peace and whose dominion will extend to the ends of the earth. The fact that the text has Jesus' disciples putting their cloaks on two animals and Jesus sitting on two animals seems a clear indication that a literal depiction of what happened is not the writer's intent. Rather, Jesus is being honored; the cloaks of his disciples provide a cushion and the crowds' cloaks provide a carpet. Psalm 118:27 proclaims: "The LORD is God, and he has given us light. Bind the festal procession with branches, up to the horns of the altar." And so Matthew's author incorporates branches into Jesus' festal procession up to Jerusalem. When the crowds chant referring to Jesus as Son of David, they evoke his identity as descendant of the great king and therefore himself a king.

THE LITURGY THAT INTRODUCES A JESUS BEING HONORED BY THE PEOPLE CONCLUDES WITH A JESUS BEING TAKEN INTO CUSTODY—AND THE MOUNT OF OLIVES IS THE PLACE FROM WHICH THE TWO VERY DIFFERENT EVENTS ORIGINATE.

Surely he is the one whom Jeremiah promised, David's righteous branch whom the Lord will raise up, who will reign as king and deal wisely, the one who will execute justice and righteousness (Jer. 23:5; 33:15). The one who comes in the "name" of the Lord evokes Jesus' identity as Lord. Just as the Israelites were instructed not to take the Lord's name in vain (Exod. 20:7; 34:5; Deut. 5:11), that is, not to treat God lightly, and just as Solomon prayed that the temple contain the Lord's name (1 Kings 8:29), so Matthew's author is keen to say that Jesus is *somehow* a manifestation of God (cf. Ps. 118:26).

But who is he? "The whole city" seems unclear about precisely who this Jesus is. The reason the question arises is not just because of this triumphal procession—or maybe not even because of it at all—but rather because of the sayings and deeds of Jesus taken cumulatively. The "crowds," those who so honored him, then reply that he is a prophet, the prophet from Nazareth in Galilee. Jesus speaks and does the words of God; he is a real person with a real place of origin.

Sitting in the pew or chanting and processing with branches of palm, we hear the reading and give assent. Jesus is our king; our king rides on a donkey; our king proclaims the words and deeds of God. Yet, as we chant, we know the future: the sayings and deeds of our king's life culminate in "the whole city" seeking his death.

RESPONSIVE READING

PSALM 118:1-2, 19-29 (RCL);
PSALM 118:19-29 (BCP)

No doubt this psalm was chosen to complement the first reading. It alludes to the festal procession and the branches. Moreover, Matt. 21:26 has incorporated v. 26 of the psalm: "Blessed is the one who comes in the name of the Lord," or "Blessed in the name of the Lord is the one who comes." Still, the other verses are also most appropriate. God's *hesed* endures. The term *hesed* evokes God's faithfulness to his covenant, God's loving kindness. For this we are grateful. The acclamation is repeated because we cannot say thank you enough. We thank God for being righteous and for welcoming the righteous.

Sandwiched between affirmations of God's enduring love is the psalmist's insight that "the stone that the builders rejected has become the chief cornerstone." Anticipating Jesus' ultimate victory, the verse reinforces the appropriateness of our honoring our king. The story of Jesus' being rejected soon follows, but our faith testifies that Jesus is the foundation on which our salvation depends.

PSALM 24 (RC)

The psalm, probably chosen for its reference to the king of glory entering the gates and therefore implying a royal procession, deals also with the identity of the king. As Matt. 21:10 asks when Jesus is entering Jerusalem, "Who is this?" Psalm 24 asks, "Who is this King of glory?" This time the answer is that the Lord of Hosts is the king of glory. The placement of Ps. 24:10 following the reading from Matthew 21 confirms who Jesus is: Jesus is the Lord of Hosts; Jesus is the king of glory. To this we give assent.

THE PLACEMENT OF PS. 24:10 FOLLOWING THE READING FROM MATTHEW 21 CONFIRMS WHO JESUS IS: JESUS IS THE LORD OF HOSTS; JESUS IS THE KING OF GLORY.

PSALM 47 (RC alt.)

God is the king of all the earth (v. 7). Responding to Matt. 21:1-11 with Psalm 47 is declaring our faith that Jesus, entering Jerusalem, is not only our king but also our God. And what more fitting response to our God can there be than praise? And what more fitting way to express praise than with our hands clapping and our voices shouting and singing? And so we join those who accompany Jesus as he enters Jerusalem. With branches of palm, with declarations of praise, we acknowledge the Lord, the Most High, the one who is king of all the earth.

LITURGY OF THE PASSION
FIRST READING
ISAIAH 50:4-9a (RCL);
ISAIAH 50:4-7 (RC)

Our king rides a donkey, and though God reigns over all the earth, God empowers us for others' benefit. In this particular reading, God gives a tongue that will enable us to speak words of comfort to the weary. God gives an ear that will enable us to listen to the less powerful, the less accomplished, the less knowledgeable—not to the teacher but to the taught. God's gifts enable us to endure difficult and painful situations. Only God can empower us so that we do not shrink from pain and humiliation. The particulars are both physical and spiritual: blows to our backs and the pulling out of facial hair as well as being spat upon and insulted.

These are actions the Lord helps us to endure and, because they are the Lord's doing, they are not a source of shame or disgrace. In fact, because the Lord helps us, we will outlast those who afflict us. This is the affirmation of the psalmist's faith, and it is our affirmation also. The prophetic reading enables us to listen with a certain confidence to the details of Jesus' passion.

ISAIAH 45:21-25 (BCP)

This reading continues the theme of Matthew 21 and Psalm 118, the readings for the procession of the palms. There is no other God besides our God; God is righteous; God is strong; God is our Savior.

In declaring God's reign over all, v. 23 asserts that "every knee shall bow" to God and every tongue declare allegiance to God. The passage was chosen in conjunction with Phil. 2:10, "That at the name of Jesus every knee should bend, in heaven and on earth, and under the earth, and every tongue should confess that Jesus Christ is Lord, to the glory of God the Father." The reading was also chosen with a view to the passion narrative that follows. Jesus, the king, is our God.

ISAIAH 52:13—53:12 (BCP alt.)

Presented here as an alternate reading for Passion Sunday, the passage is also used as the first reading for Good Friday. Here it is followed by Matthew's account of the passion; on Good Friday it is followed by John's. Though the two passion accounts differ in detail, the Isaian passage serves the same function in both contexts and so is commented on below.

RESPONSIVE READING
PSALM 31:9-16 (RCL)

The psalm asks for God's help in a time of distress. The distress is then elaborated upon. It doesn't seem to be physical distress so much as psychic distress: grief, sorrow, sighing that causes fatigue. Adversaries, neighbors, and acquaintances make fun of the psalmist or avoid him or, even worse, plot his demise. In contrast to that unhappy state, the psalmist expresses trust in God and asks from God deliverance and salvation. God's compassion and steadfast love are the basis for the petitioner's confidence.

While the psalmist trusts God, the tone of the psalm sits with the petitioner's pain. This makes the psalm an appropriate response to any one of the Isaiah readings as well as an appropriate introduction to the story of Jesus' passion.

PSALM 22:1-21 (BCP);
PSALM 22:1-11 (BCP alt.);
PSALM 22:8-9, 17-18, 19-20, 23-24 (RC)

Psalm 22, like Psalm 31, makes known to God the petitioner's pain. The pain is both psychic and physical, psychic in the first section of the reading (vv. 1-8) and physical in the latter part (vv. 12-17). The psalmist experiences and articulates feelings of abandonment. Whereas Israel's history details how God delivered those who cried out to God, those who trusted God, the psalmist feels scorned and despised. Those who make fun suggest, mockingly, that the psalmist pray. The psalmist does pray. Recalling to God how God has acted protectively up to this point, he asks the one whom he said was far (v. 1), not to be far (v. 11). He desires God's presence.

The psalmist also details physical suffering. He is being attacked, as if bulls and lions were overpowering him. He names the parts of his body that are adversely affected; beginning and ending with his bones, he moves on to his mouth, his tongue, his jaws, his hands, and his feet. The psalmist then declares what we will hear minutes later, details associated with Jesus' crucifixion: "They divide my clothes among themselves, and for my clothing they cast lots" (v. 18). Again, the psalmist begs God not to be far away (v. 19).

The final verses that are included in the Roman Catholic version of the reading assume that the petitioner's prayer has been answered. The psalmist calls all who revere God, all Israelites, to praise and glorify God. God heard the cry of the afflicted.

> THE PSALMIST BEGS GOD NOT TO BE FAR AWAY.

The psalm sets a tone of suffering and pain, articulating the petitioner's trust in God. Like the psalmist, Jesus suffers psychic and physical pain. Today's Gospel details how Jesus is abandoned and then crucified.

SECOND READING

PHILIPPIANS 2:5-11 (RCL, BCP);
PHILIPPIANS 2:6-11 (RC)

The RCL and the BCP include the exhortation of v. 5 in this reading: "Let the same mind be in you that was in Christ Jesus." The Roman Catholic reading, in omitting the verse, shifts *all* the emphasis to the disposition of Christ.

Of the readings we have heard so far, this is the first that is written from the perspective of one who has died and been raised. Previous readings have asked the question, "Who is he?" Others have answered the question: "He is the Lord, our king and our God." This reading combines the previous question and answer asking a new question: "Who is the Lord, the king and our God?" The answer fits with the man on the donkey. Jesus defies the expected hierarchy. The one who was in the form of God was not concerned with being equal to God; he dispossessed himself of that which he possessed, exchanging the form of God for the form of a servant, a human form. He was willing to put himself in a subservient position, obeying another, even to the point of suffering a humiliating death.

> PAUL ARTICULATES THE FAITH OF THE EARLY CHURCH THAT JESUS LET GO OF POWER AND STATUS AND EVEN HIS VERY LIFE, AND THAT WE ARE THE RECIPIENTS OF HIS GENEROSITY.

God's response to this self-emptying behavior was to exalt Christ, placing him above all others. Christ is worthy of others' recognition, both by physical gesture and by verbal acclaim. By Christ's behavior God the Father has been glorified.

Paul articulates the faith of the early church that Jesus let go of power and status and even his very life, and that we are the recipients of his generosity. This theme runs through many—in fact, most—of the readings of Holy Week. We have been told that even when being acclaimed as king, Jesus was riding on a donkey. And we will be told that Jesus, in his last discourse with his disciples, both in Matthew's and John's versions that are read this year, spoke of a different kind of kingship and of the master being the servant. We may include v. 5 in today's reading, a verse that exhorts us to claim the attitude of Jesus, a disposition whereby we become willing servants of one another. On the other hand, our reading may begin with v. 6, in which case we focus at the beginning of this holiest of weeks exclusively on Jesus' own attitude, a disposition that would result, ultimately, in his being put to death. Both perspectives are good. What is most important is that we realize the posture of Jesus and that we express our gratitude to him.

THE GOSPEL
MATTHEW 26:14—27:66 (RCL, RC);
MATTHEW 27:11-54 (RCL alt., RC alt.);
MATTHEW (26:36-75) 27:1-54 (55-66) (BCP)

Today's Gospel reading, even in its shortest form, is long—longer than most Gospel readings for other Sundays of the year. On the other hand, it is short. For how long should it take to recall the details of a man's suffering and death, a man whose suffering and death was for our benefit? Isn't it fitting that we take a little time to hear the story again, to enter into the meaning of what is being said and to allow ourselves to be changed by what the narrative tells us?

ISN'T IT FITTING THAT WE TAKE A LITTLE TIME TO HEAR THE STORY AGAIN, TO ENTER INTO THE MEANING OF WHAT IS BEING SAID AND TO ALLOW OURSELVES TO BE CHANGED BY WHAT THE NARRATIVE TELLS US?

The Questions

Because of the dialogue between interlocutors, the account of Jesus' passion progresses with increasing insight into the hearts and souls of the characters: The questions reveal a great deal about the persons who ask them.

"What will you give me if I betray him to you?" asks Judas of the chief priests.

"Where do you want us to make the preparations for you to eat the Passover?" ask Jesus' disciples.

"Surely, not I, Lord?" asks each disciple of Jesus regarding the identity of the betrayer.

"Surely not I, Rabbi?" asks Judas of Jesus.

Jesus himself asks many questions: "So, could you not stay awake with me one hour?" "Are you still sleeping and taking your rest?" These he asks of the disciples closest to him in the garden. "Do you think that I cannot appeal to my Father, and he will at once send me more than twelve legions of angels? But how then would the Scriptures be fulfilled, which say it must happen in this way?" These he asks of Peter who has responded to what is happening with his sword.

"Have you come out with swords and clubs to arrest me as though I were a bandit?" is Jesus' question of the crowd who had come to the garden to arrest him.

More questions allow for Jesus' self-revelation and the narrative's unfolding:

"Have you no answer? What is it that they testify against you?" asks Caiaphas of Jesus after two men accuse Jesus of saying that he can destroy the temple and rebuild it in three days (cf. John 2:19). "Why do we still need further witnesses?" asks Caiaphas in response to Jesus' intimation that he is the Son of Man. "What is your verdict?" asks Caiaphas of the gathered scribes and elders after he has called Jesus' assertion blasphemy.

"Who is it that struck you?" is asked mockingly of Jesus by, in the Matthean account, some of the scribes and elders, even before Jesus is taken to Pilate. "What is that to us?" the chief priests ask Jesus in response to Judas's declaration that he has sinned by betraying an innocent man.

"Are you the king of the Jews?" is Pilate's first question to Jesus.

"Do you not hear how many accusations they make against you?" asks Pilate of Jesus in response to the accusations made against Jesus by the chief priests and elders. "Whom do you want me to release for you, Jesus Barabbas or Jesus who is called the Messiah?" asks Pilate of the crowd. "Which of the two do you want me to release for you?" repeats Pilate to the crowd, a statement perhaps intended to further distance Pilate from Jesus' condemnation. "Then what should I do with Jesus who is called the Messiah?" asks Pilate of the crowd after they have indicated that they want Barabbas's release. "Why, what evil has he done?" is Pilate's question to the crowds after they have called for Jesus to be crucified.

> FOR THOSE OF US WHO HAVE HEARD THE NARRATIVE OF JESUS' PASSION READ YEAR AFTER YEAR DURING THE HOLIEST OF WEEKS, THE QUESTIONS THAT THE CHARACTERS ASK CAN SERVE AS SHORTHAND FOR THE ENTIRE NARRATIVE.

"Eli, Eli, lema sabachthani?" "My God, my God, why have you forsaken me?" is Jesus' question of God, the first verse of Psalm 22 and the final question of today's reading.

For those of us who have heard the narrative of Jesus' passion read year after year during the holiest of weeks, the questions that the characters ask can serve as shorthand for the entire narrative. We recognize who is speaking and to whom. The questions either come from the lips of Jesus, are asked of Jesus, or at least are about Jesus; Judas, the disciples, Jesus himself, Caiaphas, scribes and elders, and Pilate speak.

Betrayal and Denial

Judas betrays Jesus for thirty pieces of silver. Afterwards, he regrets what he has done and hangs himself. Peter denies Jesus to a servant girl. Afterwards, he regrets what he has done and weeps. The Greek term for "to betray" is understood to mean both "to deliver to an enemy by treachery" and "to cause somebody to believe an untruth." What Judas did could be construed as fulfilling both of those definitions: Judas delivered Jesus by means of a kiss to those who sought to kill him. The Greek term for "to deny" can mean " to declare untrue, contradict" and "to refuse to recognize or acknowledge." What Peter did could be construed as fulfilling both of those meanings: by declaring that the servant woman was wrong, Peter refused to recognize Jesus. Similarly, what Judas did could be construed as fulfilling both meanings of the term "to deny": his kiss seems to be intended to cause Jesus to continue to believe in their friendship. And so one must ask, "Are the behaviors of the two men all that different?" If so, how? If not, then why are the outcomes so different?

Yes, Judas's action leads to Jesus' capture by the Roman soldiers, while Peter's only "betrays" his friendship with Jesus. Judas takes initiative in bringing Jesus to harm; Peter is only responding to another's question, and reluctantly at that. But from Jesus' point of view, are the two men's behaviors so different? Neither man claims Jesus as his friend; neither acts loyally; neither risks his own well-being for the sake of his friend.

Jesus seems to indicate that, although his being handed over to his enemies fulfills what is "written of him," that fact does not diminish the responsibility of the one who does the betraying. And Jesus tells Judas that he knows that Judas is his betrayer. The text depicts Jesus as knowing the future, that is, his betrayer, but as being saddened by the knowledge.

But Jesus also indicates that he knows beforehand that Peter will deny him. In response to Peter's confident protest of his loyalty, Jesus tells him that before a cock crows he will have denied Jesus three times.

That Judas hanged himself is traditionally seen as a further indication of his wrongdoing. But is it? In his world, he would be guilty of the shedding of innocent blood: a life for a life, his life for Jesus' life. Traditionally, Peter's behavior after his denial of Jesus is contrasted with that of Judas. His tears speak his regret. But both

> JESUS TAKES HUMANS' SIN, JUDAS'S SIN AS WELL AS PETER'S SIN AS WELL AS OUR SIN, UPON HIMSELF.

men regretted what they had said and done.

So again I must ask, are the two men really so different? I am reminded here of the depiction of the characters of Saul and David in the Deuteronomist History. Both men sin. Saul offered a sacrifice without waiting for Samuel to arrive (1 Sam. 13:8-13), and he failed to fulfill the demands of a Holy War (1 Sam. 15:8-11).

David had an affair with Bathsheba (2 Samuel 11) and took a census (1 Samuel 24). Nevertheless, the responses of the two men to their sins differ. Saul makes excuses while David acknowledges his sins, regrets, and repents. Obviously the outcomes for the two men are very different.

If we are able to see Judas and Peter as having a lot in common, then we must ask, "Is not what makes the difference what Jesus does?" Jesus' takes humans' sin, Judas's sin as well as Peter's sin as well as our sin, upon himself. By his death and resurrection, he redeems humankind from sin. I dare say, we have been Judas as well as Peter. We have taken the initiative in wrongdoing as well as more passively allowed our best selves to be compromised.

Celebrating the Passover

The Jews' "prime time" commemorates the story of their escape from bondage in Egypt and, most particularly, the slaying and eating of a lamb, and the spreading of its blood on the doorposts to identify them and protect them from the angel of death. Eating the sacrificed lamb led to escape from death, to life and freedom. Now, on the first day of the Feast, Jesus offers bread

> JUST AS THE JEWS COMMEMORATE THE PASSOVER, CHRISTIANS COMMEMORATE JESUS' DEATH THAT LEADS TO ESCAPE FROM DEATH, TO LIFE AND TO FREEDOM.

and wine as his body and blood; just as the lamb was sacrificed, he soon will give his body as an offering, so that those who believe in him may escape death and may have life and freedom. Just as the Jews commemorate the Passover, Christians commemorate Jesus' death that leads to escape from death, to life and to freedom.

Using Old Testament Symbols and Predictions

Jesus the king is also the shepherd. When Micaiah prophesied King Ahab's death, he said, "I saw all Israel scattered on the mountains like sheep that have no shepherd" (1 Kings 22:17). Here, the sheep are deserters; they scatter because of the shepherd's imminent death. Those who do not betray or deny Jesus merely desert him.

The Old Testament language of Holy War describes God as fighting Israel's battles; victory is thus assured. When Jesus' disciple draws his sword to protest Jesus' capture, Jesus assures him that God could fight for Jesus as he had fought for Israel, thus assuring victory. But God's doing that would prevent the fulfillment of the Scriptures.

Judas is paid thirty pieces of silver to betray Jesus to the chief priests, money that he subsequently returns because he recognizes that he got it by betraying innocent blood. The chief priests also recognize the money as blood money, and so, rather than returning it to the temple treasury, they use it to buy the potter's field, that is, the Field of Blood, as a place to bury foreigners. Many manuscripts declare that this deed fulfills one of Jeremiah's prophecies, though the connection is very loose. Jere-

miah uses a potter and his clay to denounce Judah's evils (Jeremiah 18). Other manuscripts declare that the deed fulfills one of Zechariah's prophecies. In Zechariah
11 thirty shekels of silver are given to the temple treasury before the prophet symbolically separates Judah and Israel. Matthew is keen to connect Judas's action to
the people's past. What Judas did was not a random act.

Jesus takes the opportunity to point out the inconsistency of the crowds. He used
to sit in the temple and teach and they left him alone; now they seek to arrest him.

Honest Answers

When Judas asked, "Is it I, Rabbi?" referring to the one who would betray him,
Jesus replied, "You have said so." When the high priest insisted that Jesus tell them
if he was "the Messiah, the Son of God," Jesus replied, "You have said so." When
Pilate asked Jesus directly, "Are you the king of the Jews?" he replied, "You say so."

Resistance

Pilate did not want to put Jesus to death. He allowed the chief priests and elders
to choose between "a notorious prisoner" and Jesus, in the hope that they would
choose Barabbas. Pilate's wife confirmed Pilate's reluctance to put Jesus to death,
declaring Jesus innocent and telling Pilate to have nothing to do with him, that is,
to "stay out of it." But Pilate either could not (out of fear of the crowds) or did
not (out of lack of courage) contradict the will of the Jewish leaders. He gave them
a second chance to choose Barabbas instead of Jesus, but they chose Jesus. When
he asked what they wanted to have happen to Jesus and they responded that he
should be crucified, he asked, "What evil has he done?" The question is never really
answered. They respond a second time that they want Jesus to be crucified.

Pilate wants to separate himself from any responsibility for shedding innocent
blood and publicly symbolizes this by washing his hands. In the end, however,
to satisfy the crowd, he orders that Jesus be put to death by Roman execution
(crucifixion).

The character of Pilate evokes in my mind two narratives from the Old Testament, the story of Ruth and the story of Jonah. Both narratives deal with
outsiders—the Moabite Ruth and the sailors and Ninevites. In both narratives,
the outsiders, the non-Jews, become the faithful Yahwists. Although Pilate does
allow Jesus to be crucified, in contrast to the authorities of his own people, Pilate
believes that Jesus is innocent and does not deserve to die. Symbolically he
separates himself from the will of the chief priests and elders, as does his wife.
Contemporary historical critics are concerned with the Gospel's anti-Semitic
overtones. A symbolic reading that understands the literary connections of the
Gospel with the Old Testament, however, might find here an implicit declaration
that Jesus' death is to redeem all people, not just, as what might be expected from
Jesus the Jew, the Jews.

Pilate provides a retardation of the action that is Jesus' crucifixion, a digression. He has Jesus flogged. Pilate's soldiers dress Jesus in a scarlet robe and place a crown, which they have made out of thorns, on his head. They put a reed (for a scepter) into his hand and kneel before him (see Isa. 45:23 above). Mockingly, they proclaim him the king of the Jews. But the mocking continues: they use the reed/scepter against him, striking him on the head. Before they lead him off to be crucified, they remove the scarlet robe, exchanging it for his own clothes.

The king wears a crown (of thorns). Another carries his cross (Simon of Cyrene). Arriving at Golgotha, they offer him bitter wine that he tastes but then rejects. They hang him on the cross, then they cast lots for his clothing (see Ps. 22:18 above), and finally they identify him: "This is Jesus, the king of the Jews."

Two others are being crucified at the same time and in the same place with Jesus. They, one on Jesus' right and the other on his left, mock Jesus along with passers-by, the chief priests, scribes, and elders. They goad him to save himself. After all, he said he could rebuild the temple in three days; if he really is the Son of God, he should come down from the cross; since he saved others, he should save himself. They profess that they would then believe in him. One is reminded of Jesus' telling them in the garden that he been with them daily teaching and they hadn't indicated any problem, but now they are out to get him (Matt. 26:55).

A SYMBOLIC READING THAT UNDERSTANDS THE LITERARY CONNECTIONS OF THE GOSPEL WITH THE OLD TESTAMENT, HOWEVER, MIGHT FIND HERE AN IMPLICIT DECLARATION THAT JESUS' DEATH IS TO REDEEM ALL PEOPLE, NOT JUST, AS WHAT MIGHT BE EXPECTED FROM JESUS THE JEW, THE JEWS.

While Jesus hung on the cross, there was darkness. When Jesus cried out the opening verse of Psalm 22, "My God, my God, why have you forsaken me?" the bystanders misunderstood. They thought he was calling for Elijah. Would they believe if Elijah came (see Mal. 4:5-6)? Again he is treated to sour wine, but Jesus dies.

At Jesus' death, the curtain of the temple is torn in two. That which separated the people from the Holy of Holies is ruptured forever. Jesus has definitively broken through any separation between humanity and God; he is returning to the Father. As with many Old Testament theophanies, the earth shakes and the rocks are split; God's creation reacts dramatically. The tombs of many people who have died are opened and they are raised from the dead. In fact, after Jesus has himself been raised from the dead, many of these saints leave their tombs, go into Jerusalem, and make themselves known to many.

The centurion and the other Roman soldiers witness the dramatic changes in nature and realize that Jesus is truly who he said he was. Many women who had been followers of Jesus to the end also witness these events.

In the evening, Joseph of Arimathea, who was a disciple of Jesus, asks Pilate for

Jesus' body; he provides it with a clean linen cloth and a tomb. The two Marys persevere to the end, through Jesus' burial.

The next day, the chief priests and the Pharisees approach Pilate. Concerned that even in death Jesus could still be a threat to their status and prestige, since he said that after three days he would rise again (the taunting of v. 40), they request that Pilate see to it that Jesus' tomb be made secure. Pilate agrees to give them a guard of soldiers so that they can make it "as secure as you can." The guard seals the stone.

Today's liturgy began with the reading of Jesus' entry into Jerusalem accompanied by the praise of many of the people who had heard his words and seen his deeds, many who had come to believe in him. Today's liturgy ends with Jesus, deserted by the crowds who had praised him and deserted also by his own disciples, dead and buried. For those who are unable to attend liturgy during the week, Jesus remains in the tomb until the Easter Vigil. The week is spent reflecting on central tenets of our faith: Jesus loved us to the end . . . and love is costly.

JESUS LOVED US TO THE END . . . AND LOVE IS COSTLY.

MONDAY OF HOLY WEEK

MARCH 21, 2005

REVISED COMMON	EPISCOPAL (BCP)	ROMAN CATHOLIC
Isa. 42:1-9	Isa. 42:1-9	Isa. 42:1-7
Ps. 36:5-11	Ps. 36:5-10	Ps. 27:1, 2, 3, 13-14
Heb. 9:11-15	Heb. 11:39—12:3	
John 12:1-11	John 12:1-11 or	John 12:1-11
	Mark 14:3-9	

The readings for Monday through Friday of Holy Week do not change from year to year, as the Sunday readings do. What this means, in effect, is that if you bought Year B or Year C of the Proclamation series (2002–2003 and 2003–2004), you have read comments on these same readings. For this reason, I have commented more extensively on the Sunday readings. However, each of us is at a different place than we were a year or two ago, and we will hear the readings differently. Also, I am a different commentator than previous commentators on the Holy Week readings, and so it is likely that I will highlight different aspects of the texts. I, for example, will comment on those texts that space limitations required be omitted last year, verses of Psalms 27 and 36, verses from the letter to the Hebrews, Matthew 9–10 and verses from chapter 26, and Mark 11.

During the week, we walk with Jesus from his triumphal entry into Jerusalem to his final supper with his friends, to his prayer of lament and petition in the garden, to his capture and condemnation, to his humiliating torture, and finally, to his crucifixion. The week begins on a high and ends with the loss of Jesus' life. Those who support him during his glory days abandon him when the going gets rough—a not unfamiliar scenario. But this year we will stay; we will walk beside him through these readings.

FIRST READING

ISAIAH 42:1-9 (RCL, BCP);
ISAIAH 42:1-7 (RC)

Known as a "Servant Song," these verses identify God's Servant as the one who brings forth justice (vv. 1, 3, 4). The Lord's Servant's manner is gentle, not breaking a bruised reed or quenching a dimly burning wick. But he is also determined and persevering. He will not grow faint or be crushed until he has established justice. The Lord who is the Creator has called the Servant, who becomes a covenant to the people, a light to the nations. His actions are liberating, enabling the blind to see and freeing prisoners from darkness. The one who sends the servant is the Lord; there is no God but the Lord. This proclamation, God declares through the prophet, is a prediction of the future (v. 9).

FOR US WHO READ THE PASSAGE IN THE CONTEXT OF HOLY WEEK, IT IS A PERFECT DESCRIPTION OF WHAT WE BELIEVE JESUS TO HAVE DONE. JESUS ACCEPTED THE WILL OF GOD AND BY SO DOING BRINGS FORTH JUSTICE.

Who is the Servant? Is it Israel, by whose redemption from exile the nations can be led to Israel's God? Is it an individual, whose righteous leadership is transforming, who inspires hope in an exiled and despairing people? Is it Jesus, a text understood by those who have faith in Jesus as perfectly descriptive of what he accomplished? For us who read the passage in the context of Holy Week, it is a perfect description of what we believe Jesus to have done. Jesus accepted the will of God and by so doing brings forth justice.

RESPONSIVE READING

PSALM 36:5-10 (RCL);
PSALM 36:5-11 (BCP);
PSALM 27:1, 2, 3, 13-14 (RC)

The psalm reading opens by celebrating God's *hesed*, that is, God's enduring love but also God's faithfulness, God's righteousness, God's judgments, and God's work of saving all living things. God provides that which is absolutely essential for life, water and light. The psalmist then asks God to continue showing that enduring love and salvation, protecting the psalmist from the wicked who is identified as arrogant.

Within the context of Holy Week, it is God's enduring love and faithfulness that lead Jesus to the garden and to his arrest, the steadfast faithfulness that will bring him to the cross. We ask not to be identified with the wicked who are arrogant, with those who were jealous of Jesus and would seek his death.

The same themes that occur in Psalm 36 are found in Psalm 27: God provides light and salvation. The psalmist consequently proclaims repeatedly that he therefore has no reason to fear (twice in v. 1 and twice in v. 3). Confident that God's goodness will emerge, the psalmist exhorts those who hear him to "wait for the LORD" (twice in v. 14), to be strong and courageous. The verse is reminiscent of Hab. 2:3, a text that encourages those who experience suffering to persevere in their faithfulness to God, confident that their patience will be rewarded.

As we set aside this time as the holiest of weeks in 2005 to walk with Jesus in his suffering and to his death, we are encouraged to remain confident. Death is not the final word. Whatever suffering we endure this year or in the future—rejection, betrayal, physical or mental sickness—we have no need to fear. Nor does such an

> THIS READING AND HOLY WEEK IN GENERAL ASSURE US THAT OUR SUFFERING IS BOUND TO THE REDEMPTIVE SUFFERING AND DEATH OF JESUS, AND THEREFORE WILL BE OVERCOME.

assertion belittle our suffering. Rather, this reading and Holy Week in general assure us that our suffering is bound to the redemptive suffering and death of Jesus and therefore will be overcome. This is the basis of our confidence.

SECOND READING
HEBREWS 9:11-15 (RCL);
HEBREWS 11:39—12:3 (BCP)

The author of Hebrews picks up on the sin offering that was so important to Jewish self-understanding and worship referred to throughout Leviticus, and the author identifies Jesus as the final sin offering. The effects of the Jew's animal offerings and Jesus' self-offering are the same, except that the effect of Jesus' offering is permanent. Having offered himself once, no more sin offerings are necessary. But Christ is not just the sacrificial victim that has no choice; he is also the high priest who does the offering. He chooses

> WHATEVER SHAME AND HOSTILITY WE ENDURE, WE SHOULD TAKE COURAGE FROM JESUS' EXAMPLE AND PERSEVERE IN OUR FIDELITY TO GOD.

the will of the Father (Matt. 26:42) and thus, as a sinless victim, becomes the mediator between God and humankind.

Hebrews 11 celebrates the major Old Testament figures whose lives are understood as a faithful response to God—Abel, Enoch, Noah, Abraham, Isaac, Jacob, Joseph, Moses, Rahab, Gideon, Barak, Samson, Jephthah, David, Samuel, the prophets, and others. Their lives have served as an inspiration for others and are not to be valued lightly. Yet today's passage points to someone even more inspiring than they—Jesus. We are encouraged to persevere in our faith and to live our lives looking to Jesus who, for the sake of God, endured the cross, disregarding its shame and enduring sinners' hostility. Whatever shame and hostility we endure, we should take courage from Jesus' example and persevere in our fidelity to God.

Who are our role models? Who are the role models of our culture? Are they inspiring? Who and what do they inspire us to become? Is Jesus our primary role model? How successful are we—or do we try to be—in living in accord with his values? What if living in accord with his values will cause us to be ostracized or rejected? What if "doing the right thing" will lead to some form of the cross? Will we persevere in faith in following our role model? Clearly the author of Hebrews encourages us to do so. As we walk through Holy Week, we are reminded that Jesus was willing to become the offering for our sins.

The Gospel
JOHN 12:1-11 (RCL, BCP, RC);
MARK 14:3-9 (BCP alt.)

It is an extravagant gesture of love to waste precious perfume on another's feet. In her own way, Mary does what Jesus soon will do; she performs an extravagant gesture of love. She "wastes" what might be used more sparingly, saved for special occasions, sold, and turned into money for a more practical exchange.

But how do we express our love? I am reminded of O. Henry's short story *The Gift of the Magi*, when husband and wife give to the other at great personal sacrifice the most precious thing they possess. Who cannot appreciate such a generous gesture of love bestowed by one human being on another? One who is jealous, perhaps? One who has no appreciation of symbols, what gifts say, one who sees only monetary value?

The text tells us a little about the character of Judas. Rather than giving generously to another what was his (as Mary had done), he took for himself what was not his; he was a thief.

Jesus defends Mary's action and perhaps says more about it than even Mary knew. It is fitting to anoint a dead body before burial. Jesus would soon no longer be among them as he had been; he would soon be crucified. As such, it was fitting to honor him now. There is always time to give generously to the poor because, as Jesus says and as we know, there are always poor who need our generosity.

The final verses of the unit turn their attention to Lazarus, whom Jesus had raised from the dead. Surely he was a symbol of the power of God working in Jesus. The chief priests, jealous of Jesus' power and resenting it, intended to put Lazarus to death "as well." A living Lazarus was living testimony of God's power in Jesus. When power used for good is experienced as a threat to one's own power, those who are evil seek to eliminate the good. I am reminded of Saul's jealousy of David, for which reason he tried to kill David (1 Sam. 18:9).

The alternative reading from Mark's Gospel also takes place at Bethany and also involves a woman anointing Jesus. In this version, the woman anoints Jesus' head, reminiscent of the anointing of kings. Here too the ointment is costly nard, and here too onlookers, missing the point, protest the waste. And here as well Jesus silences those who criticize the woman's generosity, affirming her gesture and assuring those who complain that they can always act generously toward the poor. Jesus describes her action as anointing his body beforehand for his burial. Missing in the Johannine version is Jesus' comment in Mark that she will be remembered for her generous gesture of love.

This reading takes my mind in two directions. The first is toward the holocausts of the Old Testament. As whole-burnt sacrifices, these offerings were completely destroyed as a way of giving them to God and preventing their use by others. Mary's "wasting" of the ointment offers it to Jesus in a way that prevents its sale. The recipient of the ointment, Jesus, and the woman's love that prompts her lavishness make the gesture very appropriate.

If you are reading this commentary in the United States, your context is one of relative affluence. We waste food every day; we buy more than we need, our wants become our needs. This is true of our culture. Sometimes wasteful attitudes and behaviors even affect the poorer members of our society. Yet most of us would agree that generosity is

> WE WHO ARE RICH, RELATIVELY SPEAKING, ARE CALLED TO BE HABITUALLY GENEROUS AND HABITUALLY MINDFUL OF THE POOR.

good and waste is not. It is possible to interpret Mary's generosity as waste, and Judas does so. However, sometimes it is appropriate to be so extravagant that some might describe it as imprudent or wasteful. I am reminded of the extravagant generosity of the widow who contributed to the temple treasury "everything she had, all she had to live on" (Mark 12:41-44). Jesus taught that her two small copper coins were of greater value than the large sums that the rich people put into the treasury. We who are rich, relatively speaking, are called to be habitually generous and habitually mindful of the poor. And yet, with Mary and the widow as role models, sometimes we may even be called to behave in such extravagantly generous ways that some might think we are imprudent or even wasteful, when in fact we are only making generous gestures of love.

TUESDAY OF HOLY WEEK

MARCH 22, 2005

REVISED COMMON	EPISCOPAL (BCP)	ROMAN CATHOLIC
Isa. 49:1-7	Isa. 49:1-6	Isa. 49:1-6
Ps. 71:1-14	Ps. 71:1-12	Ps. 71:1-2, 3-4a,
		5ab-6ab, 15, 17
1 Cor. 1:18-31	1 Cor. 1:18-31	
John 12:20-36	John 12:37-38, 42-50	John 13:21-33, 36-38
	or Mark 11:15-19	

FIRST READING

ISAIAH 49:1-7 (RCL);
ISAIAH 49:1-6 (BCP, RC)

The prophet calls on peoples of other nations, peoples living along the coastlands and people who live far away, to listen to this testimony. He then gives his credentials—why they should listen. He was called by God before he was born, and his mouth was prepared by God to deliver God's message. Still, the prophet is a bit discouraged because his message was not heeded. Nevertheless, he knows that God will reward his faithfulness. At this point God intervenes, addressing the prophet whom God "formed in the womb to be his servant" (v. 5). God assures the prophet that his message is destined not just for Israel but for the nations; Israel will become "a light to the nations" (v. 6b). God's salvation will reach to the ends of the earth; that is, God ultimately wills everyone's salvation. Even more, God assures Israel, despised and in exile, that God has chosen them, and that restoration will include a reversal of their situation; they who had been scorned and enslaved will be the recipients of respect from other nations.

Hearing this passage during Holy Week affirms Christian faith that just as Israel's suffering in exile would benefit others, peoples of the coastlands and the peoples far away, so Jesus' suffering is for others. And just as the despised and exiled Israelites would be restored to a place of honor, so Jesus would be raised to new life. His humiliating suffering and death are not the final word; instead, a new beginning is at hand.

PSALM 71:1–14 (RCL);
PSALM 71:1–12 (BCP);
PSALM 71:1–2, 3–4a, 5ab–6ab, 15, 17 (RC)

The psalm opens with several requests of God:

may the petitioner never be put to shame but, rather,
may his accusers be put to shame instead;
may the psalmist be delivered and rescued but
may his enemies be disgraced;
may God hear him and save him and not cast him off in his old age;
may God never be far from him.

These requests are based on the psalmist's relationship with God. God is the petitioner's rock, fortress, hope, trust, and refuge. The psalmist reminds God that he has consistently proclaimed God's praise.

Such a covenant relationship, while affirming the psalmist's trust in God, asserts his knowledge and acceptance that he is dependent on God. As such, the psalm is appropriate for Holy Week. We are dependent on, and we wish to acknowledge that we know we are dependent on, the generous love of Jesus that led him to accept the cross.

Acknowledging dependence is a difficult thing to do in our culture. Lack of power and independence makes our poor youth angry. Diminishing power and independence make our elderly depressed. Lesser power and independence make our men feel emasculated. Having power, not being dependent on others, is accepted, often unqualifiedly, as a good. But the reading, in its liturgical context within Holy Week, presents us with a paradox. It reminds us that we are dependent on God, and yet Jesus acts out his power by accepting death on a cross at the hands of those who were jealous of his power.

> WHAT DOES IT MEAN, PRACTICALLY SPEAKING IN OUR LIVES, TO DELIBERATELY LET GO OF POWER AS JESUS DID?

What is the relationship between God's power, which effects what we cannot, our acknowledgment of that power, and God's power acting in us? What does it mean, practically speaking in our lives, to deliberately let go of power as Jesus did? To exchange being right for being loving? What does it mean to deliberately allow ourselves to become vulnerable and to depend on one another?

(I assume here and in other comments about the psalms that are used during the liturgies of Holy Week that their authors were men. Ancient Israel, after all, was a patriarchal culture. Further, the attributions that are explicit in the biblical text ascribe the psalms to male authorship. That does not mean that contemporary women cannot put themselves in the place of the psalmist and pray the prayer that he authored. His sentiments are human.)

SECOND READING

1 CORINTHIANS 1:18-31 (RCL, BCP)

How can suffering a humiliating death lead to victory? God's wisdom confounds the wise. God's foolishness is wiser than human wisdom, and God's weakness is stronger than human strength. Herein lies the paradox and the test of faith. What will we risk to believe? The grain of wheat must first fall into the ground and die if it is to produce much fruit (John 12:24). But that doesn't seem rational. Giving one's life for those who betray you (à la Judas), for those who deny you (à la Peter), for those who are suspicious of you (à la the chief priests and elders) just doesn't make sense. Such a generous gesture of love goes beyond a woman's anointing with precious ointment (John 12:1-11, see above). It's not rational. I am reminded of "the pig and chicken story," at which we laugh. A breakfast of bacon and eggs represents a gift from the chicken but "total commitment" from the pig. Jesus extends total commitment to sinners. Such forgiveness is outrageous yet is at the core of what we believe, what makes us Christians. It is not worldly wisdom that gives meaning to our lives, though it may put money in our wallet. The wisdom of God is indescribably better than worldly wisdom. It is the source of our hope.

> THEIR LOWLINESS HELPS TO REMIND THEM THAT THE SOURCE OF THEIR LIFE AND WELL-BEING IS CHRIST, AND CHRIST IS THE WISDOM OF GOD.

Paul goes on to comment on his audience. Most are not "wise by human standards" (v. 26). Most are foolish, weak, lowly, despised, nobodies, when measured by the world's standards, but that is their protection. Lest they take themselves too seriously, lest they think they are responsible for their achievements, their lowliness helps to remind them that the source of their life and well-being is Christ, and Christ is the wisdom of God. God is responsible for our achievements.

The reading echoes Psalm 71 and my comments above. We are dependent on God, and that is not such a bad thing after all.

JOHN 12:20-36 (RCL);
JOHN 12:37-38, 42-50 (BCP);
MARK 11:15-19 (BCP alt.);
JOHN 13:21-33, 36-38 (RC)

What function do the Greeks have in this reading? Are they "the coastlands" and "the peoples from far away" to which the first reading refers? Do they then become hearers of Jesus' prediction of his death?

Connected to the preceding reading, Jesus here proclaims what is about to happen. Just as a grain of wheat must die to produce much fruit, Jesus must be willing to die to redeem humankind. And those who follow him must be willing to die also. Jesus, here as in Matt. 26:42, articulates his willingness to suffer and die for the salvation of humankind. Just as the grain of wheat will produce much fruit, Jesus' death produces new life. The extravagant gift of love that is Jesus' death and resurrection glorifies God. Those who hear Jesus say this hear also a confirmation—whether by the words of an angel or by thunder—of what Jesus said.

Jesus then proclaims sentiments similar to those asserted in 1 Corinthians 1 that God's wisdom surpasses human wisdom. The ruler of this world is replaced by a crucified Jesus, who will draw all to himself. But Jesus' listeners, responding with worldly wisdom, cannot understand. How can Jesus be the Anointed One (Messiah), the Son of Man (Ezekiel), and yet be crucified? It is their understanding that the Messiah will be triumphant, and yet Jesus speaks of his death. How can this be? To them the contradiction is obvious.

Jesus, as is often the case (see the comments on the Gospel for the Easter Vigil, below), did not directly answer their question about the identity of the Son of Man. Rather, speaking of himself as the light, he again (see yesterday's Gospel) says that he will not be among them for much longer, but that while he is among them, they should take advantage of his presence. He is the light, and he advises his listeners to walk in the light while they have the light, to believe in the light, and to become children of light. The ending of this passage recalls the Gospel's prologue: "the life was the light of all people. The light shines in the darkness, and the darkness did not overcome it" (John 1:4b-5).

Today's BCP reading reminds us that, in spite of so many indications of Jesus' identity, many still did not believe. However, some, even some of the authorities, did. Yet acknowledging that one believed in Jesus was a risk that could potentially have harmful consequences. Fearing that they would be removed from the synagogue, some people kept their faith in Jesus hidden.

The text is written from the perspective of lack of sympathy for these people, probably because, by the time the text was written, there had been a rupture between Jews faithful to temple worship and the early Christians. But within the world of the literary text, one might not be totally unsympathetic to these people. It was not necessarily only the desire to retain status that prevented them from publicly acknowledging their allegiance to Jesus. They may also quite legitimately have considered important their allegiance as Jews to their religious identity, tradition, and authority. Whatever their motivation, Jesus would stretch the faith of believers in him even further. He taught that those who came to believe in him were actually believing in his Father, that he had been sent by the Father. Again, Jesus identifies himself as the light (cf. vv. 35-36).

Then Jesus says that he is not about judging but about saving. Those who reject what Jesus has taught, however, may be judged by the teaching itself. It is the word that the Father has sent Jesus to teach and it is the Father's commandment that is eternal life. A couple of chapters later in John's Gospel, we learn the content of that commandment: "As the Father has *loved* me, so I have *loved* you; abide in my *love*. If you keep my commandments, you will abide in my *love*, just as I have kept my Father's commandments and abide in His *love*. . . . This is my commandment, that you *love* one another as I have *loved* you. No one has greater *love* than this, to lay down one's life for one's friends" (John 15:9-13).

It is love that causes Jesus to accept suffering and death, and it is love that he requires from those who would believe in him. Some simply do not believe; some believe but are unwilling to be publicly identified with Jesus; worldly wisdom hinders their acceptance of the wisdom of God. Finally, there are those who do believe and whose faith propels them to accept Jesus' death as an act of love, to be willing to follow Jesus even to death as an act of love; their faith makes it unnecessary for them to separate themselves from a dying Messiah.

These are the categories of people this reading addresses; Jews and Greeks can be found in each category. In which category are we to be found? Where do we want to be found?

In the BCP alternate reading from Mark's Gospel, Jesus spends the day in Jerusalem. His declaration against turning the temple into a place of commerce combines the assertion in Isa. 56:7 that God's "house shall be called a house of prayer for all nations" with Jeremiah's condemnation of behaviors taking place in the temple that were not expressions of covenant faithfulness (Jeremiah 7).

The exilic or postexilic Isaian passage envisions all peoples recognizing the Jews' God. In the Jeremian passage, it is not the buying and selling of animals per se but hypocrisy, executing sacrifices as if the Israelites are practicing other behaviors consistent with faithfulness to God, that generates the condemnation. For Mark in this passage as for Matthew in its passion account, the chief priests and scribes experience Jesus as challenging their status and power as well as their control over the temple. If they could, they would kill him; they don't kill him only because they fear a backlash from the crowd. Here as elsewhere in passages we read this week, the supposed insiders are the problem. Jesus' theology, on the other hand, at least according to the author of Mark's Gospel, supports a more inclusive worshiping community.

The passage prompts me to ask myself how I behave when my power is threatened. How do I respond when (1) a woman is promoted and not I? (2) A person of color is promoted and not I? (3) A younger person exceeds my accomplishments? (4) I as an American experience that the United States no longer commands the respect it once did in the world? Do my sentiments resemble those of the chief priests and scribes? Must I participate in the Holy Week liturgies as one who would also like to kill Jesus, in fact, as one who does so all too often in my daily life?

> THE PASSAGE PROMPTS ME TO ASK MYSELF HOW I BEHAVE WHEN MY POWER IS THREATENED.

John's version of Jesus' betrayal by Judas contains several significant differences from the Matthean account that was read on Palm/Passion Sunday. John's version adds a comment about Jesus' reaction to what was about to take place: he "was deeply troubled" (13:21). Whereas the Matthean account has each of the disciples incredulous, wondering if he might be the betrayer, the Johannine version places "the disciple whom Jesus loved" and Peter in the forefront. Peter asks the beloved disciple to ask Jesus to reveal the traitor's identity. In the Matthean account, Jesus identifies his betrayer as "the one who has dipped his hand into the bowl with [him]" (26:23). In contrast, in today's reading, Jesus identifies his betrayer as "the one to whom I hand the morsel after I have dipped it" (13:26), the narrator then indicating that Jesus dipped the morsel and handed it to Judas. Only after Jesus had done this, as if giving permission for what would follow, did Satan enter into Judas.

In the Matthean account, Jesus then gives bread and wine to his disciples as his body and blood; the Johannine account omits these gestures. Rather, the bread is dipped and then given to the betrayer. In the Matthean account, there is no indication that Judas was not present when Jesus gave the disciples his body and blood; in the Johannine account, which lacks Jesus giving the disciples his body and blood, Judas leaves the supper immediately after Jesus identifies him. The scene in John then turns to Jesus' pronouncement that the Son of Man, that is, the one who stands in the place of all people, is now glorified and that God is glorified in him and that God will glorify him. Again, Jesus tells them, as he had alluded at the time of his anointing, that he will be with them only "a little while" longer (John 12:1-11).

I have deliberately pointed out the discrepancy in details between the Matthean and Johannine versions of Jesus' last supper not to discredit either account but to indicate that neither is intended by its author to be an eyewitness account with absolute accuracy of every detail. The details may serve literary or theological purposes and therefore be very important, but that the events happened exactly the way they are reported is impossible, since the two versions present variations and sometimes even contradict each other. Yet as we reflect together on the readings, we do pay attention to the details; the authors constructed the narrative purposefully so that we might enter into an experience of the event, that we might be present to it, and feel and act with its characters.

Just as Judas betrayed Jesus, the reading includes Peter denying Jesus. Jesus had been referring to his death as the place where his disciples could not come (13:33), but Peter, certain of his own commitment to Jesus, assures Jesus that he will even die for him. The passage is ironic. He who rashly protests ultimate allegiance does not even render verbal allegiance—and to a servant girl at that! Here, too, as with Judas, Jesus knows with whom he is dealing; he predicts Peter's denial.

As I read and reread the texts, I know that I am Judas; I often commit the sins that Jesus died to redeem. By doing so, I hand Jesus over to be crucified. I am also Peter; I am so confident that I am faithful that I often fall into having attitudes or doing things that I don't even realize are wrong until it's too late. Does this sound familiar to you?

MARCH 23, 2005

REVISED COMMON	EPISCOPAL (BCP)	ROMAN CATHOLIC
Isa. 50:4-9a	Isa. 50:4-9a	Isa. 50:4-9a
Psalm 70	Ps. 69:7-15, 22-23	Ps. 69:8-10, 21-22, 31 and 33-34
Heb. 12:1-3	Heb. 9:11-15, 24-28	
John 13:21-32	John 13:21-35 or Matt 26:1-5, 14-25	Matt. 26:14-25

FIRST READING
ISAIAH 50:4-9a (RCL, BCP, RC)

See the comments on the first reading for the Liturgy of the Passion, Sunday, March 20, 2005, above.

RESPONSIVE READING
PSALM 70 (RCL);
PSALM 69:7-15, 22-23 (BCP);
PSALM 69:8-10, 21-22, 31 and 33-34 (RC)

Psalm 70 asks God to provide deliverance and help for the petitioner and shame, confusion, and dishonor for those who would harm the petitioner. Identifying himself as poor and needy, the petitioner communicates a sense of urgency, asking God to hurry to his aid (vv. 1, 5). The psalmist also asks that joy and gladness become the lot of those who seek God.

Within the context of Holy Week, the psalm proclaims our awareness of our vulnerability, our need of God and our faith that help is to be found in the action of God on our behalf. As combined petition and praise, the psalmist articulates his hope that those who appreciate the saving action of God will express their recognition of God as great. The feeling of combined petition and praise may not be far from our own sentiments. We declare our need of God in the very declaration of our gratitude. We need Jesus' death and glorification that has brought—will bring, liturgically speaking—new life to us.

Psalm 69 sounds very much like a description of the Suffering Servant in Isaiah. The psalmist understands his suffering not as punishment for sin but as endured for the sake of God. Those who insult God insult him. His suffering has taken many forms: reproach and shame from others and alienation from his family. Zealous for God's dwelling place, that is, for God, he has practiced the behaviors of a penitent, fasting and donning sackcloth, but these behaviors have resulted not in his being admired but in his being insulted and becoming a byword, the subject of gossip and ridicule. He names his experience as "sinking in the mire," threatened by "deep waters," "the flood," "the deep," and "the Pit" (vv. 14, 15). The psalmist asks God to deliver him at an appropriate time. The request is based on the psalmist's confidence in God's *hesed* and faithful help.

> PSALM 69 SOUNDS VERY MUCH LIKE A DESCRIPTION OF THE SUFFERING SERVANT IN ISAIAH.

Identifying with Jesus during Holy Week (or any time) means a willingness to endure, for God's sake, suffering that is not associated with our sin but with the ridicule of those who would insult God. This is the wisdom of God that is not worldly wisdom (see comments on 1 Cor. 1:18-31, above).

Verse 21 of the psalm is most likely included because it contains the clause "for my thirst they gave me vinegar to drink." This phrase may have been what the author of Matthew's Gospel was alluding to when he wrote, "they offered him wine to drink, mixed with gall" (27:34) and " . . . one of them got a sponge, filled it with sour wine . . . and gave it to him to drink" (27:48). Matthew wants in every way possible to show that what Jesus did and said, what was done to him and said of him, fulfilled the Jews' scriptures.

The additional verses at the end of the Roman Catholic reading recall appropriate worship. Faithfulness, more than the sacrifice of animals, pleases God. In addition, the psalmist confirms that the God he worships hears the needy as well as those enslaved and deserves the praise of all creation.

SECOND READING
HEBREWS 12:1-3 (RCL);
HEBREWS 9:11-15, 24-28 (BCP)

On Heb. 12:1-3 and Heb. 9:11-15, see the comments for Monday of Holy Week, above.

Hebrews 9:24-28, continuing the comparison between a sin offering and Christ's crucifixion, contrast the sanctuary of the temple and the heavenly sanctuary into which Christ entered at his death. The temple's sanctuary is human-made; Christ entered into the presence of God. Whereas the high priest annually on the Feast of the Atonement offers a sacrifice for the people's sin (see Exod. 30:10), Christ's offering was once for all. He removed sin by sacrificing himself, dying once. When Christ appears a second time, it will be to save those who believe in him.

Not only does the author of Hebrews know the Old Testament well, but he places Jesus as a Jew squarely into one of most sacred rituals, the sin offering. The similarities are obvious, but the difference cannot be overestimated. Sin offerings are repeated at regular intervals, saying symbolically that sin is repeated. Jesus' sacrificial death, on the other hand, though repeated liturgically during Holy Week, took place only once; that was all that was needed. What it accomplished it accomplished forever, for the sake of those who lived before Jesus and for us who are living now. This is the source of our gratitude and of our confidence.

THE GOSPEL

JOHN 13:21-32 (RCL);
JOHN 13:21-35 (BCP);
MATTHEW 26:1-5, 14-25 (BCP alt.);
MATTHEW 26:14-25 (RC)

John 13:21-33, 36-38 is the Gospel reading used by the Roman Catholic community for Tuesday of Holy Week (see the comments there, above). However, the BCP includes vv. 34 and 35 in its reading for today, and they are worthy of note.

After Jesus declares that he is with them only a little longer, that they will seek him but that they cannot go to where he will be, he gives them a new commandment: "Love one another. Just as I have loved you, you also should love one another. By this everyone will know that you are my disciples, if you have love for one another," that is, if you do what I have done. The identification of the content of Jesus' commandment clarifies the reference made in John 12:49-50, in which Jesus identifies the commandment as his Father's and says that "his commandment is eternal life" (v. 50). (See the comment above on the BCP reading for Tuesday of Holy Week.)

Matthew 26:1-5 set the stage for what follows. Jesus identifies the Passover with his crucifixion and reminds his disciples of its proximity. Meantime the chief priests and elders meet with the high priest, Caiaphas, to plot together how to implement their intention to kill Jesus. As elsewhere (see the comments on Mark 11:15-19, above), they recognized the place Jesus held among the people and therefore, to diffuse the possibility of a riot, determined that they would not make their move during the holy days.

Matthew 26:14-25 constituted the first part of the reading used for the Liturgy of the Passion last Sunday, March 20, 2005 (see above). Again we read of Judas's betrayal of Jesus. For Roman Catholics, this is the third time this week that an account of Judas's betrayal has been read (see the comment for Wednesday on John 13:21-30, above).

MAUNDY THURSDAY/ HOLY THURSDAY

MARCH 24, 2005

REVISED COMMON	EPISCOPAL (BCP)	ROMAN CATHOLIC
Exod. 12:1-4, (5-10) 11-14	Exod. 12:1-14a	Exod. 12:1-8, 11-14
Ps. 116:1-2, 12-19	Ps. 78:14-20, 23-25	Ps. 116:12-13, 15-16bc, 17-18
1 Cor. 11:23-26	1 Cor. 11:23-26 (27-32)	1 Cor. 11:23-26
John 13:1-17, 31b-35	John 13:1-15 or Luke 22:14-30	John 13:1-15

FIRST READING
EXODUS 12:1-4, (5-10) 11-14 (RCL);
EXODUS 12:1-14a (BCP);
EXODUS 12:1-8, 11-14 (RC)

Exodus 12:1-14 describes how the Jewish feast of Passover is to be celebrated. Whether the passage is late in authorship, dated to the time of Israel's exile, or earlier is not nearly as important as its contents. The passage remembers, recalls, reenacts, and makes present the story of the Hebrews' definitive deliverance from bondage in Egypt. The event is to herald a new beginning; the time is to be understood as the first month, ushering in a new year. On the tenth day of the first month, each family or household is to take a one-year-old unblemished lamb or goat—or two families living in close proximity are to take one lamb together, if a lamb is too much for one family. They are to divide the lamb according to the number of people who will eat it, and on the fourteenth day of the month at twilight, they are to slaughter it, roast it, and eat it along with unleavened bread and bitter herbs. Some of the blood of the lamb is to be placed on the two doorposts and the lintel of the houses in which they will eat the lamb. No part of the lamb is to be eaten raw or boiled in water; the head, legs, and inner organs can be eaten. The entire lamb is to be eaten on the fourteenth day, that is, on the day it is slaughtered. If there are leftovers that are not consumed, they are not to be eaten the following day but are to be burned.

In describing how the lamb is to be eaten, the ritual provides that the Hebrews are to eat it quickly as if they are about to set out at any moment on a journey. They are to be dressed, shoes and all, with staff in hand.

The Lord then identifies the day and the ritual action as the Passover of the Lord, with the Lord passing over the houses where the lamb has been eaten, and where the blood has been smeared on the doorposts and the lintel. The other houses the Lord will not pass over; rather, God will strike down every firstborn, both human and animal, in those households. The blood, which to the people of Israel symbolized life, was to serve as the sign; where there was blood, the lives of the firstborn would be spared. The passage provides that this ritual should take place every year and that every year the Israelites should remember how the Lord delivered them.

> EARLY CHRISTIAN WRITERS SAW THE ACTION OF THE PASSOVER AS A TYPE OF JESUS' SAVING ACTION ON THE CROSS.

Early Christian writers saw the action of the Passover as a type of Jesus' saving action on the cross. Just as God delivered the Hebrews from bondage in Egypt by the shedding of the blood of the Passover lamb, Jesus is understood to be God's lamb who by the shedding of his blood delivers all people from the slavery of sin.

RESPONSIVE READING

PSALM 116:1-2, 12-19 (RCL);
PSALM 78:14-20, 23-25 (BCP);
PSALM 116:12-13, 15-16bc, 17-18 (RC)

In Psalm 116, a thanksgiving psalm, the author proclaims that the Lord has heard his pleading and his requests. The response of the psalmist to God's action on his behalf is love, gratitude, and fidelity. Rhetorically, he asks how he can repay the Lord for God's goodness. He will pray, and twice he professes that he will publicly make a vowed commitment to God (vv. 14, 18). He will be willing to die for God. The psalmist reiterates that God has liberated him, and that his response is to offer a sacrifice of thanksgiving and to pray to the Lord.

Jesus would have prayed this psalm. Identifying himself toward the end as possessing some of the qualities of those who had taken a Nazirite vow (see Numbers 6; Matt. 2:23; 26:29), Jesus also was willing to die and did die to fulfill God's will and effect our redemption. We whom God has liberated (liturgically, will liberate) should surely respond with thanksgiving and praise.

Psalm 78 narrates the exodus experience. Connected with the first reading, the psalm recalls the cloud that led the Hebrews through the desert by day and the pillar of fire that led them by night. The psalm then refers to the incident at Meribah

(Num. 20:11), where Moses brought water from a rock. Nevertheless, as the book of Numbers recounts in much greater detail, the people continued to sin. They demanded food and meat, questioning God's ability to provide for them though God had delivered them. The psalmist recounts how God provided what they requested, manna and food in abundance. Praising the action of God on Israel's behalf, the psalmist refers to God's gift in the desert as "the bread of angels" (v. 25).

God provides; the people have no reason to fear; yet they lack trust. Though they doubt, God takes care of them. Is this a pattern of behavior that we recognize, one that is all too common in our own lives? We have been definitively delivered, not from Egypt but from sin. God has provided for us, satisfying our needs and desires in a myriad of ways. Still, we complain.

SECOND READING
1 CORINTHIANS 11:23-26 (RCL, RC);
1 CORINTHIANS 11:23-26 (27-32) (BCP)

This reading, building on today's first reading from Exodus 12, provides Paul's version of Jesus' eating the Passover with his disciples. Paul identifies the evening as "the night when [Jesus] was betrayed" (v. 23) and then recounts how Jesus offered bread as his body that he would offer for them, and the cup (wine) as his blood that would effect the new covenant. Jesus instructed the disciples to reenact the ritual in memory of him and informed them that, whenever they did so, they would be proclaiming his death "until [he] comes" (v. 26). Moreover, Jesus taught that they must distinguish his body and blood in the eating and drinking of the bread and wine.

Distinguishing Jesus' body and blood is connected with judgment. Those who fail to distinguish Jesus' body and blood judge themselves. (One is reminded of John 12:47, commented on above, in which Jesus assures his followers that he does not judge them, though the word he speaks may.) Here Jesus tells his disciples that those who do distinguish the Lord's body and blood, the Lord does judge. Though the Lord disciplines them, God does not condemn them.

> TO EAT THE PASSOVER IS TO EAT THE PASSOVER LAMB; TO EAT THE BODY OF CHRIST IS TO EAT THE PASCHAL LAMB.

This reading is best understood within the larger context of chapter 11. According to Paul, the community does not always accord the Lord's body and blood sufficient reverence. Sometimes there is not sharing of food so that some are hungry; sometimes wine is drunk to excess (v. 21). Sometimes eating the bread or drinking the cup of the Lord is done in an unworthy manner (v. 27). These behaviors seem to constitute failing to distinguish the body and blood of the Lord, and those who behave in such a manner judge themselves. The others, though not perfect, may, when judged by the Lord, be in need of discipline, but they will not be condemned.

To eat the Passover is to eat the Passover lamb; to eat the body of Christ is to eat the Paschal lamb. On Holy Thursday, the bread-become-body is offered to us; on Good Friday, the body-become-lamb is sacrificed for us. "As often as [we] eat this bread and drink the cup [we] proclaim the Lord's death until he comes" (v. 26). This theology makes the celebration of the Eucharist central to our faith.

The Gospel
JOHN 13:1-17, 31b-35 (RCL);
JOHN 13:1-15 (BCP, RC);
LUKE 22:14-30 (BCP alt.)

Today's reading from the first verses of John 13 precedes yesterday's reading, vv. 21-32 or 35, from the BCP and RCL, respectively. This passage opens with an indication of timing: Jesus' "hour" (v. 1) is connected to the time shortly before the festival of the Passover. Again, reference is made to Jesus' love—love "to the end" (v. 1), that is, even to death. (Recall the irony between Peter's protest that he will die with Jesus, then his denial of Jesus, and Jesus' love because of which he does in fact die.) The devil (Satan, v. 27) has already put it into the heart of Judas to betray Jesus.

The passage details Jesus' washing of the disciples' feet. Peter emerges consistent with his character as presented in the passage in which he protests that he will never desert Jesus (Matt. 26:33, see comment above). He resists allowing Jesus to wash his feet. Jesus assures Peter that it is absolutely necessary that Peter allow him to wash his feet if Peter is to be allied with Jesus. This becomes clear a few lines later when Jesus tells his disciples that as he has washed their feet, they are to wash one other's feet. Just as he had told them to love one another as he had loved them (v. 34), here too they are to follow his example.

Washing feet, though a symbol for the service one was to offer the other, was, in fact, necessary activity for the sandal-clad feet that walked the sandy streets of Palestine. They were in need of cleansing. But just as Peter, symbolically, did not need to have his head and hands washed—Jesus' activity of foot-washing was symbolic—so one among them was, symbolically, not clean. In veiled language, Jesus was referring to Judas (cf. vv. 2).

Curiously enough, Jesus says the obvious—or what should be obvious. Servants are not greater than their master. This is not news to us who live in a hierarchical world. But would it have been possible for Jesus' disciples to forget this insight, since Jesus had provided them with an example of being master that was not hier-archical? Jesus assures them that they must be willing to wash feet, that is, they must be willing not just to serve but to be others' servants. He assures them, too, that they are not greater than he, the one who will send them when they become messengers. It's one thing to know this, but does one always put such knowledge into practice? Is not modern idolatry treating other things—money, material possessions, status, prestige, power—as more important than God? It seems so obvious that God is more important than these things, but we do not always behave accordingly.

Comments on the remainder of the passage can be found above at the BCP Gospel reading for Wednesday of Holy Week.

The hour to which John refers (v. 1, commented on immediately above) also opens the reading from Luke. A variation of the account of the celebration of the Eucharist found in 1 Cor. 11:23-26, today's second reading, this passage from Luke's Gospel combines the Passover with Jesus' suffering. Jesus declares that this is his last Passover until "it is fulfilled" (Luke 22:16) in the kingdom of God. What is fulfilled? The Father's will, that he should suffer and die for humankind's sin? The Passover, that he, as the sacrificial lamb (see the comments on Exodus 14, above), will enact in his body?

> JESUS ASSURES THEM THAT THEY MUST BE WILLING TO WASH FEET, THAT IS, THEY MUST BE WILLING NOT JUST TO SERVE BUT TO BE OTHERS' SERVANTS.

In this account, Jesus takes two cups of wine. When he asks the disciples to share the first cup among themselves, he identifies with the Nazirite who refrains from wine (see Numbers 6), proclaiming that he will not drink wine until the kingdom of God comes. He then gives bread to the disciples, identifies it as his body that will be given for them, and asks them to repeat the ritual gesture in his memory. The second cup of wine, taken after the meal, Jesus declares is the new covenant in his blood poured out for them. Just as covenants were cut in ancient Israel and described in the Old Testament by the pouring out of the blood of a sacrificed animal, Jesus here identifies with that animal. His own blood is about to be shed on our behalf.

Jesus then alerts his disciples to the presence of his betrayer but, using traditional prophetic language, warns the one who is his betrayer. A slight variant of the Matthean account, the disciples do not ask Jesus if they are the betrayer, but rather they discuss here among themselves who it might be.

Juxtaposed with uncertainty about which of them is the betrayer is a dispute over which of them is the greatest. Jesus uses the opportunity to challenge their aspirations; the text serves the same function, that is, it conveys the same message as John 13:16: the servant is not greater than his master or the messenger than the one who sent him. Jesus tells them that, unlike the kings of the Gentiles (recall the wisdom of the foolish, Tuesday of Holy Week's second reading, 1 Cor. 1:18-31), the greatest among them is to become like the youngest and the leader as one who serves (again, John 13:16, see above). Jesus then asks them rhetorically whether the one who is at table or the one who serves is the greater. Surely, according to worldly wisdom, the one who is at table is the greater. But Jesus points out his conformity to the wisdom of the foolish, the wisdom of God that confounds the wise: "I am among you as one who serves" (v. 27).

Jesus then expresses his love and appreciation for his disciples' loyalty. He confers on his disciples a kingdom, just as his Father had given him a kingdom (see vv. 16 and 18). Jesus promises that they will eat and drink in his kingdom and sit on thrones judging the twelve tribes of Israel. But Jesus' kingdom came through his death, and they are not to be like the kings of the Gentiles. Surely this is a different kind of kingdom!

Today's Gospel reading, whether from John or Luke, intends to record Jesus' last meal with his disciples. Though scholars are quick to point out the difference between the Synoptic Gospels' accounts of the institution of the Eucharist and its absence from John's Gospel, it is perhaps as important if not even more important to point out what is present in both of today's readings. Immediately before Jesus accepted his sufferings and death, he taught his disciples about power. Although he possesses power, being the teacher and Lord (John 13:13), the master (v. 16) and the one who sends the messengers (v. 16), he nevertheless, despite the protests of Peter, washed their feet; that is, he became their servant. And he told them explicitly that he had set them an example, that as he had done, they also should do (v. 15).

Luke's version emphasizes the same attitude. They are not to be like the kings of the Gentiles or even like those in authority who "lord it over" (v. 25) others. To the contrary, the greatest among them is to become like the youngest, and the leader like the one who serves. Jesus assures them that although Jesus is the greater, "the one who is at table" (v. 27), he is nevertheless like the one who serves those at table; he is among them as one who serves.

And I am back to the wisdom of God that is foolishness. Those who follow Jesus are not to covet the power of kings or masters or the great. They are to serve. They, like Jesus, are to give their lives in the service of others. Anything less shortchanges the events we liturgically reenact during Holy Week.

GOOD FRIDAY

MARCH 25, 2005

REVISED COMMON	EPISCOPAL (BCP)	ROMAN CATHOLIC
Isa. 52:13—53:12	Isa. 52:13—53:12 or Gen. 22:1-18 or Wisd. of Sol. 2:1, 12-24	Isa. 52:13—53:12
Psalm 22	Ps. 22:1-21 or 22:1-11 or 40:1-14 or 69:1-23	Ps. 31:2, 6, 12-13, 15-16, 17, 25
Heb. 10:16-25 or 4:14-16; 5:7-9	Heb. 10:1-25	Heb. 4:14-16; 5:7-9
John 18:1—19:42	John (18:1-40) 19:1-37	John 18:1—19:42

FIRST READING

ISAIAH 52:13—53:12 (RCL, BCP, RC);
GENESIS 22:1-18 (BCP alt.);
WISDOM OF SOLOMON 2:1, 12-24 (BCP alt.)

Today's reading is the longest of Second Isaiah's Suffering Servant poems, produced during the exile. Again, historians ask about the identity of the Servant whom the prophet describes. Is he an individual? Does he represent the people of Israel? Early Christian commentators understood the passage to be a description of Jesus who was "the Servant," and, within the context of this Good Friday liturgy, Jesus is unquestionably the Servant to which the passage refers.

A biography in poetry, the passage declares that "he will be exalted and lifted up" (52:13), terms used later by the author of John's Gospel to describe Jesus' death and resurrection. On the journey to his crucifixion, Jesus' appearance was certainly "marred" (v. 14). Recall the beating to which Pilate's soldiers subjected him. Yet his triumph, that is, Jesus' victory over death, "shall startle many nations" (v. 15) and bring kings to silence. Jesus reverses human expectations; the people see and contemplate the totally unexpected. There was nothing special about Jesus in his youth; he was simply the son of a carpenter from Nazareth. In fact, his lot was unenviable: "he was despised and rejected by many" (53:3). But what makes the

Servant different, what makes the passage resonate with the life, sufferings, and death of Jesus is that he bore *our* infirmities and carried *our* diseases; he was wounded for *our* transgressions, crushed for *our* infirmities, the punishment he underwent benefited *us*, his bruises healed *us*.

The passage then describes human sinfulness: we are like sheep that go astray; in contrast he is like a lamb that is led to the slaughter. Recall the Passover lamb of Exodus 12. He was sacrificed not because he deserved it; in fact, to sacrifice that lamb was unjust, a perversion of justice. Although he was innocent, it was the will of the Lord to crush him with pain. Recall the garden scene in which Jesus accepts the Father's will.

WHAT MAKES THE SERVANT DIFFERENT, WHAT MAKES THE PASSAGE RESONATE WITH THE LIFE, SUFFERINGS, AND DEATH OF JESUS IS THAT HE BORE OUR INFIRMITIES AND CARRIED OUR DISEASES.

But for the Servant, as for Jesus, suffering and death are not the final word. He shall be blessed by God. In ancient Israel blessings from God meant a long life and many progeny. Reading the text from a Christian perspective, the blessing Jesus received from God included his resurrection and exaltation.

Through him the will of God shall prosper; he himself shall find light and satisfaction. Moreover, the Servant, now described as "the righteous one" (v. 11), will make many righteous. Not only is his suffering vicarious, so also is the sin he bears. Because the Servant was willing to die, to be thought a wrongdoer, he shall be vindicated.

The poem speaks of taking on the sins of others and their sufferings; it speaks of being rejected and an object of scorn, but it also speaks of eventual vindication. The sheep went astray; the lamb did not object to being sacrificed. Whoever the ancient writer meant to describe, it is an accurate portrayal of the life of Jesus.

Genesis 22:1-18 appears as an alternate BCP reading for Good Friday. Because it is an integral part of the Easter Vigil, it is commented on below.

Finally, calling on a reading from the deuterocanonical books of the Old Testament, the BCP proposes yet another alternative passage. The reading from the book of Wisdom deals explicitly with death as the end and the intention of evil men to put the righteous to death. Reading the text, one recalls the scene in Pilate's house. Clearly Jesus is not deserving of death, and yet his very righteousness makes those who are jealous of him seek his life. In this passage, the wicked clearly misunderstand the intent of God: God created us for incorruption and made us in the image of his own nature. Death entered the world through the devil's envy, and those who are envious experience death.

PSALM 22 (RCL);
PSALM 22:1-21 or 22:1-11 (BCP);
PSALM 40:1-14 (BCP alt.);
PSALM 69:1-23 (BCP alt.);
PSALM 31:2, 6, 12-13, 15-16, 17, 25 (RC)

The first twenty-one verses of Psalm 22 appear as an alternative response in the BCP Liturgy of the Word on Palm/Passion Sunday and are therefore commented on above. The psalm, however, contains thirty-one verses. The first part of the psalm expresses a lament and calls on God for deliverance. In these latter verses, the psalmist, certain that the help sought will be forthcoming, praises God, promises to praise God publicly, and calls others to praise God. He declares how God heard the prayer of the afflicted and responded. The psalmist is certain of God's benevolence to the poor. God is the God of all nations whom all peoples, including those who have died and those yet to be born, shall praise.

The strength of the psalm lies in its ability to convey the depth of the psalmist's pain in its first verses, the intensity with which the psalmist calls to God for deliverance, and the conviction that praise, from everyone everywhere is fitting for God who has heard the psalmist's prayer.

The psalm is appropriate as a response on Good Friday because of its intensity. Jesus calls out to God, naming his pain, asking for God's support, and praising God for the victory he knows is certain.

Psalm 40 is one of praise and thanksgiving, filled with declarations of the Lord's goodness. The Lord delivered the psalmist who is grateful. Those who put their trust in God rather than in the arrogant or in idols are far better off; nothing can compare with the wondrous and innumerable deeds of God. God is not interested in sacrificial offerings but in the one who listens and responds and does God's will. The psalmist declares how he has proclaimed God's goodness and then asks God to continue protecting him, extending steadfast love (*hesed*) and faithfulness. Even now the psalmist feels burdened but asks God to deliver him and to keep in check those who would harm him. This is the prayer of a person of faith who looks to God with confidence and gratitude.

Verses 7-15 and 21-23 of Psalm 69 are included in alternative readings for Wednesday of Holy Week. This alternative reading includes the first twenty-three verses of the psalm. The psalm opens with a description of the experience of the psalmist. He uses the symbol of water to depict his suffering. He is drowning; he is being swallowed up by quicksand; a flood of deep waters is sweeping over him

(vv. 1, 2). He is exhausted from calling for help; he is feeling overwhelmed by the number of his enemies, by those who slander him (vv. 3, 4). Still, he admits that he is not faultless and God knows his wrongdoing (v. 5).

The psalmist does not want his behavior to result in shame or dishonor to those who seek God and hope in God (vv. 5, 6).

The psalmist continues his petition, asking God to hear his prayer. He counts on God because of God's *hesed* (steadfast love) and God's abundant mercy. He prays: draw near to me, redeem me, save me (vv. 16-18). He then returns to expressions of his pain: he receives insults and is the object of shame and dishonor at the hands of his enemies. He is alone without human support (vv. 19, 20). The final half of v. 20, that he looked for comforters but found none, evokes a line repeated often in the book of Lamentations (1:2, 9, 16, 17, 21). There the narrator describes the widow Jerusalem during the exile. This psalm then like many others may originally have been written by a psalmist but prayed not so much by an individual as by the collective people Israel. Whoever the suppliant, the psalm pours out to God the suppliant's pain.

> ANY OF THESE PSALMS IS APPROPRIATE FOR HOLY WEEK, BECAUSE THEY ALL NAME SOME SORT OF SUFFERING AND DECLARE WITH CONFIDENCE THAT GOD WILL DELIVER THE SUFFERER.

Psalm 31 opens with a prayer of petition: hear me and rescue me; be a source of strength for me. The petitioner identifies himself as one who trusts in the Lord, not one who worships idols. The speaker then goes on to tell God how he experiences his life as threatened by enemies. Alluding to God's *hesed*, the psalmist repeats the request: deliver me; save me.

Any of these psalms is appropriate for Holy Week, because they all name some sort of suffering and declare with confidence that God will deliver the sufferer. They were appropriate to their own historical context; they are also appropriate here during Holy Week, read liturgically, as Jesus' prayer, and prayed now also by us. We are knowledgeable of our sin, but we also are confident of God's deliverance of us from sin through the death and resurrection of Jesus.

SECOND READING

HEBREWS 10:16–25 (RCL);
HEBREWS 10:1–25 (BCP);
HEBREWS 4:14–16; 5:7–9 (BCP, RCL, RC)

Hebrews 10 opens with a description of Jewish sacrificial practices; they must be repeated year after year because they are not lastingly effective. For the author, bulls and goats are incapable of removing sin. Christ, on the other hand,

came to do God's will (cf. the garden, Matt. 26:42). The offering of the body of
Jesus Christ once for all, in fulfillment of God's will, is what has sanctified us.
Christ sits now at God's right hand; his enemies will become his footstool.

Jeremiah 31:31, dated to Judah's exile, promises a new covenant. Understood
in the late sixth century B.C.E. as a promise of return and restoration to Judah from
Babylon, the law is now internalized, and the sins and offenses that led to the exile
are eliminated.

The verse, inserted into this passage, refers to the new covenant in Jesus' blood,
by which sin is forgiven. There is no need
to have additional sin offerings, because our
sin has been forgiven once and for all. For
this author, the blood of Jesus allows us to
enter into the sanctuary through the cur-
tain, a reference to the temple's Holy of Holies in which was the Ark of the
Covenant (Exod. 26:33), and into which only priests could enter (1 Kings 8:6).
Christ has become our high priest.

> WE ARE PRODDED TO ENCOURAGE ONE ANOTHER TO
> ACT IN LOVING WAYS, TO DO GOOD DEEDS, AND TO
> MEET TOGETHER FOR MUTUAL SUPPORT.

Reminiscent of selected psalms, we are encouraged to have confidence and to
remain steadfast in our faith. Further, we are prodded to encourage one another
to act in loving ways, to do good deeds, and to meet together for mutual support.
The future holds the "Day," a term used by several of the prophets to refer to the
advent of God. We anticipate with increasing eagerness the union to come.

Hebrews 4:14-16; 5:7-9 identify Christ as high priest. But Christ is not only a
high priest (just as he is not only the sacrificial victim). Here he is described as
being like us: he can sympathize with our weakness, and he was tested like we are.
Though he is different from us—he is without sin—we are encouraged to
approach him so that we may receive mercy and help.

Jesus prayed to his Father and his prayer was heard. He obeyed his Father's will,
suffered, and was made perfect through his suffering, so that he has become the
source of salvation for all who obey him. We accept this truth in faith, and it
becomes the consolation of Good Friday.

THE GOSPEL
JOHN 18:1—19:42 (RCL, RC);
JOHN (18:1-40) 19:1-37 (BCP)

The reading begins with Jesus going to the garden. John's version of the
story omits Jesus' prayer to the Father. Judas also knows the place and goes to the
garden—with a detachment of soldiers and police from the chief priests and
the Pharisees.

Jesus asks them a rhetorical question, "Whom are you looking for?" (v. 4). They answer, "Jesus of Nazareth" (v. 5), and Jesus acknowledges that is who he is. Their response is illogical: they step back and fall to the ground. This is hardly the expected behavior of those who had come to arrest "Jesus of Nazareth."

Jesus asks the rhetorical question a second time: "Whom are you looking for?" (v. 7), and they respond again as they did the first time. Jesus says that he already told them that he is Jesus. He then expresses concern about the well-being of his disciples. Peter, not identified by name in Matthew's account (read on Passion Sunday), then cuts off the right ear, identified in Matthew's account simply as an ear, of the high priest's slave, Malchus (unnamed in the Matthean account). Jesus tells Peter with a third rhetorical question that he is to drink the cup his Father has given him.

In contrast to the Matthean account, Jesus is taken to Annas, the father-in-law of the high priest, Caiaphas, and Caiaphas is identified here, but not in the Matthean account, as the one who alerted the Jews that it was better to have one person die for the people.

John's account records another disciple, thought to be John himself, accompanying Peter. Both follow Jesus. The other disciple was known to Caiaphas and entered the courtyard with Jesus, while Peter stood outside at the gate. The disciple intervened with the gatekeeper so that Peter was able to come inside. The gatekeeper asked Peter, with a negative question—"you aren't, are you?" (v. 17), that is, whether or not he was one of Jesus' disciples. Peter said no.

The scene then moves to where Jesus is being questioned. Asked about his preaching, Jesus replied in his defense that there was nothing secretive about it, that he had taught openly in the synagogues and the temple, and that those who had heard him could speak to the content of his preaching. This self-confident response triggered the anger of a policeman who struck Jesus, but Jesus defended himself. What wrong had he done? But if he had done no wrong, why was he struck? In John's account, it is at this point that Jesus is taken to Caiaphas.

While Jesus' interrogation was taking place, Peter was warming himself by a fire with the slaves and the police. They asked him the same question the gatekeeper had asked and in the same manner. Again Peter said no. This occasioned a third question from one of the relatives of Malchus, about whether or not Peter was in the garden with Jesus. A third time Peter said no. And then the cock crowed, a reference to John 13:38, Jesus' prediction that Peter would deny him three times before a cock crowed. (Roman Catholics read the passage containing John 13:38 on Tuesday of Holy Week.)

Jesus is then taken from Caiaphas to Pilate. In the Johannine account, the narrative does not develop while Jesus is with Caiaphas; he simply is taken from Annas, to Caiaphas, to Pilate. Perhaps the detail of Jesus' being led to three officials, three being a symbolic number for completion, is intended to indicate that Jesus came progressively from one official to the next, each one more important than the last. Finally, Jesus appeared before Pilate, the governor. He alone of the three had the power to put Jesus to death.

Those who had brought Jesus to Pilate are described as being very conscientious about ritual purification; they do not enter Pilate's house lest they become contaminated and be prevented from eating the Passover. Pilate, an outsider to the Jews, therefore goes outside to them and asks what Jesus has done wrong. Their answer begs the question. Instead of naming a crime of which Jesus was guilty, they, ironically, appeal to their own credibility: would they, after all, have handed Jesus over to Pilate if he were not a criminal? Pilate directs the people to deal with Jesus themselves. They respond, however, that they are unable to put anyone to death and they want Jesus to be put to death.

Pilate went inside and asked Jesus if he was the king of the Jews. Jesus' answer, like the crowd's answer to Pilate, sidesteps Pilate's question. Jesus asks if Pilate is asking the question on his own or because of what he has heard from others (cf. John 12:13).

Jesus' question seems to exasperate Pilate. He is not a Jew; it is the Jews who are condemning Jesus. Pilate wants to know what Jesus has done that might possibly be deserving of death. Jesus answers that his kingdom is not of this world and explains that that is the reason why his followers are not here trying to prevent his being handed over to the Jews. Pilate concludes that Jesus has admitted to being a king. Jesus concurs, saying that he has been sent to testify to the truth, to which Pilate asks, "What is truth?"

(John 18:33-37, the part of today's reading wherein Pilate questions Jesus about being king of the Jews, is used as the Gospel reading for the Feast of Christ the King, year B. I include this information here because the content of the verses, placed within their larger literary context,

THE GUILTY IS SET FREE; THE INNOCENT CONDEMNED.

move Jesus closer to death. The liturgical celebration of the Feast of Christ the King may emphasize Jesus' power, that is, his power to destroy death and therefore his victory and exaltation. However, the king of the Jews is, first of all, a king who accepts to be crucified, as this reading for Good Friday makes clear.)

The encounter between Jesus and Pilate convinced Pilate that Jesus was innocent. He therefore proceeded to go outside to tell the Jews his findings. Appealing to the Jews' custom that a prisoner be released at Passover, Pilate offered to release Jesus. They replied, calling instead for the release of the bandit Barabbas. The guilty is set free; the innocent condemned.

Pilate then orders that Jesus be flogged. John's report of Jesus' flogging is more succinct than the Matthean account. The crown of thorns, the purple robe, and the taunt "Hail, King of the Jews" (19:3) are recorded but with little drama. A few details are added: they struck Jesus on the face; Pilate, after declaring that he could not identify the man's crime, brought Jesus out to the people, wearing the crown of thorns and the purple robe. The chief priests and police wanted him crucified, but Pilate asserted yet again that he could not identify the man's crime.

The Jews then told Pilate that, according to their law, Jesus was guilty of a crime punishable by death because he had claimed to be the Son of God. This information concerned Pilate who then asked Jesus where he was from. Jesus didn't answer (see Matt. 27:14, where Jesus gives Pilate no answer to the accusations made against him). Whereas in the Matthean account, Jesus' seemingly impertinent answer caused Pilate, to be amazed, here his failure to answer causes Pilate to remind Jesus of Pilate's power over life and death. Jesus calmly and confidently responds, however, that the source of Pilate's power is "from above" and that Judas has the greater culpability (19:11).

Pilate, who has found "no cause against him" (19: 4, 6), from that point on wants to release him. The chief priests and police continue to press their point that Jesus deserves to be crucified and even intimate Pilate's disloyalty to Caesar if he does not authorize the crucifixion, since anyone claiming to be king challenges Caesar's authority.

A dramatic dialogue ensues. Pilate brings Jesus out and presents him to the Jews; they demand his crucifixion. Pilate asks, "Shall I crucify your king?" (19:15). The chief priests respond that they have no king, only the emperor. Pilate apparently recognizes that his behavior, if he doesn't allow Jesus to be crucified, may well be interpreted as disloyalty to the emperor. On the other hand, the Jews have proved their loyalty by demanding Jesus' crucifixion. Pilate responds by handing Jesus over to the people.

In contrast to the Matthean account in which Simon of Cyrene carries Jesus' cross (Matt. 27:32), here the point is made that Jesus carried his own cross. At the "place of the skull," a place likely named for the deaths of those crucified there, Jesus was crucified between two others.

Pilate had the inscription "Jesus of Nazareth, King of the Jews" (19:19) put on the cross, written in Hebrew, Latin, and Greek, clearly intending that the inscription be intelligible to all. When the Jews asked that the inscription be changed and that it be replaced by one that undercut Jesus' identity, Pilate refused.

Four soldiers crucified Jesus. Four, like three, is a symbolic number, signifying fullness or completion. The soldiers divided up Jesus' clothing except for his seamless tunic; for that they cast lots. The author explicitly identifies this detail as fulfilling v. 8 of Psalm 22. This, then, is not an unconnected single man's crucifixion; this death builds on and completes the promises and the contents of the Old Testament.

John, again in contrast to the Matthean account, in which three women are standing at a distance, portrays three women (all named Mary) near the cross. Just as the account after the garden depicts the disciple whom Jesus loved following after Jesus with Peter, here, also in contrast to Matthew's version, the disciple whom Jesus loved emerges. He is standing beside Jesus' mother and causes Jesus to address Mary, entrusting to her the beloved disciple, and to address the beloved disciple, entrusting his mother to him. Jesus, dying, provides for the well-being of his mother who, lacking a husband and now a son, would be destitute. The beloved disciple "from that hour" (19:27) takes Mary into his home. Jesus is a good Jew. The gesture recalls the Levirate practice, according to which the closest of kin of a dead husband claims and provides for the dead man's wife. Jesus' beloved disciple claims and provides for the dead man's mother.

The Gospel, resonating here with Matthew's account, details Jesus' request for wine (Jesus accepted the offer of wine in Matthew), identifying it here, as in Matthew, with the fulfillment of the scriptures. Finally, declaring that he had accomplished the Father's will, Jesus dies.

Jesus is distinguished from the two men who die with him. Since he is already dead, they do not break Jesus' legs; instead, they pierce his side. The Gospel tells us yet again that this happened to connect Jesus' death with the Jewish scriptures, indicating that none of his bones were broken (Exod. 12:46) and that they had pierced him (Zech. 12:10).

Joseph of Arimathea, here as in Matthew, identified as a secret disciple of Jesus, requested and received Jesus' body. John adds Nicodemus (see John 3), one of the disciples who, like Joseph, had come to Jesus secretly. Nicodemus provides the myrrh and aloes for Jesus' anointing according to Jewish custom. In contrast to the Matthean account, according to which they lay Jesus' body in Joseph's new tomb, here they lay Jesus' body in a new tomb that was in a garden near where Jesus was crucified. In both accounts, because Jesus' death took place so close to Passover, they were anxious to have the bodies removed from their respective crosses and buried.

THE WOMEN, THE LOW ONES ON THE SOCIAL SCALE, ARE PRESENT IN BOTH ACCOUNTS OF JESUS' PASSION READ THIS YEAR. THE WOMEN STAY WITH JESUS TO THE END.

I can't help but notice that Peter, who so vehemently declared that he would defend Jesus to the death, is nowhere to be found. Three women, along with Joseph of Arimathea, play prominently; Nicodemus is added in John's account. Most of the disciples and apostles whom one might expect to be loyal and to be with Jesus through his sufferings and death, given their place in relation to Jesus in the rest of the Gospels, were nowhere to be found. Rather, those who had first been fearful of identifying with Jesus, who recognized the risks and the cost, now came forward. And the women, the low ones on the social scale, are present in both accounts of Jesus' passion read this year. The women stay with Jesus to the end.

The Gospel reading for Good Friday ends with Jesus' burial. He is in the tomb, and not until the vigil of Easter will the light dawn and the resurrection triumph. We are left to feel what our sins cost; there is time between now and the Easter Vigil, time to experience Jesus in the grave, time to mourn, time to grieve, time to repent. Even as we believe that this is not the end, we believe that Jesus' death is a tragedy, a tragedy caused by our sins. Greater love than this has no one, than to lay down one's life for a friend. We should never forget, no matter how rough the going gets, that we are greatly loved. Jesus loved us to the end, and that love empowers us to love one another and to know for certain that resurrection and new life are just around the corner.

THE GREAT VIGIL OF EASTER / HOLY SATURDAY

MARCH 26, 2005

REVISED COMMON	EPISCOPAL (BCP) *Service of Readings*	ROMAN CATHOLIC
Gen. 1:1—2:4a	Gen. 1:1—2:2	Gen. 1:1—2:2 or Gen. 1:1, 26-31a
Gen. 7:1-5, 11-18; 8:6-18; 9:8-13	Gen. 7:1-5, 11-18; 8:6-18; 9:8-13	
Gen. 22:1-18	Gen. 22:1-18	Gen. 22:1-18 or Gen 22:1-2, 9a, 10-13, 15-18
Exod. 14:10-31; 15:20-21	Exod. 14:10—15:1	Exod. 14:15—15:1
	Isa. 4:2-6	Isa. 54:5-14
Isa. 55:1-11	Isa. 55:1-11	Isa. 55:1-11
Prov. 8:1-8, 19-21; 9:4b-6 or Bar. 3:9-15, 32—4:4		Bar. 3:9-15, 32—4:4
Ezek. 36:24-28	Ezek. 36:24-28	Ezek. 36:16-17a, 18-28
Ezek. 37:1-14	Ezek. 37:1-14	
Zeph. 3:14-20	Zeph. 3:12-20	
Lutheran lectionary adds:		
Jon. 3:1-10		
Deut. 31:19-30		
Dan. 3:1-29		
New Testament Reading		
Rom. 6:3-11	Rom. 6:3-11	Rom. 6:3-11
The Psalm		
Psalm 114	Psalm 114	Ps.118:1-2, 16-17, 22-23
The Gospel		
Matt. 28:1-10	Matt 28:1-10	Matt. 28:1-10

At the Easter Vigil service, which in many churches is held at midnight, or at least after dark, the community begins in darkness, but the darkness is transformed into light. Darkness symbolizes death, the bosom of the earth, the tomb, while light nourishes life. We who are sinners, who have walked in darkness, receive now the light and life that Jesus' death and resurrection make possible. Participating in an Easter Vigil service is a public proclamation that we reject sin, that we, with Christ, have died to sin, and that, through Jesus' triumph over sin and death, we have been born to new life.

SERVICE OF READINGS
GENESIS 1:1—2:4a (RCL);
GENESIS 1:1—2:2 (BCP, RC);
GENESIS 1:1, 26-31a (RC alt.)

Genesis: in the beginning. God is the source of everything: the heavens, the earth, the darkness, the wind, the waters. When God speaks, His word is effective; that which God says is accomplished. God creates light/day and separates it from darkness/night. God creates a dome to separate the waters and calls the dome sky. God creates the dry land/earth that puts forth vegetation; God separates the dry land from the waters under the dome/seas.

> PARTICIPATING IN AN EASTER VIGIL SERVICE IS A PUBLIC PROCLAMATION THAT WE REJECT SIN, THAT WE, WITH CHRIST, HAVE DIED TO SIN, AND THAT, THROUGH JESUS' TRIUMPH OVER SIN AND DEATH, WE HAVE BEEN BORN TO NEW LIFE.

God creates light in the sky, the sun, the moon, and the stars. These determine days and seasons and years. God creates swarms of living creatures in the seas and birds in the sky; God orders them to multiply. God also creates earth's living creatures, including humankind, and orders them to multiply. Humankind is to fill the earth and have dominion over it and over all that is in it. To all humans, and to beasts, birds, and all living things, God gives plants for food. When God has created all that is, God rests. In six days, God created, and on the seventh day, God rested.

For the believing community that celebrates this liturgy, God is the source of all that is, the Alpha. Somehow all creation owes its existence to God, the source of life. Beginning the Easter Vigil celebration with this reminder provides a context. Jesus, by his death and resurrection, becomes the source of new life, the source of the fullness of life. Easter is a new creation.

GENESIS 7:1-5, 11-18; 8:6-18; 9:8-13 (RCL, BCP)

Because of humankind's sinfulness, God directs righteous Noah to build an ark and in it to preserve himself and his family and representatives of all the species of God's creation (male and female) from the devastation of a flood, so that eventually they can reproduce and repopulate the earth. Noah has seven days' warning, and the flood lasts forty days. Both numbers are symbolic and signify completion. Noah had sufficient time to build the ark, and the flood had sufficient time to destroy the earth. At the end of the time for preparation, the rain began. At the end of the time for the flood, the rain stopped.

At the end of "forty days," Noah sent out a raven; it didn't return to the ark, but that wasn't a firm indication that the waters had subsided. Noah sent out a dove, but it returned to the ark; it found no place to land. Seven days later, Noah sent the dove out again; it returned again, but this time it brought an olive branch. Seven days later, Noah sent the dove out a third time—three is also a symbolic number signifying completion. This time the dove did not return.

The first year after six hundred years, the first month of that year, the first day of that month, the waters were dried up from the earth. Approximately two months later, the earth was dry and God instructed Noah to leave the ark, along with his family and all the other living things he had brought into the ark. God directed that they reproduce.

God then made a covenant, not just with Noah and his family, but also with all of the living creatures that had come out of the ark. God promised never again to destroy the earth with a flood. God set a rainbow in the sky as a sign of this covenant that God had made with all of creation.

Just as Gen.1:1—2:4a, the account of creation produced during Israel's exile, says in stylized fashion that God is the source of life, so Noah's story confirms the Genesis creation account. However, in this version of creation, there has already been the rejection of God that is sin. Whereas sin leads to death, righteousness leads to life. God creates again; the episode anticipates Easter as a new creation.

GENESIS 22:1-18 (RC, RCL, BCP); GENESIS 22:1-2, 9a, 10-13, 15-18 (RC alt.)

God tested Abraham, as God would later allow Satan to test Job. Would Abraham be willing to sacrifice his beloved son, the one whom God had promised would be Abraham's heir, the one whom God, overcoming a seemingly insurmountable obstacle, allowed Sarah to conceive in her old age? Just how much faith and trust in God did Abraham have to do what must have seemed irrational and counterproductive?

When God called Abraham, Abraham answered, "Here I am," the same words that Samuel would later answer to God's call (1 Sam. 3:4). God directed Abraham to offer his son as a burnt offering on a mountain that God would show him. The passage recalls Gen. 12:1, when God promised to take Abraham to the land he would show him. Similar to Abraham's response at that time, not knowing the future, he set out to obey God. The next morning, Abraham saddled a donkey, took two young men and his own son, cut wood for the sacrifice, and proceeded toward the place God would show him. On the third day, Abraham saw the place in the distance. Recall that three is a symbolic number signifying completion; recall also that, in last Sunday's Gospel reading, Jesus was accused of saying that he could rebuild the temple in three days; recall also that Jonah was enclosed within the belly of a fish for three days. When sufficient time has passed, a new phase or stage begins.

Abraham directed the young men to stay at a distance with the donkey. Recall Jesus telling Peter, James, and John in the garden to stay at a slight distance from where Jesus would go to pray (Matt. 26:37–38), and recall also that the priests proceeded only so far up the mountain with Moses (Exod. 24:1–2). Abraham, leaving the two young men behind and carrying the fire and the knife, went with Isaac, who carried the wood for the burnt offering.

> RECALL THAT THREE IS A SYMBOLIC NUMBER SIGNI-FYING COMPLETION.

When Isaac called to his father, Abraham replied with the same words he had used to respond to God: "Here I am." At this point, Isaac asked his father where the lamb was that should constitute their offering. Abraham responded that God would provide the lamb. For those who know the narrative, Abraham's answer is reminiscent of Deborah's to Barak; the narrative turns out differently from what is implied. Whereas Barak is led to conclude that the enemy will fall to Deborah, another female emerges as victor (Judg. 4:9). Here, Abraham thinks that God intends Isaac to be the offering, but the narrative will reveal another lamb.

Abraham bound his son and placed him on the wood that had already been placed on the altar. When Abraham was about to strike Isaac with the knife, the angel of the Lord called to Abraham from heaven. For a third time in this literary unit, Abraham answered, "Here I am." This time the command would reverse God's original direction: Don't harm the boy; you have shown fear of God. You hold God in awe and you reverence God. This is clear from you not having withheld your son. Though Abraham had been willing to comply with the directive of God, he was not required to do so.

Because God provided a lamb/ram for the burnt offering, Abraham named the site, "The LORD will provide"; "on the mount of the LORD it shall be provided." The angel of the Lord who had told Abraham not to harm Isaac called again from heaven, reiterating God's acknowledgment of Abraham's willingness not to withhold from God even his only son. The angel confirms that because of Abraham's obedience, he will be blessed with progeny and with security, and that other nations will receive blessings because of their association with his descendants.

The narrative evokes many connections to the account of Jesus' passion. (1) Isaac is identified as his father's only son, the beloved son. (For the purposes of this narrative, Ishmael recedes; he is not the heir.) (2) Isaac becomes the lamb about to be sacrificed. Jesus becomes the Paschal lamb, the Lamb of God, by whose death sin is overcome and freedom achieved. (3) Abraham conforms his behavior to the will of God, as Jesus does, even (in Abraham's case, "almost") to the point of death.

EXODUS 14:10-31; 15:20-21 (RCL)

The narrative begins with fear and blame. Because the Israelites fear the advancing Egyptians, they blame Moses for leading their escape. Any hesitation they may have had risking the unknown comes to the fore. Moses reassures them with words that will later be used by God to Joshua and then by Joshua to the people: "Do not be afraid, stand firm." The Lord will accomplish your deliverance today; the Lord will fight for you. Let it unfold. In other words, "Hang in there and trust God."

Just as the people had questioned Moses, blaming him for getting them into what they perceived as a precarious situation, and he had responded with assurance, the Lord responds in somewhat the same way to Moses. God asks Moses, "What's your problem?" and then tells Moses what to do. The Israelites are to continue on course; Moses is to divide the sea by raising his staff with his hand outstretched over it. This will result in the Israelites being able to pass through the sea on the dry land that has been created between the waters. Meantime, God tells Moses that he will harden the Egyptians' hearts so that they will follow after the Israelites. Recall that God had hardened the Pharaoh's heart several times so that he changed his mind and prevented the Hebrews from leaving Egypt (Exod. 8:15, 32). Now the "hardening of the heart" will allow the enemy to pursue—but the goal of impeding the Egyptians is the same. The angel of God and the pillar of cloud went from in front of the Israelites to behind them, separating the Israelites from the pursuing Egyptians.

The narrative records that events unfolded as God had told Moses. The Egyptians realized too late what was happening. They fell into a panic and tried to flee because they realized that the Lord was fighting for the Hebrews against them.

At this point the Lord gave Moses a second directive. Again he was to stretch out his hand over the sea; this time the separated waters would flow together. Again the narrative records that events unfolded as God had told Moses. Pharaoh's entire army, which had followed the Israelites into the sea, was destroyed.

THE WATER PROVES TO BE LIFE-GIVING FOR THE HEBREWS AS IS THE WATER OF BAPTISM BY WHICH WE DIE TO SIN AND RISE TO NEW LIFE WITH CHRIST.

The contrast is stark. The Israelites were protected by separated waters and were saved; the Egyptians who were pursuing the Israelites were drowned when the waters came together. God's work against the Egyptians inspired the Hebrews to fear God and to have faith in both God and Moses. Moses' sister, Miriam, recognizing God's victory over Israel's enemies, began a victory song that gave God the credit for the victory: the Lord destroyed Israel's enemies and triumphed.

Why is this reading appropriate tonight? God delivers the Hebrews from Egyptian bondage to freedom; Christ, by his death and resurrection, delivers us from the bondage of sin to the freedom of the children of God. The water proves to be life-giving for the Hebrews as is the water of baptism by which we die to sin and rise to new life with Christ.

EXODUS 14:10—15:1 (RC, BCP)

Whereas the RCL combines the texts so that Miriam and the women lead the victory song (15:20-21), the BCP and RC versions of this reading proceed in sequence, according to which it is Moses and the Israelites who sing the song. Feminist exegetes posit that the original version of the text had the women leading the victory song, partly because of women's singing in ritual celebrations elsewhere in the Old Testament, but that a later redactor, wishing to strengthen Moses' authority, accorded him the leadership role. Recall the women chanting, "Saul has killed his thousands, and David his ten thousands" (1 Sam. 18:7, 8); or Deborah's victory song (Judg. 5:1).

ISAIAH 4:2-6 (BCP)

Who or what is the "branch of the LORD"? Is it the extension of "God's holy arm," that is, God's strength? The prophet looks forward to a time of purification and restoration. At that time the survivors of the exile will be proud of the land's produce. The imagery is reminiscent of the exodus when a pillar of cloud led the Israelites by day and a pillar of fire by night . In this passage, the Lord will create over the whole site of Mount Zion and over its places of assembly, that is, over the temple, a cloud by day and smoke and the shining of a flaming fire by night.

The Lord had provided presence and protection for the Hebrews as they traveled through the desert, including protection from the potentially threatening aspects of nature. The imagery identifies the potentially threatening aspects of nature as heat, storm, and rain. Here the Lord will provide protection from all that is threatening and potentially harmful.

Assertions of God's presence and protection, at the time of the Hebrews' deliverance from Egypt and at the time of their deliverance from exile, are consistent with the meaning of the events reenacted during Holy Week. The community of believers professes its faith in Jesus whose suffering, death, and resurrection have definitely delivered us from sin and death and brought us to new life with God. God is with us.

ISAIAH 54:5-14 (RC)

The first verse of this reading is reminiscent of Jer. 31:32, which refers to the covenant that Judah broke with God though "I was your *husband*, says the LORD." Here the prophet declares to the exiles that the one who made them is, in fact, their husband, their redeemer, all creation's God. The Lord's calling Judah in the same way that a husband calls "a wife forsaken and grieved in spirit," a wife "cast off," contains echoes of Ezekiel 16. There, God, despite the detailed infidelities practiced by the lewd women and God's punishment, continues to care for them, will remember the covenant with them, and will make a new and lasting one (v. 60). The passage especially contains echoes of Hosea 1–3, in which Hosea, like God, continues to love his faithless spouse.

Contemporary feminist scholarship decries the male-female imagery in which the male is God and the female, "his" sinful people. Such scholarship is accurate insofar as the culture that produced these texts was patriarchal. However, the imagery is symbolic. It is not women of the sixth century B.C.E. or the twenty-first century C.E. who are the wife and lewd women to which the texts refer, but *the people* (in contrast to God), men and women alike. In fact, ironically enough, because the culture of ancient Israel was patriarchal, the text originally was referring to men even more than to women.

Though the Lord confesses to a brief abandonment of the people, God now extends everlasting love (*hesed*) and great compassion. The text itself recalls the promise God makes that is recorded in Gen. 9:15. Never again will there be total destruction. Appealing to the certainty of nature, even if nature would act contrary to its being (mountains depart and hills be removed), God promises that neither *hesed* nor compassion nor God's covenant of peace will depart from the people. Such an appeal is also made in Jer. 31:35-37 with similar intent: Only if the "fixed order"—identified as "the sun for light by day" and "the moon and the stars for light by night"—were to cease from God's presence, only then would Israel cease to be a nation. Similarly, only if the heavens could be measured and the foundations of the earth explored would the Lord reject Israel because of their sin. For the prophet/poet, nature is certain, as is God's faithfulness.

Turning to the image of a building, God declares that he will soon rebuild Jerusalem with precious jewels. The Lord will teach the children who will be prosperous. The people shall not be oppressed nor shall they have reason to fear.

Confident assertions by an exilic prophet that loss and uncertainty are short-lived, are especially appropriate for the believing community to hear on Holy Saturday evening. After all, it is during this night, at this very time, that our deepest being knows that restoration, a new beginning, is at hand. Jesus has been raised from the dead; liturgically speaking, Jesus *is being raised* from the dead. Our redemption is at hand.

ISAIAH 55:1-11 (RCL, BCP, RC)

The original setting for this text is probably Babylon during Judah's exile there. Water, money, food, power, and autonomy are scarce and no doubt sought after. The prophet suggests, however, that those things are not what are needed and what are important. Ultimately they cannot satisfy. He suggests an alternative that is life-giving, sustaining, and nourishing. God will make a lasting covenant with the people. God will see to it that the people are restored and even sought out by other nations. Their part of the covenant is to seek the Lord. The wicked and the unrighteous—both words used in poetic parallelism but actually one and the same group of people—are to change their behavior and return to God. God will in turn pardon them. God will not treat them with "eye for eye" justice or as they deserve; God, in that regard, is not like humans!

The exiles can be certain of this new covenant. God's word functions with as much certainty as nature. Just as nature can be counted on to behave in certain ways and that behavior counted on to yield certain effects, so God can be counted on to accomplish what God promises and intends. God's new covenant is certain and can be trusted.

Hearing this reading within the context of Holy Week, the assertion that God is forgiving and will not punish as the people's sins deserve prepares for the narrative of Jesus' passion. The sinless one suffers the personal pain of rejection by friends, the physical pain of being beaten, and the ultimate sacrifice of his life, not because he deserved these things, but to achieve the good of others, their redemption and restoration. In today's world, who would claim this behavior as rational? Consider your workplace. Who goes the extra mile without any expectation of reward? Who takes the blame for someone else's failure? Who assumes responsibility to try to effect reconciliation? Do you?

PROVERBS 8:1-8, 19-21; 9:4b-6 (RCL)

Wisdom, personified as a woman, goes to the heights, to the crossroads, to the city gates—in other words, to everywhere she can be heard, to everywhere people gather, to proclaim her message. She directs her message first to "the simple ones" (v. 5), telling them to learn prudence and acquire intelligence. She will speak noble things, what is right, truth, and righteous words. She assures her listeners that what she produces is better than gold and silver; it is the fruit of righteousness and justice, so indeed they will become wealthy.

Wisdom then directs her message to "those who lack sense" (9:4b), encouraging them to eat of her food and drink of her wine, telling them to opt for insight, her food, rather than immaturity.

Looking at the reading within its historical context allows for an appreciation of two-way theology (wisdom and folly, both personified as women who seek to gain a following) or the more contemporary studies of wisdom as female. In contrast to the women of Ezekiel 16 and 23, Hosea 1–3, or even Isaiah 54 (commented on above), Wisdom is to be pursued and has very valuable things to offer. Elsewhere, it is even by wisdom that the Lord founded the earth (Prov. 3:19); wisdom was created before anything else (Sir. 1:4).

However, as I look at this reading in its present liturgical context, I am reminded of the passage read this year on Tuesday of Holy Week, 1 Cor 1:18-31. Historically, the passage predates Jesus, and yet it calls its listeners to value wisdom more than gold and silver and the power and material objects that gold and silver can buy. The Corinthian passage assures us that God's wisdom differs from the wisdom of the world. Whereas worldly wisdom can lead to power and the material objects that gold and silver can buy, God's wisdom is foolishness. Tonight, in this liturgical context, God's wisdom has effected our redemption, the sinless one has accepted the will of his Father, has suffered death, and is now being raised triumphant. Indeed, we are encouraged to seek prudence, intelligence, truth, righteousness, and noble things.

> GOD'S WISDOM HAS EFFECTED OUR REDEMPTION, THE SINLESS ONE HAS ACCEPTED THE WILL OF HIS FATHER, HAS SUFFERED DEATH, AND IS NOW BEING RAISED TRIUMPHANT.

BARUCH 3:9-15, 32—4:4 (RCL alt., RC)

This passage also celebrates wisdom and encourages its hearers to pursue wisdom. It is another of the passages proclaimed from the perspective of exile. The scribe questions why the people of Israel are in exile in the first place and immediately answers his own question: They had forsaken wisdom. Baruch then counsels that they seek wisdom, and strength, and understanding; finding them, they will also find life, light, and peace.

Now the Creator is the source of wisdom. Baruch recalls how God gave wisdom to Jacob and to Israel, and he exhorts everyone to hold fast to wisdom. Seeking wisdom, seeking the Creator, is for the exiles a new beginning. We this night are certain of a new beginning.

EZEKIEL 36:24-28 (RCL, BCP)

In this passage directed to the exiles, to those who had sinned and had consequently been estranged from God, the prophet proclaims deliverance and hope. The Lord will return the exiles to their own land. The Lord will purify the people from the pollution of their idolatry and make them clean. The new beginning involves a new heart and a new spirit. Having removed the people's heart of stone, the Lord will replace it with a heart of flesh. When the spirit of God dwells in them, they will obey God and live in their ancestors' land. Moreover, their covenant identity shall be restored: they will be the Lord's people, and the Lord will again be their God. The restoration of this covenant identity is a new beginning.

This week we reenact Jesus' sealing of the new covenant in his blood, the covenant by which sin and death are definitely destroyed, the covenant by which we have been redeemed, the covenant that restores us, all people, to God. The hope that Ezekiel inspires in the exiles foreshadows the hope and certainty in faith that are ours.

EZEKIEL 36:16-17a, 18-28 (RC)

The passage is divided into two parts. The Lord directs Ezekiel to proclaim to the people of Israel their recent history as God sees it: their sinfulness and its consequent punishment landing them in exile; their continuing sin in exile which God understands as further insulting him, this time in front of other peoples. Because God is concerned for his name, that is, for his identity, as people would come to understand or misunderstand it because of Israel's behavior, the Lord decides to take action.

The second part of the passage describes that action and is commented on immediately above. For the sake of God's name, the Lord will restore the people. Again, the restoration of the people's covenant identity is a new beginning.

One of the particularly interesting details about this text is its acknowledgment that even in exile the people continued to sin. As I write these comments, I am fully aware of myself as a sinner and of the sin that permeates our world. Yes, Jesus' death and resurrection triumphed over sin, and yes, I continue to sin. Yet, our continued sinfulness does not diminish the fact that we have been redeemed, that we are called to renounce sin, and that forgiveness is certain. What Jesus' resurrection accomplished, what we celebrate this evening, puts us all at a different place with respect to sin. Sin no longer has to lead to our condemnation but rather to forgiveness and restoration and eternal life.

> OUR CONTINUED SINFULNESS DOES NOT DIMINISH THE FACT THAT WE HAVE BEEN REDEEMED, THAT WE ARE CALLED TO RENOUNCE SIN, AND THAT FORGIVENESS IS CERTAIN.

EZEKIEL 37:1-14 (RCL, BCP)

This famous passage, often read at funerals, describes the resurrection of dead bones, the dead/exiled people of Israel. First is the vision of the bones and the question of the prophet, "Can these bones live?" (v. 3). The prophet's reply indicates his submission to God. He does not know; God knows. Only God knows whether or not God is capable of making the dead bones live.

The Lord directs the prophet to tell the bones that God will cause breath to enter them so that they will live, that God will lay sinews and flesh on them, cover them with flesh and give them breath. When this has occurred, Ezekiel will know what he had said only God knew, whether or not the dead bones could live. God further declares that, because of such occurrences at the Lord's direction, the people will know that God is the Lord.

The prophet did as God had directed him, and what the prophet proclaimed came to pass. Then God identified the bones to the prophet: they are the whole house of Israel.

The house of Israel was at that time in a state of hopelessness, but God ordered Ezekiel to tell the people that God was going to open their graves and restore them to life and to their land. That would enable them to know that God is the Lord. The Lord tells the people that when that has happened, God will put God's spirit into them and they will live. (See the promise of God's spirit in Ezek. 36:26, commented on above.) I am reminded of Jesus' cure of the paralytic: so that the people would know that Jesus had the power to forgive sins, he cured the physical ailment of the one who had come to him. Which was harder to do (Mark 2:2-12; cf. Matt. 9:1-8; Luke 5:18-26)? Here God causes dead bones to come to life, but the real event, the miraculous deed so to speak, is the infusion of God's spirit. That will change the people of Israel; that will restore them and make them new. Just as in several of the other passages commented on above, this text promises new life and a new beginning.

ZEPHANIAH 3:14-20 (RCL);
ZEPHANIAH 3:12-20 (BCP)

This passage, presumed to have been produced during Judah's exile, also provides consolation and hope. The prophet is directed to proclaim that the Lord has taken away the punishments for the people's sin and has removed their enemies. No longer is there a human king of Judah, but God is their king. He is with them and they have no need to fear. Their God is a warrior; they have no need to fear any enemies.

HOLY SATURDAY EVENING, THE EASTER VIGIL, IS A NIGHT OF REVERSALS.

In describing Judah's restoration, the poet describes rejoicing and loud singing appropriate to a festival—no disaster, no reproach, no oppression. Restoration will include making those usually the recipients of shame (e.g., the lame) the recipients of praise and recognition instead. Expectations will be reversed. Not only will Judah's exiles return to their own land, they shall become recipients of recognition and praise from other nations. Again, expectations will be reversed. Their disgrace will be transformed into honor—a new beginning is at hand!

Like shame and honor, so death and life are opposites. Jesus died to sin so that we might live to God. The old is replaced with the new. Liturgically speaking, Holy Saturday evening, the Easter Vigil, is a night of reversals.

JONAH 3:1-10 (LUTH.)

The first time Jonah was asked by God to go to Nineveh and preach, he refused. However, he obeyed God's second request. He went to Nineveh. (It took three days to cross the city; note the use of the symbolic number three.) One day's walk into the city, Jonah began to prophesy that after forty more days (reminiscent of the flood story recounted above; three and forty are both symbolic numbers for completion), Nineveh would be overthrown.

The Ninevites believed the prophet's proclamation of the word of God and responded by proclaiming a fast and donning sackcloth. The king himself exchanged his robe for sackcloth and sat in ashes and ordered that all the people and animals of Nineveh fast, taking neither food nor water, and that they don sackcloth. These gestures represent mourning and grieving. They recall the gestures associated with the repentance the prophets had urged upon a sinful Israel (e.g., Joel 1:13-14; Jer. 6:26).

The king also ordered that the Ninevites pray and change their sinful and violent behaviors. The king hoped that the people's repentance would cause God to repent of the destruction God was planning to inflict. In fact, God was swayed by their efforts and did not destroy them. Sorrow and repentance caused God to change and forgive.

Read in the context of the Easter Vigil liturgy, the passage reminds us that God's redemption is for all people, our enemies as well as our friends. The hated Ninevites obey God and repent, and God forgives. We also have received God's forgiveness; we have not been destroyed but rather brought to new life, and we look forward to the life to come.

DEUTERONOMY 31:19-30 (LUTH.)

Moses wants to record for posterity what he believes will be Israel's future unfaithfulness. Knowing the people all too well, he foresees a time when they will no longer experience a need to be dependent on God. When that time comes, they will practice idolatry, reject the Lord, and break the covenant. But after they have rejected God and consequently experience suffering, Moses directs that they be confronted with the words he is speaking as a witness. In other words, Moses wants the people to be presented with what he had predicted. Implicitly he will be saying, "I told you so."

The Book of the Law was to be placed beside the Ark of the Lord. It also was to serve as a witness against the Israelites. Moses, then, having called the elders, recited the words of the Law in their hearing; he called on heaven and earth to witness against the Israelites if they violated its content. But Moses told them that he knew they would; they already had done so even before he was dead.

Finally, Moses had the people assemble their elders and officials so that he could recite for their benefit the teachings, and so they too could serve as witnesses of the people's unfaithfulness. Moses predicted what he had every reason to believe would prove true: affluence and security would diminish the people's dependence on God and would promote idolatry.

The passage allows for three separate witnesses against the Israelites: Moses' own words recorded for future reference, the contents of the Book of the Law, and the witness of the elders and officials. Moses knew the people well, or else he knew well the human heart, generically speaking. He knew that when things go well, people tend to forget God, at least take God less seriously. People forget others who have contributed to their well-being—parents, teachers, those who cared for and otherwise inspired them. Sometimes they tend to replace God with other values—idols, power, status, money. Moses was very sure the people would become unfaithful.

Reading the text historically, we suspect that it was written as a theological judgment that helped to explain theologically why Israel went into exile. Read liturgically, the text serves as a record of our history that includes sin and also as a subtle and sober reminder that in spite of Jesus' triumph over sin, we are likely to sin again.

DEUTERONOMY 3:1-29 (LUTH.)

Recalling the Israelites' history, Moses details what happened to them in their proximate efforts to enter Canaan. Told as a variation of the Holy War story (not everything is destroyed), God is depicted as doing the fighting on Israel's behalf. Two kings of the Amorites, King Sihon of Heshbon and King Og of Bashan, have been struck down. The devastation has been complete, with all the human beings having been killed and their cities destroyed. The livestock and the plunder have become the Israelites' booty. These victories have enabled the Israelites to claim the land east of the Jordan River as their own. The text then details the distribution of the land, to the Gadites, to the Reubenites, and to the half-tribe of Manasseh, as well as to several delineated families.

Moses required of those given land east of the Jordan that they cross the Jordan with their fellow Israelites—except the women and children—in order to help their fellow Israelites take possession of that land. Again, they were instructed not to fear; the Lord would be fighting for them. When Moses asked the Lord to allow him to cross the Jordan to see the land the people would possess, the Lord denied him. As a compromise, Moses would be able to see the land from Mount Pisgah, but it would be Joshua who would lead the people into the land.

Heard during the Easter Vigil, the passage contains relevant themes. It is God who accomplishes the victories—over the kings of the Amorites, and we know from the book of Joshua, over the people's entrance into the remainder of the land. It is God through Jesus who accomplishes the victory over sin that we celebrate tonight. Second, entrance into the new land is a new beginning. We also begin anew, rising to new life with the risen Lord.

New Testament Reading
ROMANS 6:3-11 (RCL, BCP, RC)

Christian baptism means being baptized into Christ's death and burial so that like him, we can be raised from the dead to new life. Baptism into Jesus' death means the death of sin, that we no longer be controlled by sin. Baptism into Jesus' death also means baptism into his life, and his life is God's life. Participating in Christ's passion, death, and resurrection involves dying to sin and living to God. Faith in Jesus' death and resurrection, in his ultimate triumph over sin, is what Holy Week is all about. We ritually reenact what Christ did once for all. Easter is a new beginning and brings with it new life.

The Psalm
PSALM 114 (RCL, BCP)

This psalm recalls and celebrates the Exodus. When Israel departed Egypt, they became God's special people. The sea separated for them so they could flee the pursuing Egyptians; the Jordan separated for them so they could enter the land God had promised them. Nature behaved to the benefit of God's people. These marvelous events, as well as the miracle at Meribah where Moses drew water from a rock (Num. 20:11), took place because of the presence (and power) of God.

The psalm recalls the Israelites' deliverance from bondage in Egypt and celebrates the God whose power controlled nature for the protection and benefit of the people. What better connection to the Easter Vigil liturgy, during which we recall our deliverance from bondage to sin and celebrate the God whose power raised Jesus from the dead?

PSALM 118:1-2, 16-17, 22-23 (RC)

Parts of this psalm are used as readings for Palm/Passion Sunday (vv. 1-2 and 19-29 in the RCL and vv. 19-29 in the BCP). The Roman Catholic liturgy saves the psalm until the Easter Vigil and uses it very selectively, including vv. 16-17. A psalm of thanksgiving for God's steadfast and enduring love (*hesed*), the psalm testifies that because of God, the psalmist, that is, the one or ones praying the psalm, will not die but live. The use of the psalm in connection with Jesus' triumph over death and resurrection is obvious. In

> THE PSALM TESTIFIES THAT BECAUSE OF GOD, THE PSALMIST, THAT IS, THE ONE OR ONES PRAYING THE PSALM, WILL NOT DIE BUT LIVE.

addition, the one rejected (here understood as Jesus crucified) becomes the cornerstone (the source of Christianity). The psalm concludes with a declaration that God is the one who makes this marvelous event possible.

THE GOSPEL
MATTHEW 28:1-10 (RCL, BCP, RC)

The Gospel reading picks up where the Gospel reading for Palm/Passion Sunday left off. After the Sabbath, at dawn on the first day of the week, the two Marys returned to the tomb. There was another earthquake; the first had been at the time of Jesus' death (27:54). This time an angel of the Lord came down from heaven, rolled back the stone, and sat on it. Recall that Pilate's guard of soldiers had sealed the stone. The angel's appearance was "like lightening" (v. 3); the image recalls the face of the man in Daniel's vision (10:6). Moreover, the angel's clothing was as "white as snow." The image "white as snow" recalls Isa. 1:18 where

> DEATH IS NOT THE FINAL WORD: CHRIST ROSE FROM THE DEAD, AND WE HAVE BEEN REDEEMED AND GIVEN NEW LIFE. IT IS THAT NEW LIFE THAT WE ARE CALLED TO BRING INTO THE WORLD. LET US LOVE ONE ANOTHER.

the Lord, addressing the sinful people of Judah, promises that their scarlet sins will become "white as snow" (RSV). The guards feared the angel, shook, and became like dead men. Note that Jesus was alive; the guards were "dead," if only traumatized.

The angel seems to have ignored the guards. He spoke to the women, telling them not to be afraid. The angel announced to the women that he knew that they sought Jesus who was crucified but that he was not here; he had been raised (see 27:53). The angel shows them the place in the tomb where Jesus' body had lain and then instructs them to go and tell Jesus' disciples that he has been raised and that he is going ahead of them to Galilee where they will see him.

The women, both fearful and joyful, set off to take the news to Jesus' disciples. En route, Jesus met them and said, "Greetings!" The women "came to him, took hold of his feet, and worshiped him" (v. 9). Jesus repeated the angel's message, telling the women not to fear, but to tell his brothers to go to Galilee where they would see him.

Matthew's version of Jesus' crucifixion has no faithful apostles at the foot of the cross, only a few women "who had followed Jesus from Galilee" (27:55), that is, from the beginning, and who had provided for him. They had stood at a distance. When Joseph of Arimathea, one of Jesus' disciples, buried Jesus' body, the women were there. The next morning when the women came to the tomb, they were greeted by the angel and shown the empty tomb; finally, they were greeted by the risen Lord.

Many Americans today, having read *The Da Vinci Code*, are now convinced that texts favorable to women were suppressed by the early church. Yet when one reads Matthew's account of Jesus' passion, death, and resurrection, one can't miss the central role played by women. Matthew 27–28 reminds us that it is not always the canonical texts but rather the later interpretation of those texts by men that have served to denigrate women.

"Unless a grain of wheat falls into the earth and dies, it remains just a single grain; but if it dies, it bears much fruit" (John 12:24). Jesus' death was necessary so that all of humankind could be redeemed. The seed will not be alone, but it shall bear much fruit.

When we leave the Easter Vigil liturgy, we go forth as grateful, joyous redeemed people. We have been transformed. We are not the same people who entered the church awhile ago. I am finishing this commentary on January 4, 2004, the feast of the Epiphany. The world that I left the church to enter this morning is a world at war, in Israel and in Iraq and almost everywhere. We continue to sin and to harm one another, and we avoid repentance; we continue to be sinned against and harmed, and we refuse forgiveness. The world that we will leave the church to enter on March 26, 2005, will likely also be a world at war, though we cannot now predict the details. It is a world into which Christ came to forgive sins. He did so by his death, and he died because he loves us and because he also loves those who sin against us, because he wanted our sins forgiven and for us to forgive others' sins, because he conformed his will to God's will. Death is not the final word: Christ rose from the dead, and we have been redeemed and given new life. It is that new life that we are called to bring into the world. Let us love one another.

DECEMBER 2004

Sunday	Monday	Tuesday	Wednesday	Thursday	Friday	Saturday
			1	2	3	4
5 2 Advent	6	7	8	9	10	11
12 3 Advent	13	14	15	16	17	18
19 4 Advent	20	21	22	23	24 Christmas Eve	25 Christmas Day
26 1 Christmas / St. Stephen	27	28	29	30	31 New Year's Eve	

254

JANUARY 2005

Sunday	Monday	Tuesday	Wednesday	Thursday	Friday	Saturday
						1
2 Christmas / Epiphany	3	4	5	6	7	8
9 1 Epiphany / Baptism of Christ	10	11	12	13	14	15
16 2 Epiphany	17	18	19	20	21	22
23 3 Epiphany	24	25	26	27	28	29
30 4 Epiphany	31					

FEBRUARY 2005

Sunday	Monday	Tuesday	Wednesday	Thursday	Friday	Saturday
		1	2	3	4	5
6 5 Epiphany / Transfiguration	7	8	9 Ash Wednesday	10	11	12
13 1 Lent	14	15	16	17	18	19
20 2 Lent	21	22	23	24	25	26
27 3 Lent	28					

MARCH 2005

Sunday	Monday	Tuesday	Wednesday	Thursday	Friday	Saturday
		1	2	3	4	5
6 4 Lent	7	8	9	10	11	12
13 5 Lent	14	15	16	17	18	19
20 Palm Sunday / Passion Sunday	21	22	23	24 Holy Thursday	25 Good Friday	26 Holy Saturday
27 Easter Day	28	29	30	31		